Placing the Dead

Seminar Studies in Anthropology

Placing the Dead

Tombs, Ancestral Villages, and Kinship
Organization in Madagascar

Maurice Bloch

*The London School of Economics
and Political Science*

1971
SEMINAR PRESS
London and New York

Seminar Press Limited
Berkeley Square House
Berkeley Square, London W1X 6BA

U.S. edition published by
SEMINAR PRESS INC.
111 Fifth Avenue,
New York, New York 10003

Library of Congress Catalog Card Number: 70–162375
ISBN: 0–12–809150–9

PRINTED IN GREAT BRITAIN BY
W & J MACKAY & CO LTD, CHATHAM, KENT

Preface

There are over one million Merina and I have studied only about five thousand of them in two villages and this can in no way be considered a typical sample; a fact which must be borne in mind by the reader.

The information on which the study is based was for the most part obtained during field work in Imerina between October 1964 and April 1966. Of this, four months were spent in a small village in old Imerina in the canton of Fieferana[1] and a year in the canton of Ambatomanoina where most of the villages of the canton were studied. In addition, I was able to make occasional visits to a number of villages in other parts of Imerina and was thus able to gain a more general impression.[2]

Quite clearly there was insufficient time for a definitive study of Merina culture as a whole and, in any case, it is impossible for one worker to produce a complete study of such a numerous and varied population. Hence I was presented with a difficult problem: either I could base my study on the villages which I have examined in detail and reach conclusions which might have little significance for Imerina as a whole, or I could try to give a widely based but very little documented account of Merina society in general. In fact, I have tried to steer a middle course. I have not limited myself to conclusions about the particular villages in which I worked because Merina society is in many aspects not bounded by the locality. This I hope will become apparent during the course of my analysis. On the other hand, it would not be acceptable to assume that all aspects of social organization in the villages in which I worked were typical of rural Imerina. Indeed, the comparisons I was able to make with other villages brought this home to me. Merina society is extremely diverse and even if we ignore the completely different

---

[1] Andrainarivo (see Map 3).
[2] An account of the technique employed is given in Bloch (1968b).

situation in large urban centres such as Tananarive, the historical and economic background varies radically from one place to another. In many ways some of the villages which I studied were exceptional for Merina society both in their remoteness from Tananarive and in their ecology. In spite of this the general pattern of attachment to the *tanindrazana*, balanced against the necessity for the Merina to form links with the village in which he lives, is basic to Merina society and always takes the same form. Studies carried out in other parts of Imerina will, I hope, confirm this. However, the description of the organization of the Ambatomanoina district and the details of ceremonies which I give are applicable only in varying degrees to the rest of Imerina. The figures in Chapters 3 and 5 apply only to the specific areas studied.

It is in the light of continuing research on Merina society that I feel that the course I have taken is justifiable. It gives the framework of what is probably the most important aspect of Merina life; a framework which will facilitate the understanding of Merina society as a whole and which is therefore verifiable by studies in any other part of Imerina. Furthermore, the more detailed ethnographic data includes information which may be used with similar information from other districts in a more detailed and all-embracing study of the whole of Imerina. Even during the preparation of this book further work was in progress, some of it supporting my own findings, some elaborating upon them, and some dealing with topics which I have not touched upon.

March 1971   MAURICE BLOCH

Acknowledgements

I was introduced to the villagers of Andrainarivo by my friends Arsene Rataimbazafy and Pasteur Vahinimalala and was therefore very soon accepted in the village. R. P. Blot, SJ, took me to Ambatomanoina and there introduced me to R. P. de Batz, SJ, who found accommodation for myself and my wife and befriended us throughout.

The work was financed by The Nuffield Foundation of Great Britain and additional help, both financial and material, was provided by The Henry Oliver Foundation, The E. Horniman Foundation and the University of Tananarive.

So many people helped me in numerous different ways that it would be impossible to thank them all individually here, but I am particularly grateful to Professor J. Poirier for his practical assistance and hospitality, and also for giving me the opportunity to discuss the progress of my work with him and his staff. I would like to thank Mr and Mrs Gilbey of the LMS, R. P. Papov, SJ, Mr A. Rakotomanga, and M and Mme P. Vérin for the assistance which they so willingly gave to me. I am also most grateful to the Malagasy Government for granting permission for me to carry out this field work. Finally, I owe much to the people of Ambatomanoina and Andrainarivo for their patience, understanding and trust.

The substance of this book was earlier presented at the University of Cambridge as a thesis. The project was first suggested by Professor M. Fortes and his interest and encouragement, both in practical and academic matters, was a great inspiration to me. Dr S. J. Tambiah guided me in the preparation of the manuscript as well as assisting with certain aspects of the work. I am grateful to Dr R. Abrahams for commenting on Parts 1 and 2, to Dr J. Goody for criticizing an earlier version of Chapter 2, and to Mr G. Whittington for helping with the statistics in Part 3. Indeed, there is no member of staff or research student in the Department of Social Anthropology at Cambridge with whom I have not had useful and enlightening discussions about the project either in seminars or privately.

The work has also profited greatly through comments I have received from Dr J. Loudon, Dr La Fontaine, Professor A. Southall, Professor P. Ottino, Miss Anne Akeroyd, Dr J. Woodburn, and Mr A. Forge.

Lastly, I am deeply indebted to my wife for sharing with me the experience of field work; in a way it can be said that we obtained much of the information jointly. I must thank her also for her help in the preparation of this book.

Contents

PART I

The Background to Merina Rural Society

1

Introduction[1]

The Merina, who are sometimes referred to as the Hova, live in the northern part of the central plateau of Madagascar. They number approximately 1¼ million, and speak one of the many dialects of the Malayo-Polynesian language spoken throughout the island (Dahl, 1951). The Merina divide themselves into two categories based on physical differences. The first, which they call *fotsy* (white), refers principally to the descendants of the "free" Merina; the other, which they call *mainty* (black), refers principally to the descendants of slaves who are usually described as negroid. The casual observer can easily distinguish the extremes of these two types, but some individuals cannot be classified in one or other of these groups on physical criteria alone. The division is ultimately a social one, although normally appearance is a sufficient guide to group membership (see Plates 1a and 1b).

How far these social divisions correspond to different origin is difficult to say. It is obvious that the majority of whites have physical characteristics which link them to the Indonesian and Malay peoples. The untrained observer immediately sees the similarity in physical appearance of some Malagasy and the Malay and this is borne out by the, as yet somewhat scanty, work of physical anthropologists. Rakoto Ratsimamanga is quoted as considering that 60 per cent of the Merina are of an "Indonesian-mongoloid type" which he defines as "characterized

---

[1] As recent histories and geographies of Madagascar have given much of the background necessary for a study of Merina society, I shall limit myself here to the minimum necessary for the understanding of the argument. H. Deschamps, *Histoire de Madagascar*, 1961. H. Isnard, *Madagascar*, 1955. J. Faublée, *L'Ethnographie de Madagascar*, 1946.

by low stature, light yellow skin, straight flat hair, low pilosity, a prominent nose and a long narrow skull (dolichocephalic)"—Faublée, 1946, pp. 130–131. The rest of the population is described as European type (30 per cent), oceanian negroid type (8 per cent) and African negroid (2 per cent). This kind of description is obviously insufficient, especially as we are told little of sampling procedures, and, as I suspect must be the case, it only refers to "whites".

The "white" Merina are the people in which the "Indonesian" ethnic element is clearest. This element is also frequently present in the Merina's north-east neighbours, the Sihanaka, and the people who are closest to them in culture, economy and habitat, the Betsileo, who live to the south and with whom the Merina share the central plateau.

The "blacks" are for the most part descendants of slaves captured by the Merina in other parts of Madagascar and also of some other aboriginal peoples from the area now dominated by the Merina. Some of the "blacks" whom I knew could remember ancestors of Betsileo, Artaifasy, Bara and Betsimisaraka origin and others would call themselves by the names of people who had traditionally always lived in the area where they are now. However, I was unable to get a satisfactory picture of the origin of the "blacks" as a whole. This was because there are many difficulties in obtaining this kind of information, as the unwillingness to admit slave origin leads many descendants of slaves to claim origin from non-Merina peoples in order to stress their, ultimately, free descent. This may lead in some cases to unjustified claims to be, for example, Betsileo, since the Betsileo have great prestige and are, after the Merina, the best educated people in Madagascar.

It is not surprising that the "blacks" are closer in physical type to the non-Merina Malagasy as most of them are their descendants, and among them the "Indonesian-mongoloid" type is much rarer and the negroid types commoner. The ethnic affinity of this negroid type is far from clear and it should not be assumed that it is necessarily of African origin. The theories concerning the origin of these peoples are conflicting and until we have much more evidence it seems to me pointless to come down on one side or the other (Valette, 1965).

The ethnological history of the Merina and indeed of all the Malagasy is problematical. This is surprising when we know so much already. The linguistic and ethnic affinities with the Malayo-Polynesian peoples are clear, but we do not know with any degree of certainty when and for how long contact and migration occurred. We do not know the nature

Plate 1a. A boy of free descent, classified as *fotsy* (white) by the Merina.

Plate 1b. Children of slave descent, classified as *mainty* (black) by the Merina.

of the contact and what proportion of the present Malagasy have a South-east Asian origin. It does not seem that a cultural or sociological study such as this will help us very much in this direction. Only archaeology, with the help of physical anthropology, can settle the matter. Having said this it must be admitted, however, that many of the features that will be discussed here offer confirmation of the cultural affinities of the Merina with South-East Asia.

The Country

The country of the Merina is called Imerina, but this can mean two things. For the peasant it means a relatively small area corresponding to the size of the Merina Kingdom as it was at the time of its unification at the end of the 18th century. Imerina in this sense is a folk concept and is not very exactly defined.[1] It does not extend further than about 40 miles north, 35 miles south, 30 miles east and 30 miles west of Tananarive. Tananarive was the capital of the kingdom and is now the capital of the whole of Madagascar (Callet, 1908, p. 683ff.). For the administration, however, Imerina refers to the government division called the *"Province de Tananarive"*. Here, I am concerned with the first of these two meanings and when I speak of Imerina, I mean old or traditional Imerina (see Map 1).

Two sharply distinct seasons divide the year. The one, lasting from mid-October to April, is hot and very wet, the other, from May to October, is colder and dry. During the dry season there is only occasional cyclonic rain, but during the wet season violent storms occur almost every evening causing violent precipitation for a few hours. It is during the wet season that most of the time-consuming agricultural work is done, and during the dry season that there is most time for ceremonies.

The part of Madagascar inhabited by the Merina is commonly referred to as the plateau area. The word plateau is, however, misleading since almost no large expanse of flat land is found on it. It is really a very broad top of a mountain range averaging in height around 1300 meters above sea level (Hatzfeld, 1960, p. 9). The general effect is of a succession of hills separated by flat valley bottoms. The hills consist of an extremely poor hard lateritic clay of surprisingly bright and varied red

---

[1] Some writers have referred to this concept by the phrase *Imerina enin-toko* (six-part Imerina)— see p. 47.

hues and they are normally bare with little or no top soil. Their natural vegetation is a dry scanty grass which offers poor pasture for cattle. In some places fields are made on this land and such plants as groundnuts, beans, *voandzeia* and maize may be grown on them with liberal manure. Even so, the soil is rapidly exhausted, and the fields must be moved every

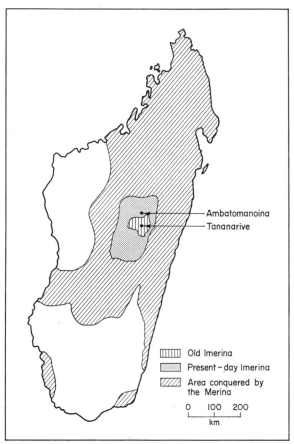

Map 1. Madagascar

year. Traditionally the grass was burnt before cultivation and this is still common, in spite of government restrictions. The hills are naturally bare which gives them an ascetic beauty heightened by the great gashes of erosion due to the torrential rain. They stand out in bright red against the grey-green hill-sides. The French and now the Malagasy government have been anxious to halt this erosion by planting trees, mainly eucalyptus, which now cover a number of the slopes around Tananarive and near some of the villages. None the less, Imerina still generally affords a treeless aspect which, combined with the bare hills and great erosive scars, gives it an almost lunar appearance.

The valleys are very different. The soil is richer and well irrigated by numerous streams throughout the year. The natural vegetation is lush and varied, but usually it is replaced by irrigated and terraced rice fields which provide the Merina with their principal livelihood. Around the edges of the rice field one commonly finds small gardens with fruit trees such as orange, banana, plantain, plum, mango; many vegetables: maize, beans, greens of many kinds, tomatoes, onions, taro, *voondzeia*, sweet potatoes, melons, cucumbers, gourds and various exclusively Malagasy plants. The rice fields cut up the slopes into level fields surrounded by small mud walls with here and there heavier dykes. They are irrigated by channels which divert the streams that flow in the middle of the valleys.

The Merina also obtain significant resources from livestock. Cattle are kept in all parts, although the number of heads of cattle to the population varies so widely that it is impossible to generalize. Everywhere cattle are used to draw the carts or sledges of those fortunate enough to possess them, as well as for harrowing, ploughing and trampling the rice and the rice fields. They are, of course, also kept for meat, but their skins are not usually used. Cattle manure is used when dry in those areas where the soil is of low fertility. They are also of significance in articulating the economy and for such things as capital accumulation and credit. Apart from cattle, pigs, sheep, geese, turkeys and, above all, chickens, are either kept for meat or sold. But the chickens produce few eggs and the sheep have no wool.

Man has left his mark irrevocably in other ways than by cultivation. The traditional central part of Imerina everywhere bears witness to the past and the Merina are continually aware of the remains of a previous age, as indeed I myself became aware after various historical features were repeatedly pointed out to me. This made me realize the extent to which old fortifications, remains of enclosures and old village sites act as the framework of present-day life. The existence of the past in the present is very much more real in Imerina than it is anywhere else I know. The summit of almost every dominating hill is encircled by rows of parallel moats and walls which once formed the fortifications of an old fort or village. These are largely overgrown and sometimes almost completely obliterated. However, I soon grew accustomed to recognizing the traces of the past and to feeling the presence of *Malagasy* times in the way the Merina themselves did, by attaching importance to pointing out these remains and retelling histories and myths associated with them. Everywhere there are traces of ancient dwellings marked by deep moats of 30 feet or more which surrounded them. Some of the present-day villages too are still surrounded by such moats (Plate 3). It is impossible to know from simple inspection how old these remains of fortifications are and the Merina willingly over-exaggerate their age. It seems, however, quite clear that many are of considerable antiquity, but for the Merina of today this is not the point; they are proof of a glorious *Malagasy* past.

As striking as the old fortifications are the tombs, but as these form an important part of this study I shall only mention them briefly here. Some are linked with the fortifications, often being the only edifices which remain standing within their walls. Some of the older ones are immense squat buildings, sometimes made of earth blocks and largely overgrown, but most commonly made from megaliths. Some are no longer visible but their position is remembered and they are sometimes discovered accidentally in low bush or completely buried below ground. Of more recent origin and often near villages are extremely elaborate 19th century tombs with arcades, clearly inspired by the style of funerary edifices built for the Merina monarchs and "Prime Ministers" by a few European artisans associated with the diplomatic and religious missions of the time. They are mainly small, highly decorated stone granite buildings of exceptional solidity. All travellers unacquainted with Merina culture cannot but be struck by their solidity and importance which contrasts with the impermanence of the houses of the living.

Another type of funerary monument which proclaim the past are the monolithic dolmens (*tsangan-bato*—standing stones). These, it is assumed, were raised, as they are today, to substitute for those whose bodies had been lost and who consequently could not be buried in the tombs. These tall stones are to be found in all parts of Imerina. A few of them are 10 feet or more in height. These very large dolmens are not necessarily associated with the lost dead but may commemorate a treaty or have some other memonic purpose. The Merina consider some of them to be of extreme antiquity and this claim may well be justified in some cases.

The People

The Merina see themselves as a people whose society and culture is in the process of radical change. They see themselves as faced by two totally different principles of life and their every action involves a choice of one or the other principle. This belief is a historical belief; in the past in "*Malagasy* times", as they say, things were done according to "*Malagasy* custom" but since then foreigners, *vazaha*, have come. Missionaries and colonialists have introduced new ways of doing things, *fomba vazaha*, and the present time is the time of the *vazaha*. This is an oversimplification of a complex and subtle system of belief which it is the purpose of this book to illustrate. It is essential as a preliminary statement to even the most elementary description of what the Merina look like and where they live, since the meaning of these things is underlined by this distinction.

Dress

The great variety in dress among the Merina is interpreted in terms of this *Malagasy–vazaha* contrast.

As is the case for the nearby Betsileo, the most striking fact about Merina dress is the great variety of styles to be seen even in one small village, but this variety seems simple if we see it as a continuum from the *Malagasy* extreme to the *vazaha* or Tananarive extreme.

The most characteristic feature of this wide range can be seen in hats. These are made in almost as many varieties of vegetable materials and colours as is possible. On the whole the most favoured types are broad rimmed and offer a suitable shield from the sun, but the rich and especially the town dwellers replace the *Malagasy* with *vazaha* types such as Tyrolean and homberg hats. The same sort of variety exists in clothing. In Tananarive richer men dress much as they would in Paris and London but the great majority have to be satisfied with imitations made of various types of Japanese and French cottons as well as with the large quantity of assorted second-hand jumble which seems to be imported from a number of industrialized countries. More typically *Malagasy* are suits made of light flannel such as is used for pyjamas. The top part consists of a smock which reaches down to the knees and the bottom part consists of loose trousers. Shoes and sandals are a rare luxury except in Tananarive and other big centres. Very often men wear a large cloth, which is often white, over their shoulders, or sometimes a cotton blanket. This is hitched up on the shoulders so as to hang in a triangle front and back. When it is cold it is allowed to fall giving a complete toga-like cover. This cloth is a clear sign of *Malagasy* type dress and may be worn by some people just to make a point about their *Malagasy* orientation, but in the more rural areas its great usefulness reduces its symbolic importance. Finally, among the poorer men and commonly in more remote areas a long skirt tucked in at the waist replaces the trousers.

Apart from the very rich town dwellers who might have ready-made or tailored clothes, women wear home-made Western-type dresses made from the many cheap cotton prints available. There the style and the length of the hem are significant, a modest style and a long full skirt being more *Malagasy*. Two features of women's dress are most significant: the hair-style and the cloth shawl, *lamba*, which is worn over the dress. The *lamba* is a shawl worn over the shoulders in which babies can be carried. For everyday wear in the villages it is often a piece of rough cloth, but is replaced by strikingly attractive silk or at least cotton cloth on Sunday. These clothes more than anything else are *Malagasy* and only a woman who wanted to demonstrate her total rejection of *Malagasy* life would not wear one. The richest and most Europeanized wear this shawl, clearly, only for its symbolical value. Much the same can be said about the way the women wear their hair. They never cut it but wear it in long plaits arranged in a variety of elegant styles. Only a very few women, usually those who have lived in Europe, will make the dramatic declaration involved in cutting their hair and thereby completely disassociating themselves from their traditional culture.

Except in Tananarive most clothes are inevitably very worn, tattered and discoloured, because of the poor quality of the material and the fact that new clothes are often "jumble", and also because agricultural work and vigorous washing with unpurified soap in cold water leads to rapid deterioration. However, to complete the picture one other fact must be imagined. There is nothing more striking than the transformation in appearance of those people who go to church on Sunday. Women who have even the most tattered clothes appear clean and strikingly dignified with their white *lambas* and the gold jewellery which most of them possess after their marriage. This is largely made by Merina craftsmen who have learnt their style from Indian immigrants.

Houses

Merina houses vary tremendously from small mud and bamboo huts covered with grass to much more elaborate structures. Typical Merina houses are two storied, and made of large blocks of mud or in some cases smaller mud bricks. They are rectangular, tall and narrow and the steeply sloping roof is covered by grass. Normally there are only openings on the west side and all houses must be orientated from north to south. This gives a peculiar appearance to many Merina villages which seem to lack a centre since the streets are lined on one side with the backs of houses. The houses, built of the earth that surrounds them, are usually of the same striking red colour, but sometimes this is covered by chalk. The walls are massive to support a storey of unbaked clay. Not only the houses but everything within them is placed in relation to the points of the compass, a practice which is linked with astrological beliefs (Bloch, 1968, p. 291).

In the two-storied houses the kitchen is upstairs. The hearth consists of three stones on which pots are placed and it is always on the west side. To the east of the hearth is the big water storage jar. Above the hearth may hang meat which is being smoked and some melon or maize seeds which are being dried for the next season. Small baskets for salt, spoons and other cooking necessities hang on the wall. The fire is produced by grass and sticks. Downstairs there are normally two rooms. The western one is often used as a silo or for keeping animals. The northern one is the reception room of the house. The earth floor and walls are normally covered by mats. The clay quickly rots the floor mats and they are continually covered by cleaner mats which rapidly soil and perish so that inumerable layers of mats cover some floors. The furniture varies. It may include a few chairs and a table, but will always include at least the chest which a bride brings at her marriage (see p. 180). Normally the room will also contain the bed of the head of the house. This will be in the honoured north-east corner while in the north-east itself will be hung a little of the rice from the previous year's harvest, as well as some medicines.

The type of house I have just described can be considered as average. There are poorer, smaller houses, especially in those areas where the soil is not suitable for two-storied houses. There are also better, larger houses. The larger villages contain a number of these which belong to richer peasants but also, most commonly, to shopkeepers and government employees. The traditional house can first be improved by replacing the permeable and perishable grass roof by a tin roof. The next improvement gives many Malagasy houses their typical appearance. It consists in the building of a portico in front of the house. This is formed by four brick columns which support a balcony at first floor level and a forward projection of the roof. The balcony may have a decorated balustrade. This type of structure makes an ordinary Merina house surprisingly impressive; it protects the front from the rain and permits the window and door openings to be much larger. The significance of these porticoes as status symbols was brought home to me when my wife set an essay in a missionary school with the title "If I were rich". The *lavarangana* (from the word "verandah") was the outstanding desired material item to occur regularly, even in the essays of those children whose homes already had one. Houses with porticoes and tin roofs are usually the grandest to be found in villages but in the larger towns the windows may be glazed and mud bricks may be replaced by baked bricks. In Tananarive there may even be running water and electricity.

Tananarive

The tremendous diversity in clothing and housing is only one of the aspects of the major fact about Imerina. Imerina is inhabited by peasants using a type of cultivation little changed since our earliest records (Mayeur, 1777), a type of cultivation leading to a subsistence economy, yet in the very centre of the territory is a modern city which is both the administrative and trading centre of the whole of Madagascar. It is a city with running water and electricity in its centre. There are office blocks, cinemas and a few small factories. It is served by a railway station and an international airport and it houses diplomatic missions from many countries and international organizations. Tananarive itself, however, is for the peasants of the countryside a paradox. On the one hand it is the embodiment of an international modernity which is both desired and threateningly intrusive—the heart of things *vazaha*. It is also the centre of the old kingdom of Imerina, the very symbol of things *Malagasy*. It is impossible to ignore this aspect, in spite of the office blocks and the street lighting, as the city is dominated by the ancient palaces of the Merina monarchs and of their "Prime Ministers". Even these are ambiguous and unintentionally symbolic. The part of the town in which the palaces of the monarchs are to be found contains both traditional tombs and some of the oldest palaces in traditional style, but these are encircled and dominated by buildings of the 19th century French craftsman, Laborde, and of the Scotsman, Cameron, both of whom were brought to Madagascar by competing French and British interests in the hope that their architectural and technical feats would favourably influence the Merina monarchs. The city of Tananarive too is deeply marked by traditional Imerina. Old tombs and dolmens are found everywhere. Few buildings are modern concrete structures. Indeed, when I had been in Tananarive for a time it became clear to me that most of it was a conglomeration of Merina villages with houses little different from those of the countryside, but more insalubrious and depressing because of their overcrowding.

It is not my purpose here to present a study of Tananarive, or even of those villages which live in a close symbiotic relation with Tananarive, but to understand many aspects of the rural Merina's concepts we must understand the concept of Tananarive. Tananarive is the home of the petrol engine, especially of the lorries and the *taxis-brousse*—converted delivery vans which act as buses. It is the place where all highly desired manufactured goods originate, such as bicycles, sewing machines, watches, transistor radios, and kerosene lamps, and it is the place where those who are in control of these goods live. From the point of view of the villager the ambiguity of this very control underlines the problem of Tananarive and the problem of the contrast of things *vazaha* and things *Malagasy*. The control of things *vazaha* is obtained by people "who know things" (*mahay zavatra*) but this knowledge of things is separate from knowledge of things *Malagasy*, the knowledge of custom (*mahay fomba*). This is reserved by various devices to the elders with traditional authority (Bloch, 1968, pp. 292–294). Knowledge of things *"vazaha"* is by contrast not restricted and is therefore to a certain extent illegitimate. To know custom is to be wise, but to know things is to be crafty. Tananarive, the capital of the Merina state, the source of wisdom, is also the place of people who know things. The Merina peasant will often stress the point by saying that although the *vazaha* know things they are *kamo*. *Kamo*—usually translated as lazy—is better translated as someone who is slack in performing his traditional *Malagasy* duties.

There are, however, certain aspects of life which complicate and seem to contradict this clear contrast. Three such features are worth noting— the Christian Churches, the political parties, and education.

The Christian Churches

Firstly the position of the Christian churches and especially the Protestant Church has added a new complication. One of the words which has been taken over from French into Malagasy is *barbare* (savage, barbaric).

The contrast with being a *barbare* is being a Christian. People continually pointed out to me how they were not *barbare* but Christian, while other people with less access to *vazaha* goods and culture were *barbare*. It was not just a simple reaction to the presence of an anthropologist, although obviously this is difficult to judge, but the frequency of the occurrence of this concept in conversations which I overheard makes me have no doubt that not being *barbare* is a major preoccupation of the Merina. The exact reference of the concept is not so easy to isolate as might at first appear. The objects most strongly attacked by missionaries such as traditional medicines and charms are definitely *barbare*. Being *barbare* diminishes with identification with the Churches, but also with European dress and generally with wealth. The possession and understanding of manufactured goods is also a sign. Not being *barbare*, however, is not just following Western ideas, although this is how the Merina look upon it. The extreme emphasis on politeness in verbal exchange and the avoidance of the display of aggressive emotions such as anger (all qualities which are traditionally *Malagasy* and indeed contrast strikingly with those of Western culture) show that one is not *barbare*.

The notion of what is *barbare* and what is "Christian" is incompatible with the primary contrast between things *Malagasy* and things *vazaha*, since there something morally good is identified with a foreign introduction, namely the Church. The contradiction is never fully resolved but the historical concepts on which it is based offer a kind of solution. That is the way the Protestant Church can be described as "the religion of the ancestors", something "*Malagasy*" as opposed to something "*vazaha*". This possibility is open to the Protestants who contrast Protestantism which came first to Imerina, which uses Malagasy clergy and which can be associated (and often is) with the traditional Merina kingdom, with Catholicism which is a more recent introduction with a largely European clergy and is associated with the forces that destroyed the Merina kingdom. The strange equation of Protestantism and *Malagasy* things is further strengthened by the political situation, or rather by the simplified and somewhat distorted political situation as it appears to the peasants. The present government and its party, the "*Parti Social Democrate*" or PSD, is associated by many Merina with anti-Merina forces and its political support for people traditionally subject to the Merina explains its hostile attitude to Merina expansionist traditions. The main opposition party in Imerina (politically to the left of the PSD) is the AKFM, which draws its support more from the Merina of free descent and is therefore believed to be traditionally orientated. Because Protestantism is associated with the Merina and the Merina kingdom and Catholicism with the ex-subjects and slaves of the Merina, and also because the leaders of the AKFM are often ministers of the Protestant Church, it is possible for the Merina peasant to equate the PSD with *vazaha* things and Catholicism, and the AKFM with traditionalism and Protestantism. This is a misleading simplification but it contributes to resolving the problem discussed above by joining the Christian "good" with the *Malagasy* ancestral "good". (This neat and somewhat surprising answer to a logical problem is not open to Catholics.) The resolution none the less is temporary and the relationship of Protestant Christianity with traditional society remains basically ambiguous. The pastors and the evangelists of the Protestant churches are significant people in rural Imerina. Usually they are more closely associated with Tananarive than the rest of the villagers. They go to meetings in Tananarive and may be in touch or have been in touch with European missionaries. Their houses are likely to contain much of the furniture and ornaments which are bought there. They are likely to be zealous in their desire to exterminate *Malagasy* elements. Indeed, the main message of many Merina sermons is how necessary it is to get rid of old superstitions and practices of whatever kind. Thus the obvious organization for maintaining things *Malagasy*, the Protestant Church, turns out to be in another context their greatest enemy, but by calling the *Malagasy* things when attacked *barbare* again reduces the difficulty. The ambiguous position of the Protestant Church is in fact more of a problem for its officers, pastors and evangelists and their close followers than for their flock. This is because for them the Protestant Church is associated with the traditional past and has had a vested interest for a long time in combating change, which means the encroachment of Roman Catholicism. The Protestant Church is radical and conservative in different contexts and each individual must make his uncomfortable adjustment between these two tendencies.

Education

The difficulty which we have just noted involved in placing the Church and the political parties in the contrast between things *Malagasy* and things *vazaha* also occurs in another field, that of education. Modern education is also regarded by the Merina as an intrusive force, a thing from Tananarive, a source of authority which conflicts with traditional authority. Nevertheless, because it is associated with wisdom in its widest sense, I do not think it is regarded as potentially evil and destructive in the same way as the Merina view other *vazaha* innovations. It is such a source of potential advantage that it cannot be dismissed as simply wicked.

Outline of Merina History

This brief description of the appearance of the people, of the countryside and of Tananarive shows how the present is interpreted in historical terms by the Merina and indeed the purpose of this book is to show the significance of this for social organization. The contrast between *vazaha* and *Malagasy* is a historical one and I now turn to its place in the history of the Merina.

The early history of the Merina is, as might be expected, unclear. The obvious link which the Merina have with peoples on the other side of the Indian Ocean really tells us little. For example, we do not know whether they came alone or with all the other, or at least some of the other, peoples of Madagascar, or which of them came first. The most obvious solution and that suggested by Murdoch (1959) is that the majority of the Malagasy are descendants of a group of Africans of Arab-Bantu ancestry who had already mixed with Indonesian elements on the African coast and who then came over at various times. Sometimes purer African groups came over; at other times purer Indonesian groups came. This ingenious theory, which is similar to that postulated by Deschamps (1961), although clearly attractive, is supported by only very flimsy evidence and still raises many difficulties, one of the main ones being the strength of the Indonesian side of the culture in some parts and the weakness of any other influences. (For another view see Kent, 1968). Whatever the actual case may be, the tradition of many of the "free" groups tells how they arrived from "overseas" on the east coast near the present-day town of Maronsetra and how they moved slowly through the forest towards the central plateau (Ramilison, 1951–52). There are the remains of fortified hill-tops deep into the forest which are said to have been intermediary stopping places of the Merina on their way towards the plateau. These sites are still commemorated at certain ceremonies as are many of the sites of the villages of origin of famous kings, but here again it is difficult to decide just how much significance should be attached to these traditions. It was only when the Merina were clearly established in Imerina that historical traditions began to abound. These have been recorded extensively (Callet, 1878) and the evaluation of all this information would require a book in itself. We have long genealogies of Merina monarchs and petty princes, some of whom appear to have been rulers of all Merina, some of one or a few villages only. The general picture to emerge is that of a very fluid situation in terms of chieftains and kingdoms, restricted to a distinct limited area inhabited by Merina cultivators. However, in spite of the turmoil and discontinuity which existed, a tendency towards greater unification and expansion was emerging. Expansion at this stage was probably principally directed against some previous occupants who are referred to by the traditions as *vazimba*.[1] A name for aborigines to whom supernatural features are often attributed.

It was only during the 17th century that the Merina state as it was to emerge began to appear. The semi-mythical king Ralambo, traditionally buried north of Tananarive in the village of Ambohitrabiby, was clearly a centralizer and unified a great part of traditional Imerina. Significantly he is reported to have been the first Merina king to have obtained guns. In spite of the promise of the kingdom under Ralambo and under his successors Andriamjaka and Andriamasinavalona, it was to divide again. Not until the reign of the legendary and heroic king Andrianampoinimerina can we see the beginning of the type of state which was to enable the Merina to conquer most of Madagascar.

Andrianampoinimerina came to the throne of one of the four petty kingdoms into which Imerina had been divided. His accession, which took place probably in the year 1787 (this is the date accepted by Deschamps, 1961, p. 121), was the result of a minor rebellion. After a period of relative peace[2] Andrianampoinimerina succeeded in conquering and unifying the various people who considered themselves Merina. (The notion of being Merina was probably defined in terms of having previously been part of a unified kingdom and subsequently being ruled by chiefs and kings related among themselves by kinship.)

---

[1] I feel that we should not presume that these people were necessarily very different from other Merina. They might even have been another group of Merina since a Merina deme, the *Antehiroka*, are usually described as *vazimba* but are physically and culturally identical with other Merina. The problem of who or what the *vazimba* were is most complex.

[2] This period is, according to tradition, one of seven years but, quite clearly, because of the significance of the number seven for the Merina this is most unlikely to be accurate.

It is in cultural terms that the Merina were a unit. The Merina shared a unified culture which contrasted with that of most of their neighbours, with the exception of the Betsileo to the south, and they were separated from this people by the Vakinankaratra mountains.

The significance of this is that the Merina nation was not just the result of an accident of conquest. The idea of a cultural unit corresponding to Imerina was clear and well known throughout Madagascar by the 18th century. That the Merina[1] lived in a number of settled groups with a distinctive culture and quite advanced technology whose identity was clear is evident from the writing of the first European to reach Imerina—a Frenchman by the name of Mayeur. This is how he described a market as he saw it in 1777, a time of great political disorganization:

> The present King has created a market in each province for every day of the week. Saturday is market day in the capital. I have briefly mentioned this when describing my arrival. However, I feel it is necessary to return to this topic. A list of the things available will make the reader realize the nature of the crafts practised in this country and what type of people the inhabitants are. Apart from the animals I have mentioned above, we find the following articles: silk in cocoons, silk in yarn, silk in threads, silk dyed and made up into loin cloths and into three kinds of *lamba*, banana fibre cloth, raffia cloth, made of raffia leaves imported from the east coast; iron ore, pig-iron, iron made into spades, axes, knives of all sizes, spear heads; pears from Ambravataeo, white and red apricots, bananas and taro both cooked and uncooked; wood for building, reeds for fencing or for roofs or to burn. Finally, beef is sold in small quantities just as it is in a butcher's shop. This can be obtained from even a 120th part of a thaler if one cannot afford more . . .

This wealth explains what in many ways is a paradox in the Merina's view of the *Malagasy* past. The past was a turbulent story of wars, of successful conquests and of the death of kingdoms. It was also a period when social organization hardly changed, when local groups perpetuated themselves, and when a settled, highly organized agricultural system flourished. In a sense both these points of view are a part of the truth. The affairs of chiefs and kings were largely dominated by the flux of power, but peasant organization continued, in spite of the turbulence of the rulers.

In a somewhat different way this apparent paradox also applies to the reign of Andrianampoinimerina and of his successors. We are particularly fortunate in the amount we know about his reign, though this

---

[1] Early writers do not use the word Merina but other words with similar referent, e.g. Mayeur uses Ankova (the place of the Hova).

is mainly from oral traditions collected twenty or so years later. Naturally the evaluation of this type of information is a difficult task which would need to be undertaken with the care suggested by Vansina (1961). Nevertheless, a general pattern emerges clearly. On the one hand there was great administrative innovation marked by the extension of central government control in Imerina by means of various local delegates (*Vadin-tany*, spouses of the earth) (Callet, 1909, p. 936). On the other hand Andrianampoinimerina seems to have been extremely conservative in policy, only strengthening what were clearly the traditional laws of the Merina by giving them the sanction of force. It has been repeatedly pointed out how Andrianampoinimerina's emphasis on the importance of the *Fokon'olona*, the traditional local councils, was in fact a recognition of the *status quo* (Julien, 1909, p. 298). However, behind Andrianampoinimerina's legislation is clearly the intention not just to maintain what he had found, but to maintain it through his authority. This was thus an attempt to change the source of power behind traditional institutions without changing their form. Thus the *Fokon'olona*, the council formed by the people of a given area to regulate their own affairs for their own convenience, became a council with the same purpose and still administering the same laws but by the authority of Andrianampoinimerina. In fact nothing was changed but an attempt had been made to alter the source of legitimacy of the system (Bloch, 1971). The same pattern is also evident in the way the traditional kinship groupings were handled. Their traditional territory was declared as their own by decree, the traditional rules of marriage were also made the subject of royal decrees (Callet, 1878, p. 710ff). However, there were some innovations. The attempt to define territories was also an attempt to enforce central law within the territory. The adoption of the *Fokon'olona* by the central administration was also such an attempt. Traditionally the *Fokon'olona* mobilized for mutual help and for undertaking work for the benefit of the community. This it continued to do, but because the *Fokon'olona* was seen as acting by the grace of the king, rather than just as a mutual aid association, it became possible for the king to use the *Fokon'olona* for performing tasks for himself. Government service became an important part of the duties of these local associations as they provided both services for the state internally and were mobilized for military service. Andrianampoinimerina's ability to control labour, which was probably the basis of his success, was due to administrative organization and to charismatic leadership. Internally, this authority was used for the organization of irrigation and drainage schemes so as to extend the area where rice could be cultivated. The most spectacular of these hydraulic reforms was the draining of the large plain which surrounds Tananarive on three sides. Indeed, the traditions of Andrianampoini-merina's reign were as much concerned with irrigation works as with foreign wars (Callet, 1878, p. 746). It has been argued by Isnard that the draining of the Tananarive marshes and the rice surplus it produced was the key to the success of Andrianampoinimerina and his successors and explains his ability to support the administrators and soldiers necessary for these tasks (Isnard, 1954).

European Contact

The internal policy of Andrianampoinimerina was conservative in content but radical in the way it was carried out. The external policy by contrast is clearly expansionist and innovatory. It seems unnecessary here to go over the process and history of the conquests of Andrianampoinimerina and his successors; suffice to say that it was the result of a mixture of astute matrimonial alliances, trickery and conquest. The total result was rapid territorial conquest. Under Andrianampoinimerina the territory of Imerina was first expanded to the disputed territory around traditional Imerina, and then the Betsileo to the south were conquered. The military successes of the Merina are perhaps understandable when we consider the technological sophistication of the Mcrina described by Mayeur, together with the administrative sophistication of this reign. There is, however, another factor. The fact that during the reigns of Andrianam-poinimerina and his successor the Merina succeeded in capturing the lucrative trade that was beginning to develop between the island and the external world. This trade was particularly significant in another way because it enabled the Merina to obtain guns, and much of their subse-quent success can be attributed to their control of firearms. This control was a direct result of the channelling of foreign trade through their hands.

Andrianampoinimerina was succeeded by his son Radama I or Lehidama as the Malagasy themselves called him. His reign really marks the beginning of the direct contact of the Merina kingdom with Europe and especially with Britain and France. From this period on we have full documentary information on the administrative and legal aspects of the Merina kingdom until its downfall in 1895. In fact, the very wealth of information we possess makes a detailed description of this period impossible in a study mainly concerned with contemporary Merina culture. I shall limit myself therefore to a summary of the general conclusions of historians which seem particularly relevant here.

The first and most striking aspect of Merina history during that period was the continued expansion of the kingdom along the same lines as those initiated by Andrianampoinimerina. The extraordinary thing about this expansion is its success and extent. By the time of the French conquest, the Merina were in nominal control of almost the whole of Madagascar and in very real control of most of this immense empire. They had established government garrison posts and small trading towns throughout the country. They attempted to tax the whole of their empire either directly or indirectly by means of forced labour. They also established a rudimentary judiciary to deal with disputes between Merina and non-Merina.

This type of administration required an extensive control of new techniques by the Merina which acquired through contact with Europe, especially England and France. During the reign of Radama I the king was visited by various emissaries and missionaries of the two countries and open competition for influence developed and became acute during the whole period until the French conquest. This was, in fact, mixed up with the religious rivalry between the London Missionary Society and the British Protestant missions which followed them, and the Jesuits, who were mainly French. However, as part of the general European influence on the Merina kingdom, the missionaries were to have significant influence. By cleverly playing one side against the other, Radama, and less successfully his successors, managed to obtain considerable technical aid with the minimum loss of sovereignty. A few British and French craftsmen taught the Merina a large number of techniques, from superior iron smelting to new types of architecture. The general impression one gets from this period is of an extremely fast development of arts and crafts which did not produce an industrial economy because the manufactures and skills were used only to produce luxuries for the court and were supported and financed from abroad for what were ultimately political purposes: a type of "prestige help" with which we are more familiar today. It is, however, interesting to note that the "temptation of Tamtalus", which is characteristic of the present-day peasants' relation with Tananarive and the Western goods it contains, has been in existence for a long time in Imerina.

The European influence did not limit itself to industrial techniques. Perhaps one of the most significant innovations was the introduction of the Roman alphabet and the subsequent spread of writing as an administrative tool (Bloch, 1968). In this way it soon became possible to publish written laws and to this end written codes were formulated. This development of administrative techniques was accompanied by a conscious attempt to establish a government with ministers and a Prime Minister after the British model. In fact, at no time was this a realistic attempt in that these "ministers" had no departments, no civil servants etc. Nevertheless, the attempt at this rather slavish imitation shows clearly the influence and prestige of France and England. The army too was given a European terminology with names for ranks derived from the British and French armies. Old uniforms from these armies were in great demand and of course weapons, although the Merina found it difficult to get much in this line from their European "friends".

The extraordinary hold European ideas gained in Imerina during the 19th century and the idolization of all things European is only one side of the picture. During the reign of Radama and more markedly later, two trends of opinion emerged. There was the pro-European trend, whole-heartedly accepting change, trying to imitate closely the manners and beliefs of the Europeans. At the same time there was a reactionary trend clearly fearful of the implications of the growing importance of European cultural values and wanting to return to a past in which it seemed values were clear and defined. The clash of these two trends is revealed by the sequence of events which followed the death of Radama I. These reveal an oscillation between the two reactions to change. Radama I was followed by the reactionary Ranavalona I who for 33 years tried to contain and stem back the European influence whether technical or religious. She was followed by the short reign of Radama II, a puppet of the European Missionary party. The fall and assassination of Radama II is particularly revealing and suggestive of the main subject matter of this book. I quote at length the account given by Sibree of the mass hysteria which was the cause of Radama II's downfall.

The Imanenjana, or Dancing Mania

In the month of February 1863, the Europeans resident at Antananarivo (Tananarive), the capital of Madagascar, began to hear rumours of a new disease, which it was said had appeared in the west or south-west. The name given to it by the natives was *imanenjana*, and the dancers were called *ramanenjana*, which probably comes from a root signifying "to make tense". The name did not convey any idea of its nature, and the accounts given of it were so vague as to mystify rather than enlighten. After a time, however, it reached the capital, and in the month of March began to be common. At first, parties of two or three were to be seen, accompanied by musicians and other attendants, dancing in the public places; and in a few weeks these had increased to hundreds, so that one could not go out-of-doors without meeting bands of these dancers. It spread rapidly, as by a sort of infection, even to the most remote villages in the central province of Imerina; so that, having occasion to visit a distant part of the country in company with an Englishman, we found, even in remote hamlets, and, more wonderful still, near solitary cottages, the sound of music, indicating that the mania had spread even there.

The public mind was in a state of excitement at that time, on account of the remarkable political and social changes introduced by the late king, Radama II. A pretty strong anti-Christian, anti-European party had arisen, who were opposed to progress and change. This strange epidemic got into sympathy, especially in the capital, with this party, and the native Christians had no difficulty in recognizing it as a demoniacal possession. There was universal consternation at the spread of this remarkable disease, and the consternation favoured its propagation.

Those affected belonged chiefly, but not by any means exclusively, to the lower classes. The great majority were young women between fourteen and twenty-five years of age; there were, however, a considerable number of men to be seen amongst the dancers—but they certainly did not exceed one-fourth of the entire number—and these also belonged mostly to the lower orders of society.

Very few, indeed scarcely any, Christians came under this influence; no doubt partly because the general spirit of dissatisfaction and superstitious unrest did not affect them directly. Their sympathies were rather with those changes, political and social, which disturbed the masses. They were, so to speak, beyond the reach of the current. Their exemption may be partly explained by their superior education, mental and moral, but was also very manifestly owing to their firm conviction that the whole affair was a demoniacal possession of their heathen countrymen which could not affect them as Christians. They could thus look at it as outsiders, with the interest of observers, without the fear which, in such a malady, is one of the means of its propagation.

The patients usually complained of a weight or pain in the praecordia, and great uneasiness, sometimes a stiffness, about the nape of the neck. Others, in addition, had pains in the back and limbs, and in most cases there seems to have been an excited state of the circulation, and occasionally even mild febrile symptoms. One or more of these premonitory symptoms were frequently observed; there were numerous cases where they were absent. After complaining, it may be, one, two, or three days, they became restless and nervous, and if excited in any way, more especially if they happened to hear the sound of music or singing, they got perfectly uncontrollable, and, bursting away from all restraint, escaped from their pursuers and joined the music, when they danced, sometimes for hours together, with amazing rapidity. They moved the head from side to side with a monotonous motion, and the hands in the same way, alternately up and down. The dancers never joined in the singing, but uttered frequently a deep sighing sound. The eyes were wild, and the whole countenance assumed an indescribable abstracted expression, as if their attention was completely taken off what was going on around them. The dancing was regulated very much by the music, which was always the quickest possible—it never seemed to be quick enough. It often became more of a leaping than a dancing. They thus danced to the astonishment of all, as if possessed by some evil spirit, and with almost superhuman endurance—exhausting the patience of the musicians, who often relieved each other by turns—then fell down suddenly, as if dead; or, as often happened, if the music was interrupted, they would suddenly rush off as if seized by some new impulse, and continue running, until they fell down, almost or entirely insensible. After being completely exhausted in this way, the patients were taken home, the morbid impulse apparently, in many cases, destroyed. Sometimes the disease thus stopped never recurred, but more frequently there was a return. The sight of dancers, or the sound of music, even in the distance, or anything which, by association, seemed connected with the disease, determined a recurrence of the fit.

The patients were fond of carrying sugarcanes about with them. They held them in their hands, or carried them over the shoulder while they danced. Frequently, too, they might be seen going through their singular evolutions with a bottle of water upon their heads, which they succeeded wonderfully in balancing. The drum was the favourite instrument, but others were used, and all were acceptable. When there was no musical instrument to be had, the attendants beat time with their hands, or sung a tune which was a favourite amongst the *ramanenjana*. There is a sacred stone in a plain below the city, where many of the kings of Madagascar have been crowned. This stone was a favourite rendezvous for them. They danced there for hours together, and concluded by placing the sugarcane, as a sort of offering, upon the stone.

The tombs were also favourite places of resort for these dancers. They met in the evenings, and danced by moonlight for half the night, or longer, amongst the graves.

Many of them professed to have intercourse with the departed, and more particularly with the late queen. In describing their sensations afterwards some said that they felt as if a dead body was tied to them, so that with all their efforts they could not shake themselves clear of it; others thought that there was a heavy weight continually dragging them downwards or backwards. They disliked, above all things, hats and pigs. The very sight of these objects was so offensive that, in some cases, it threw them into a kind of convulsion that more frequently excited their rage. Still more inexplicable was their dislike of every article of dress of a black colour. Swine are reckoned unclean by several tribes in Madagascar, and might thus be an object of superstitious horror. Hats, as associated with foreigners, might similarly be objected to; but what is there in a colour to excite antipathy? Yet this caprice has been so common in this disease, in all its recorded epidemics, as to deserve attention. This phenonemon was likewise observed in the child pilgrimages of the thirteenth century, which, towards the end, began to assume some of the characteristics of choreomania.

1870, pp. 561–564

This description is remarkable as an eye-witness missionary account both in its accuracy and its insight. What Sibree fails to make clear is that the dancers apparently believed they were preparing for the return of the recently dead traditionalist queen, Ranavalona, whose determined anti-European anti-Christian stance has earned her the opprobrium of Western historians. The dancers believed they were carrying her baggage from the coast to the capital and they mimed carrying heavy loads which they passed one to the other in relay.

It would be difficult to demonstrate that this sort of outbreak was a direct result of the pressure of European culture. Probably this type of "hysteria" was endemic and may have occurred before European contact.[1] The preponderance of young women suggests the presence of other factors. However, the fact remains clear that, as Sibree saw it, this movement was both a reaction *against* and a reaction *to* foreign cultures. The movement was avowedly anti-Christian and it looked back to the anti-Christian, reactionary queen, Ranavalona. The movement was also clearly revivalist involved as it was with the "idols" the missionaries were continually attacking, with the past of the monarchy, a past which was necessarily glorious, and finally and most significantly, it emphasized those remarkable outcrops of the past the standing stones and the tombs which have already been mentioned.

Such a movement immediately brings to mind similar movements throughout the world where strikingly similar details recur (e.g. Harris, 1957), but it also recalls the famous cargo cults and other millenarian cults which it has often been convincingly argued are closely linked to violent foreign contact. In this case, however, the somewhat surprising element is the absence of any clear leaders of any kind, and perhaps the closest parallel is therefore with the ghost dancers of North America.

The significant aspect of the movement is the combination of the frenzied situation, reaffirmation of the past, the focus on tombs and the dead and the total rejection of Western influences. This element has become, in an institutionalized form, an essential aspect of the cults of the dead which form the main focus here, and I would suggest that the diachronic alternation between periods of total uncritical acceptance of new ideas followed by periods of attempted ritual rejection has, as we

---

[1] During my period of field work, I heard several reports of mass hysteria, some at girls' schools which led to their closing. In particular, an epidemic supposed to have been caused by a certain medicine, *Ambalavelona*, had spread into north Imerina from the Sihanaka country. As I was able to observe it, it was somewhat different in its symptoms from *Imanenjana* in that it only involved shaking, muttering and fits; it did not involve dancing or any group activity. It also mainly affected women. I only came across two first-hand cases of this disease and the type of explanation advanced by I. Lewis in *Spirit Possession and Deprivation Cults*, 1966, seems very reasonable in the circumstances.

shall see, its synchronic parallel in present-day Merina social organization.

The final aspect of the pre-1895 history of the mania which is particularly relevant here is the more specifically religious influence of the
missionaries. British missionaries from the London Missionary Society
first established themselves in Imerina in 1820 and were soon to obtain
great influence. They were followed by other Christian Churches,
especially the Catholics, who increased in number after the French conquest.

The Missionaries

The first LMS missionaries arrived during the reign of Radama I,
Andrianampoinimerina's son, and made a number of converts. Radama
encouraged them and was very anxious that they taught as many technical skills as possible. Later, during the reign of Ranavalona I (1828–
1861) came the period of reaction against European influence. The
Christians were persecuted and there were martyrs. The Protestant
Church was encouraged again after Ranavalona's reign, and her successors became Christian. From 1862 on, Protestantism was the official
religion of the Merina kingdom. The existence of Malagasy martyrs,
and the fact that Christianity is associated with the Merina kings,
explains why Protestantism is now thought of as a truly Merina institution. It is an integral part of Merina culture and has been modified to
fit in with this culture.

The other significant missionary influence, the Roman Catholics,
came later and was always associated with the French party at the court
in the way the LMS, the Anglicans and the Quakers were associated
with the British party. At first Roman Catholic missionaries were
mainly successful among the slaves and the subject peoples of the Merina.
It is only since the French conquest that their numbers have increased
among the free Merina. The Roman Catholic religion, however, still
remains more of a foreign implantation than Protestantism, because it
lacks the latter's association with the old monarchy, because of its association with the colonial period, and because, unlike the Protestant clergy,
most of the Catholic priests are still European. Probably the association of
the French and the Roman Catholics is something of an illusion as many
governors were firmly anti-religious (Thompson and Adloff, 1965). None
the less, the French administration often favoured the Roman Catholics,

partly because the French saw the Roman Catholics as a way of combating British influence which they identified (again not altogether justifiably) with the British missionaries. From the point of view of the ordinary Merina, the position is clear even to this day. LMS means the British and the tradition of the Merina kingdom; the Roman Catholic Church means the French. It is hardly surprising that the refinements of the relationships between governments and missionaries by and large escape them. In other words, the old opposition of traditional versus Protestant Christianity has become transformed in one of its manifestations into a Protestant–Catholic opposition.

The early missionaries directed their energies partly towards social reforms, of which the most notable was the attempt to abolish slavery, and partly towards more strictly religious matters. The religious innovations of the missionaries were really of three kinds: first, they tried to eradicate certain non-Christian beliefs; secondly, they took over some non-Christian concepts from traditional Merina religion and interpreted them in a Christian way; thirdly, they introduced completely new beliefs.

The principal Merina belief which the missionaries felt they had to remove was the cult of "idols". These "idols" (*sampy*) seem to have been powerful "medicines" of the kind common throughout Africa. The missionaries were almost completely successful in eliminating them.[1]

Apart from the few aspects of traditional religion on which they waged a frontal attack, the missionaries tried to modify and assimilate other Merina beliefs in order to make them acceptable to Christians. The Merina always had an idea of a high God, one name for which was Andriamanitra.[2] Merina notions about him were very vague and the missionaries felt able to use his name for their God. The Merina also had a belief in three "souls" the life of which continued after death. One of these, the *fanahy*, was identified with the Christian soul, and again the English word "soul" was translated as "*fanahy*" in the Malagasy Bible and Prayer Book.[3]

Finally, the missionaries introduced completely new concepts and

---

[1] On these idols see R. F. Callet, 1908, p. 173ff. For the missionary attitude towards them see J. Sibree, *Madagascar and its People*, 1870, p. 373ff.

[2] The name means "the fragrant God", or possibly "the God of the heavens" (W. E. Cousins, "The ancient theism of the Hova", *Antananarivo Annual*, Christmas 1875, and H. Dubois, "L'idee de Dieu chez les anciens Malgaches", *Anthropos*, 1929, 1934).

[3] See Chapter 4.

supernatural beings. These are completely accepted by the Merina peasants, but they seem to have little importance for them. For example, in the numerous prayers and graces I heard offered by ordinary people I never heard Christ mentioned once.

Despite the changes brought about by the missionaries, some ideas about the supernatural were unaffected. Certain non-Christian beliefs like witchcraft, astrology, and some aspects of the cult of the dead, are not thought incompatible with Christianity by the ordinary believer. Most of the Merina consider these things as so obviously real and valuable that it is difficult for them to imagine anybody not believing in them.

Christianity has come to Imerina in a gradual way and the fact that such words as Andriamanitra and *fanahy* were adopted by the missionaries means that for many people there is no sharp break between the beliefs of the ancestors and those of today. To the Merina Christianity is not something foreign which conflicts with traditional values. This explains how many Merina can describe Protestantism as "the religion of our ancestors"—in other words, something truly our own.

The French Conquest

After the coming of Christianity another element essential for our understanding of present-day Merina culture is the effect of contact with Europeans during the colonial period. This contact involved humiliation at the hands of the bearers of the culture which the Merina were in the process of accepting of their own accord because of its technical superiority. The French conquest of 1895 was surprisingly easy for reasons which are closely related to the state of the Merina empire at the time. At first the French attempted a protectorate, but the revolts which followed shortly after decided the French to adopt a policy of direct rule which continued throughout the century. The revolts, spontaneous and disorganized as they were, were clearly from one point of view a manifestation of the familiar traditionalist aspect of Merina culture which we already saw in the revolt against Radama II and which was to break out again with perhaps redoubled violence in 1947. The rebels in the years following the French occupation were called *fahavalo*. They took traditional oaths, restored "idols" and are now referred to as the "*mena lamba*", a red cloth which is also the name for shrouds, the giving of which is central to the tomb cult. Like their predecessors they not only stressed the non-Christian past and identified themselves with *Malagasy* culture but they were actively anti-Christian, murdering missionaries and converts. They believed that the conquest of the French was due to the insidious Westernization which had preceded it and the fall from the values of the ancestors. In 1897 Matthews, a Protestant catechist who had been captured by these *fahavalo*, described his experience, bringing out quite clearly the revolt's revivalist character. He quotes a leader of the *fahavalo* as saying, "The customs of our ancestors are to be followed, for the new religion is to be put down, the 'charms' are to be brought out, the idols set up and the hymns of adoration to our forefathers sung." Later he described the rebel camp: "There was dancing and singing in honour of all the different 'sacred symbols' in the camp and enquiries were made of all of them before going out to fight, or undertaking any important business . . ."

In spite of the Merina inspiration of this rebellion, they continued to keep their educational advantage over the rest of the country after the French conquest. During this period they established themselves in the various professions open to Malagasys and also in the civil service. However, they also remained the leaders of anti-French opposition and were extensively involved in the dramatic anti-colonial revolt of 1947 which was crushed with unparalleled brutality. The violence and political significance of the 1947 rebellion is so great that no account of Madagascar can ignore it. It probably ranks as the world's most bloody colonial repression, but in spite of its political character the same reactionary romantic element which was so clear in the rebellions under Radama II and after the French conquest can be seen again. Virginia Thompson and Richard Adloff, in their history of Madagascar, describe this element in the following terms:

> The malcontents were inspired in part by the same pagan and zenophobic emotions as had dominated the *fahavalo* movement in 1896. Some of the rebel bands, particularly in the forest zone, were led by fanatical sorcerers, who convinced their ignorant followers that the ancestors wanted them to destroy all agents and purveyors of modern change, and gave them amulets guaranteed to turn bullets into harmless drops of water. To this unleashing of primitive violence can be attributed the wholesale murder of officials, doctors, teachers, and the like, regardless of colour of skin.
>
> p. 55

Again we have the same elements of rejection of foreign innovations and a turn to the supposed values of the past accompanied, though this is not stated here, with a renewal of "traditional" tomb customs.

The 1947 rebellion proved fatal for the Merina. The French government's answer to what it chose to see as a Merina-inspired revolt was a deliberate turning away from the Merina on whom they had previously relied and the giving of greater power to the representatives of the peoples who had previously been subject to the Merina. This was not only a clever political move; it was easily justifiable on democratic grounds. For the Merina, however, the humiliation of conquest was made worse by the nature of the blow. After 1947 the Merina still held many of the most lucrative posts of the country but they had lost all political power. Naturally in such a situation their glorious past became all the more desirable. Their place in traditional society became of special value.

Independence

Madagascar gained her independence in 1960. It is perhaps as yet too soon to evaluate what this will mean for the Merina. It must be remembered, however, that independence has not meant the return of Merina domination. Although the present government contains leading Merina members its composition is primarily non-Merina. To some Merina this appears as the continuation of the humiliation of the colonial period.

Vazaha and *Malagasy*

The foregoing description shows in outline the historical basis of the *vazaha-Malagasy* contrast or the traditional versus innovating interpretation of events and things, but it also shows its shifting referent. Under Radama I the contrast is between innovation and tradition and especially Christianity and *Malagasy* beliefs. Then it transforms itself into a contrast between two parties at the Merina court, associated respectively with Britain and France. Then it is a contrast between Protestantism and Catholicism, only to become a contrast between colonial status and the independence of the past. It is therefore not surprising that an apparently clear conceptual contrast has become in many of its applications situational—and that it has acquired numerous accretions of meaning which we are now in a position to understand better.

The importance of the contrast can be seen in nearly every aspect of life, but we can exemplify it best perhaps by the classification of domestic plants and animals. Nearly all agricultural products have one species which is *Malagasy* and another *vazaha*. Usually, as might be expected, the believed introductions are *vazaha* while the plants believed to be aboriginal are *Malagasy*. Thus the pineapples, peanuts, rice, potatoes, chickens and most other plants and animal breeds which are qualified as *vazaha* are indeed recent introductions. This is significant because it is clear that, although in discussing the distinction I am discussing a folk category, it contains a very large element of historical truth. However, it is also significant that this classification is not always historically accurate. For example, *Malagasy* cattle and *vazaha* cattle are in fact both pre-European introductions. We are thus able to ask why species of cattle should be so distinguished and what are the principles behind this classification. The first point to notice is that *Malagasy* cattle, like all things *Malagasy*, are smaller. But, as is usually also the case, they are believed to be tougher and more resistant to disease and their meat is more tasty. Clearly, however, it is not primarily things but people who are *vazaha*, and foremost a European or rather white-skinned person, since the Chinese are included in the category. A thing is *vazaha* because it is remotely associated with Europeans or foreigners. However, *vazaha* has another shade of meaning; it means clever or *crafty*—a quality which is typical of Europeans and which is more feared than admired. A Malagasy can describe another as *vazaha* to mean that he is "dangerously full of tricks". Associated with this view of modern foreign influences is the belief that the Europeans and those who are like them in their attitudes, their way of dressing, their houses and their possessions, are *kamo*, a word which is usually translated as "lazy" but which is used by the peasants to mean rather someone who does not fulfill his traditional duties; that is, someone who does not work hard at the traditional agricultural tasks and someone who does not fulfill his kinship obligations. This was brought home to me by a father who described his son to me as *kamo*, although his son was, in fact, employed by the government in road building, an employment which is far from a sinecure; he was *kamo* because he did not work on his father's farm at rice cultivation. The *vazaha* therefore get their wealth by trickery rather than honest toil but there is no doubt in the peasant's mind that they obtain very desirable wealth in this way. Radios, bicycles, matches, kerosene lamps, etc. are highly desirable, but they are also perverted articles.

Perhaps the ambiguity of the relationship of the Merina peasant to *vazaha* goods is best expressed by the belief in "heart thieves" (*mpakafo*) or "blood thieves" (*mpakara*) which *vazaha* are universally believed to be. Europeans are typical heart thieves. At night they suddenly steal the heart or blood of any person, preferably a child, to feed themselves. The heart and the blood are the sources of power and life and in this way the European increases his own power by dreadful means at the expense of the Merina. The similarity of this idea with certain cargo cult beliefs is striking (Worsley, 1957). The Europeans possess goods and power while the Malagasy do not. The ordinary man can see no apparent reason for this. The Merina feels he has been cheated, as, in a way, he has been. The European is enjoying pleasures to which he has no right. By having more than his share, the European is detracting from the enjoyment of the Merina, but how or why he does this is inexplicable. It is easy to see how in such a situation the fantasy of the European stealing the very heart and life blood of the Merina can arise. What is interesting, however, is that the belief that people are heart thieves is rapidly being expanded to include many Malagasy and, revealingly, these are government officials and Westernized Malagasy who have obtained, or so it seems to the peasant, the mysterious unpredictable power of the European. The signs which distinguish the heart thieves are revealing; black beard, blue eyes, large dogs, all of which are typical of Europeans. There are also such things as Western suits, homburg hats, glasses, cameras, motor-cars, tape recorders, which are outward signs of a heart thief, but are more typical of the Malagasy heart thief. An indicative insight into the meaning of this notion was given to me by a Malagasy who went into one of the European supermarkets which have appeared in Tananarive. "I saw the shiny white floor, so clean, so flat, so smooth . . . that is the sort of time when I know that these people are heart thieves." The apparent *non sequitur* can be accounted for by the fact that the informant was somewhat inebriated at the time, but the juxtaposition of ideas suggests a deeper unformulated logic.

Ancestral Villages and the Present

What *vazaha* stands for to the peasant is an inevitable force which affects his life characteristically in ways which are largely incomprehensible. This fantastic power and wealth is a source of anxiety upsetting what the peasant sees as his society, yet this power and wealth is also immensely desirable and seems obtainable in part through European-like behaviour and by the purchase and control of manufactured goods. The Merina see themselves as faced by choices necessitated by two styles of life, one *vazaha* and the other *Malagasy*, but this does not mean that the actual situation is life according to *Malagasy* ancestral principles or *vazaha* principles. It is not even a simple mixture of these two elements. It is something new created by the actors having both systems of value in mind. Yet the existence of a belief in a "good" life associated with the *Malagasy* past and the belief that change, ultimately caused by foreign influences, has seduced the present-day Merina away from this "good" life, is a basic premiss for understanding the way in which the people act, and this is what we must study. However, the contrast is so basic that we must limit our study of this belief in one way. All Merina actions are interpreted in terms of traditional versus non-traditional criteria, but this is in many cases difficult to demonstrate. There is, however, one aspect of life of prime concern to the Merina where actions directed towards traditional values and those not so directed are separated in a way which simplifies description and invites analysis. That is, action directed towards ancestral villages and tombs and action directed towards the place where one lives. As we shall see, very few Merina live in the villages which they consider to be their ancestral villages and consequently the contrast between the *Malagasy* traditional way of life and the compromise of ordinary living becomes a geographical contrast between where one lives and one's ancestral village. By seeing what is involved in "belonging" to an ancestral village and in "belonging" to a village where one lives we can see the use made by Merina villagers of the basic historical contrast with which they explain their lives and which has governed their recent past. We must therefore turn briefly to the history of Merina migration away from ancestral villages in order to focus on the meaning of "traditional *Malagasy*" society as it exists for the present-day Merina peasant.

The pacification of Imerina by Andrianampoinimerina led almost immediately to territorial expansion. Andrianampoinimerina established fortresses around Imerina to protect it from surrounding peoples. As a result farmers left Imerina and began to cultivate lands which had up till then been unsafe. The conquest of other tribes also led to the placing of garrisons and administrators who were joined by small colonies of farmers who settled in the new areas. The greatest movements of population, however, were a result of the French conquest. Although the actual coming of the French was marked by little fighting, it will be recalled that this was followed by a series of rebellions which were severely repressed. These rebellions led to great movements of population, as people fled from the French soldiers and bands of rebels to more remote districts (Hellot, 1900, and Deschamps, 1962, pp. 233–234). Then came the freeing of the slaves in 1896. Many of these had to leave their masters' villages as they possessed no land there and were thus obliged to find land elsewhere (Cousins, 1899). Their masters, deprived of their labour, also left to take up the cultivation of cash crops, such as vanilla, sugarcane, etc. in areas outside Imerina, the climate of Imerina being unsuitable for the cultivation of such crops. Epidemics of plague also played a part in dislocating Merina society. Moreover, the Merina, because of their early contact with the missionaries, were the most educated group in Madagascar. The French therefore used them as administrators of all kinds, and their success in trade and the professions led to territorial dispersal. Finally the pull of Tananarive further dislocated Merina society. The result of these various factors is that today only a minority of Merina live in the villages of their ancestors.

Professor H. Deschamps, in a study of population movements in Madagascar,[1] gives a figure of 171 479 as the number of Merina living outside the province of Tananarive. This, however, represents only a small proportion of those living in new lands because of the fact that the province of Tananarive is very much larger than traditional Imerina. The province, of course, includes Tananarive itself, most of whose 156 463 Merina inhabitants are living away from the irancestral villages. Finally, many of the Merina who still live in the traditional area do not in fact live in their "own" villages. It is difficult to give an exact figure for the dislocation of Merina society as a whole and this is further complicated by the fact that there is great variation in this respect from village to village. In one of the villages of old Imerina which I studied, out of a population of 92 only four "white" people were in what they considered as their "ancestral" village. This is in no way exceptional and I am quite sure that it is safe to say that the majority of "white" Merina live away from their "ancestral" village.

Nevertheless, the "ancestral" structure of Merina society is anchored in an arrangement of localities associated with kinship groupings. This means that people feel they "belong" to the place from which their particular kinship group originated; a man feels he "belongs" to the place from which he or one of his immediate ancestors came. As we

---

[1] The figures on which this book is based are the official ones of the Government of Madagascar.

shall see this is the place where his family tomb is and where he will therefore be buried. Social movement has meant, as has already been noted, that the majority of Merina now live away from their "original" localities. These localities are called in Malagasy *tanindrazana*, which is normally translated as "the land of the ancestors".[1] The individuals who live away from their *tanindrazana* are described as *voanjo*, a word which in this context means "seeds".

To make the position of the *voanjo* clear I shall limit my analysis to a community where everybody is a *voanjo*. This is the area centred on the village of Ambatomanoina in the canton of the same name (see Map 1). Before the coming of the Merina it seems to have been a base for bands of Sihanaka marauders who have now completely disappeared. I have also limited the scope of this study to the Merina of "white" descent, although they form only half of the population. These are, by and large, the descendants of the free Merina, andriana and hova, and exclude the descendants of slaves,[2] although these represent a very significant proportion of the population of the area.[3] Although much of what follows applies equally to the ex-slaves, their somewhat different history and customs, especially marriage rules, mean that they have to be excluded for the sake of clarity.

The problem of the relation of the *voanjo* to their *tanindrazana* and to the place where they live is of basic importance to all Merina, since in a situation such as this there are two foci of action; first, the local community where the individual lives, and secondly, the *tanindrazana*. As a member of a *tanindrazana*, a Merina is part of a wider social system, which is thought of as a system of the ancestors, where he acts according to Malagasy custom. The kinship system is joined to the territorial system of traditional Imerina. The relevant aspects of this are discussed in Chapter 2. The Merina describe the system as the *fomban-drazana*," the customs of the ancestors", or the *fomba gasy*, "*Malagasy* custom". Because of this notion of the special "rightness" of the society of the *razana*, "ancestors", the present situation (Chapter 3), regulated by

---

[1] The word is discussed at greater length in Chapter 4.

[2] This is an over simplification, since there were in the past "white" slaves and "black" freemen. These, however, were a minority and by now the ex-slave "whites" are rapidly becoming assimilated in the "free white" population. Similarly, the black "freemen" and the descendants of slaves are now almost completely mixed.

[3] In the village of Ambatomanoina itself the proportion of *fotsy* to *mainty* households was 86 to 50. In the smaller villages the proportion of *mainty* was higher.

practical considerations which result from the intrusion of the *vazaha* element, is compared with the past.

As we shall see, this mental comparison leads to two different kinds of social action. The first of these leads the *voanjo* to identify himself in ritual and religious terms ever more closely with his *tanindrazana,* which he does in order to compensate for his separation from *Malagasy* things in everyday life. (This is described in Part 2.) The second kind of action consists in attempts to make the new societies in the area where he lives more traditionally *Malagasy.* This he does by trying to recreate new valued localities associated with kinship groups similar to those he has left behind. (The process is discussed in Part 3.) However, as will become clear, these two ways of acting are, in fact, contradictory. This is because identification with the *tanindrazana* means a certain separation from the place where one lives, and a ritual valuation of the place where one lives implies a separation from the *tanindrazana.* In other words, when I consider the pull of the old *tanindrazana* and the making of new *tanindrazana* I am considering the relation of two opposing forces.

In this way, by looking at the opposing pull of the *tanindrazana*, the land of the dead and of the ancestors, and of the place where a man lives I am not only considering the typical position of most Merina, but the evaluation of traditional versus non-traditional ways of action in a situation which naturally crystallizes both. By stressing the contradiction of this conservative tendency in a totally new situation I am explaining yet further innovations.

2

The Society of the Ancestors

This chapter deals with the values which the Merina consider as truly
Malagasy and which are therefore seen by them as those which regulated
the life of the ancestors (*razana*) in *Malagasy* times. I shall deal mainly
with those values concerned with social organization, not because I consider them, as many social anthropologists seem to, as having special
priority, but because social organization is here my main concern.

Certain types of values and concepts are classified as being of the
razana. In many ways it can be said that the *desirable* for the Merina is by
that very fact "of the *razana*". The values of the ancestors are moral
values and should not be modified by the actors because of the contin-
gencies of any situation. These primarily moral values, such as who is the
right person to marry, may be accompanied by practical explanations.
For example, the preference for marriage among kinsmen is explained
by the need to keep land rights inside the family. This, however, does
not mean that we can treat this type of value as resulting from a
particular believed function. If an individual can devise a more efficient
way of keeping land rights within the family, or has no land rights to
keep within the family, he will be just as much under an obligation and
marry in the preferred manner. In this way, when examining the
"ancestral" rules of social organization, it is not too much to say that all
clearly formulated concepts of social behaviour are classified as of the
razana. The hallowing of values by describing them as being "of the
ancestors" is a common feature of many cultures, but in Imerina for,
those Merina who live away from their ancestral village (the majority)

being "of the ancestors" means not only distance in time but also distance in space, because the anchoring of the individual to a particular place (his *tanindrazana*) in traditional Imerina is, as we shall see, an essential part of this system. This means that the concepts we are concerned with in this chapter are "from the ancestors when they were living in traditional Imerina".

These concepts are expressed either in statements or rules, but they are distinguished from other statements by the authoritative weight they are given and by their traditional formulation. To know these rules and to understand these concepts is to have "traditional" social wisdom. My informants understood immediately when I enquired about this type of belief, and were not surprised that I should find these rules of interest. This contrasted sharply with their surprise at my interest in actual happenings. The rules are part of the wisdom which marks out elders and which entitles a person to respect (Bloch, 1968). Everyone is anxious to learn about these things as knowing about them is one of the signs that one is a "wise man". Not only is this type of belief a recognized part of wisdom, but also the way these rules are expressed is different from the way other behaviour is described. Obtaining an idea of what happened on an occasion when I was not present was a difficult and never totally satisfactory process. The fact that my interest about the event did not correspond with the interest of my informants was only too apparent. By contrast, information about the ancestral way of behaving was elicited without difficulty in easily formulated statements, which had clearly been many times repeated. This formalization went so far that my enquiries in this field could often be answered by proverbs, "words of the ancestors" (*tenin-drazana*), which often were given the added authority of being believed to have been spoken by a Merina king, usually Andrianampoinimerina.

As field work progressed my attitude to this well-formulated social theory completely transformed itself. At first the ease with which this information could be obtained, especially from suitable "wise men", seemed to make the process of field work particularly easy. Then came a period of reaction when I realized that the social theory was completely different from what I observed was happening. My tendency was then to ignore these ancestral values and assume that even though they might once have been relevant they certainly were not any more. It was only later that I realized that however different the ancestral rules were from what was actually happening, it was only when seen within the framework of meaning of this traditional social theory that the social action witnessed became completely understandable. In other words, obeying or deviating from the ancestral system was how the actors saw what was happening, and the fact that this was how they saw it significantly affected their actions. In this book I am, in a sense, following the development of my field-work attitude. This chapter is concerned with the social theory associated with *Malagasy* times and the ancestors. The next describes the situation in the village where I worked, ignoring as far as possible the framework of traditional social theory, while the rest of the book illustrates the relation of the traditional system to what actually happens. In this chapter I am not concerned with how, in fact, these rules or values are translated into actions—which will be the subject matter of the following chapters—but only with what these rules and values are.

The "custom of the ancestors" consists of a series of beliefs. These beliefs are not independent of each other, yet their interconnectedness is more at the level of logic than of action, which means that the social system which they imply may not be able to *work*. Having said this, it would be unnecessarily cynical to consider the classification of certain values as being "of the ancestors" as just a cultural phenomenon of no historical significance, only to be explained as the result of a type of systematization. Just as with the classification of agricultural products where by and large those products described as "*Malagasy*" are aboriginal while those described as *vazaha* are recent introductions, so the placing of rules by the actors in a historical context is not without foundation. The modes of behaviour which the Merina peasants refer to as "of the ancestors" can often be attested to have been the accepted practice before the coming of the French. This can be checked against what old people remember was the case, or against some of the independent evidence found in the relatively abundant writings of missionaries who lived and worked in Imerina before the coming of the French. Also, since the peasants' explanation of the rules they classify as being ancestral refer to well attested historical facts, such as the existence of the Merina kingdom, it would be ridiculous to completely ignore the historical perspective. I have therefore, where possible, supported the description of the actors' concept of the past with historical references. In order to keep data about the past obtained from informants separate from the data obtained from independent sources, the present tense will be used for those rules of the *razana* which are felt to apply today and the past for information which is corroborated by independent evidence.[1]

Three kinds of material will therefore be used. Firstly, material obtained either directly from informants' statements or from deductions which follow logically from such statements. This is really the basis of this chapter and I shall try to show how the material for these categories was obtained. Secondly, I shall supplement and try to illustrate informants' statements by my own observations in cases where traditional rules were being followed and particularly in isolated areas of old Imerina where, because of historical circumstances, the traditional system appears to correspond to what happens better than elsewhere (e.g. Ambatomainty in the Canton of Sadabe where migration seems to have been relatively less—see Map 3). Thirdly, I shall refer to already published works on Madagascar with historical value whenever they seem relevant.[2] (These include both works based on oral traditions which add to the information I have collected myself and descriptive works by writers who knew Imerina either in the 19th century or the early part of the 20th century.)[3]

As we saw in the previous chapter, it can be said that in a way Merina society up to the time of Andrianampoinimerina seems to have been a kind of double society. There was a society of robber barons with bands of retainers living on fortified hilltops ruling over "kingdoms" composed of only a few villages. This really meant that a kind of "protection" system was operated and villages protected by rivals were pillaged. The rulers and their territories were extremely impermanent as is made clear in *Tantaran'ny Andriana* (Callet, 1908).

Their small scale is also perfectly evident from their proximity one to another. Perhaps their nature is most apparent from the position of the remains of their headquarters. High up on easily defensible hills, these

---

[1] As a historical study the following description also has some limitations. It is only a partial picture of the past. This is because only certain aspects of the past are of interest to the modern Merina. It does not follow that these aspects were the most important in the past. Indeed, there is a particular reason why the emphasis we find now differs from the one which existed in the past; the double nature of Merina society under its monarchs. This has been discussed in: G. Condominas, *Fokon'olona et Collectivités Rurales en Imerina*, 1960. F. Arbrousset, *Le Fokon'olona à Madagascar*, 1950. The administrative structure of Imerina is described in: G. Julien, *Institutions Politiques et Sociales de Madagascar*, 1909.

[2] I have discussed these sources in more detail elsewhere (Bloch, 1967).

[3] A large collection of oral traditions gathered by R. P. Callet under the title *Tantaran'ny Andriana*, 1908.

are places where settled residence and agriculture would be very difficult. The "barons" were replaced by a unified kingdom under Andrianampoinimerina and his successors (1787–1896). During this time the political organization of Imerina became more and more bureaucratic.

The petty rulers and the kings who followed them form one side of Merina society. In pre-colonial accounts we also hear of other groupings which are not so directly connected with the administrative system, such groupings as the Tsimiamboholahy, the Mandiavato, the Zanakandriambe etc., and here it is clear that we are dealing with a peasant organization separate from that of kings and rulers.[1] It is not surprising therefore that the concepts and values which we shall consider here, in so far as they have any historical significance, relate to the peasant society. Such a turbulent society as that of the rulers does not lend itself to the formulation of ancestral rules of behaviour in any but the most general terms. Furthermore, rules derived from such a society would have little relevance to a possible application to the present-day situation of the Merina peasant. The association of the past with the political systems of the past is, however, significant in another way. Because of the very real glory of the Merina past and its exaggeration through the passage of time, the rules of the society of the ancestors have all the more prestige even though these might have had little to do with such things as Radama's conquests.

Groupings and Social Categories

Apart from the fundamental division between ex-slaves and ex-freemen the Merina further divide themselves into different kinds of people. These "kinds" of people are named by the same names as those peasant groupings of historical times which we have just mentioned, e.g. Tsimiamboholahy, Mandiavato, Zanakandriambe, and the present Merina consider themselves as the contemporary representatives of these groups which they know have existed in the past for a long time and which they consider as "never dying".

---

[1] Repeatedly in *Tantaran'ny Andriana* it is made to seem that these groupings were created by various kings, especially Andrianampoinimerina (p. 732ff). Such a creation of kinship groups is clearly impossible, except in special cases like the voronmahery, individuals specially selected to people Tananarive, and the valonzatolahy, the descendants of a garrison. This is an example of a stylistic convention in Merina tradition which personalizes institutions making them innovations of great men—for example, the attribution of the introduction of the eating of beef to Ralambo.

These divisions are not as such a frequent topic of conversation. Indeed, there is a certain avoidance of mentioning them. The reason seems to be that these divisions imply, in a certain context at least, differences in rank, while most activity is carried out irrespective of these distinctions and presupposes either a different type of ranking or equality. For example, if, in terms of traditional groupings, A has precedence over B but A and B want to go on a trading expedition together, they will both naturally and studiously avoid any reference to their traditional allegiance. This would of course be much the same if B was in a superior relationship to A if, for example, B was employing A in paid work. However, even if these traditional allegiances are not often referred to, they are very well known. I had no difficulty in obtaining names of groupings for all descendants of free men in the area where I worked, either from them or their acquaintances. In fact I was often told by informants of people living in such and such a village that they belonged to a particular group when they did not even know the peoples' names and had never met them. Apart from this near universal knowledge of other people's traditional group membership there was also a certain amount of malicious gossip suggesting that although a certain person decided to belong to a certain group he was only "half" a member of that group, since one of his parents or grandparents did not belong to it.

At the beginning of my period of field work I was embarrassed in discussing this group membership, not only because of the easily sensed avoidance of the topic but also because of the difficulty of using a word to refer to these groupings. Some writers on Madagascar who refer to these groupings use the word *foko* (e.g. Condominas) and translate it as "clan", but my informants did not understand the word *foko* in this sense and only seemed to use the word in church hymns for nation or in the compound, *fokon'olona*, which roughly means "local community" (see p. 19 and Bloch, 1971). It was only when I began to use the word *karazana* that I was understood and got the information I wanted. The word *karazana* means "kind" in the sense that I could explain porridge as being "a kind of rice". It also means "species" and can be used for an animal or a plant species. Etymologically it is formed from the word *razana* which in this sense means ancestor or forebear. To ask what *karazana* a person is means, therefore, asking what kind of species he is or what kind of descendance he has; the two ideas are inseparably linked by the notion that everything breeds its own kind. The importance of understanding what this word means is that it shows how fundamental a quality is seen to be denoted by the traditional category. It is almost as if the concept is so fundamental that it is hardly worth discussing.

Although as a tactless anthropologist I often enquired directly about people's *karazana*, the Merina themselves would normally avoid such a direct reference, at least in front of the person concerned. Nevertheless, occasions do occur when they want to discuss people's *karazana*, when they do not already know it. As explained in greater detail in Chapter 4, they do this by a detour. Instead of asking what kind of person the other is they try to find out what is his ancestral village—his *tanindrazana*. The reason why this reveals a person's *karazana* is because the various types of groupings which are so described have also a local referent in traditional Imerina. In other words traditional Imerina is believed to have been, and was, according to independent evidence, divided into areas associated with traditional groupings of persons. Nowadays the village which an individual considers as his *tanindrazana* is in such an area and therefore identifies him with the grouping associated with the area in which the village is situated. From our historical evidence we can also assume that until the very violent population movements of this century referred to in the previous chapter, the association of group with territory was stronger than it is today and generally the members of a particular group actually lived in the territory with which they were associated. Anyway, this is what the Merina believe and old men have often assured me that it was indeed the case when they were young.

As a result of the attachment of Merina of free descent to their *tanindrazana*, it is possible to map out quite clearly the territorial distribution of these groups, since the association of a particular village with a particular group today is common knowledge (see Map 3). If we do this it is immediately clear that Merina peasant society is made up of groups of freemen which were once local groups. The localities from which they came were composed of a certain number of villages where the members of the group are believed to have lived and which the present-day members of the groups consider their ancestors or *razana* came from. The first feature of these named groups therefore is that they were, as it is believed, local groups and that in a special way this localization is still relevant today.

The second feature to be noted is that these groups are traditionally in-marrying. That is, informants state either that they should only marry members of their own group as their forebears had always done, or they state that they normally marry one another and that in the past their forebears normally only married within the group.

We shall return later to the question of traditional forms of marriage; here it only needs to be mentioned in so far as it helps us to understand the kind of groups we are dealing with. These local groups were usually referred to as clans by early writers such as Ellis, Grandidier, Julien etc.[1] Before proceeding further we must therefore decide what is the right term in anthropological terminology for these groups. Professor Condominas who, in his book *Fokon'olona et Collectivites Rurales*, has shown the way towards a structural understanding of Merina society, refers to the groups in question as "patricians", thus retaining the older word used by the writers already referred to, but emphasizing his view of the groups as orthodox patrilineal descent groups. In spite of a certain ideological stress on patrilinearity, it seems to me that these groups are not patrilineal (or even unilineal) and therefore not even clans in the way the word is usually understood by anthropologists.[2] I was never told anything which implied that the right of claiming to be a member of a particular group was obtained especially through patrifiliation and this despite many discussions on this subject and the fact that I was considering the norm rather than actual behaviour. Informants could never understand what I was getting at because they assumed that both mothers and fathers belonged to the same grouping and that this had always been the case. It seems that any idea of unilineal descent is irrelevant to groups which are normally thought of as in-marrying; since both father and mother should belong to the same group it is of little interest either to the anthropologist or to the actor whether children obtained membership through the father or the mother. Of course, today not all marriages are in-marriages and what really happens

---

[1] The view these writers hold on these groupings is clearly put by J. Sibree in *Madagascar, the Great African Island*, 1880, p. 182. See also A. and G. Grandidier, *Histoire . . . de Madagascar*, 1892, etc., W. Ellis, *History of Madagascar*, 1838, and J. Sibree, *Madagascar and its People*, 1870. On their permanence in changing circumstances see A. and G. Grandidier, "Histoire Politique" in *Histoire de Madagascar*, Vol. I, p. 3.

[2] A. R. Radcliffe-Brown, "Patrilineal and matrilineal succession" in *Structure and Function in Primitive Society*, 1952. For a definition of "clan" see the introduction of *African Systems of Kinship and Marriage*, A. R. Radcliffe-Brown (Ed.) A. R. Radcliffe-Brown and Daryll Forde, 1950. This work is quoted by Condominas. I am using the word here to mean descent groups to which membership is obtained exclusively by unifiliation. For certain purposes the Merina stress the father's side more than the mother's, and for others not.

will be discussed fully in Chapter 4. It has probably not always been the case, although the genealogies I collected suggested that two or three generations ago there was a very much higher rate of in-marriage than at present.[1]

There is, however, another reason why the Merina do not attempt to explain exactly how membership is established, in spite of the fact that as it stands their theory cannot account for many instances with which they are faced. The reason is that while membership of these groups implies bilateral descent it is not in terms of genealogies that it is symbolized but in terms of tombs. As we would expect in a kinship-based society the Merina are very interested in genealogies, but this interest is much weaker and very different from what we would find in a unilineal society. Genealogies are used to link up live individuals or sometimes to establish a personal link with some kind of hero of the past. Genealogies going back for many generations are not necessary to establish group membership and, primarily, the Merina are not interested in particular ancestors, but in "ancestors" as an undifferentiated category. Burial in a tomb is the ultimate criterion of membership. The tombs are one of the most striking features of the Merina countryside and they define the territories of the different so-called clans and this has always been so. Ellis, in a book published in 1838, says, "Few of the general indications of the peculiar customs of the Malagasy are more remarkable than their places of sepulchre. Most of their graves are family tombs or vaults. In their construction much time and labour, and sometimes considerable property, are expended" (p. 243). Being buried in a tomb in the area of your group is the final demonstration of membership. In the same way as the tomb is the symbol of the ancestral system and of kinship it is also the historical framework of the Merina countryside. We shall discuss this most important part of the traditional system in its social context in Chapter 4, but it must be outlined here because membership of traditional groups depends ultimately on recruitment to burial in specific tombs. If Condominas was right that these groups were patricians, then recruitment to tombs should, according to the Merina norm, be patrilineal and this is what he claims. However, as will be evident, this is certainly not the case now, and, what is more relevant, it is not as far as I was told considered the norm, nor is it

---

[1] It is difficult to know how far these genealogies can be trusted when discussing such marriages. It was obviously tempting for informants to assume that they had followed the ideal.

believed that this was so in the past. When questioned about the ideal my informants were very vague and clearly they had no ready-made answer. I was told that it had not mattered in the past because both father and mother had belonged to the same group and perhaps to the same tomb. In other words the distinctiveness of the local group seemed to remove the problems which have to be dealt with nowadays. This is doubtful evidence of what actually happened but it shows that there is no formulated rule of patrilineal descent for either group or tomb membership. The implied discreteness of the groups in question is only seen as a result of their localization and their marriage rules.

These groups are then bilateral in-marrying kinship groups. The only term which would seem to fit this case is the word "deme" as defined by Murdoch[1]—a kind of grouping which occurs, mainly in the Malayo-Polynesian area. The fact that these demes were once local groups and still have an association with their territory means that we can divide the traditional area of Imerina into the original group territories. In doing this a number of things become apparent. First of all some of the groups are segments of bigger groups. Thus the Zanak-andriambe, the Zanakandrianato and the Ambohitrabiby, along with other such groups, formed the Mandiavato and they in turn combined with the Tsimahafotsy and the Tsimiamboholahy to form Avaradrano (see Map 3). Indeed, other levels of segmentation are also sometimes referred to. It is, therefore, clear that we are dealing with a segmentary system made up of corporate groups, in the sense that they have a common territory and a common name.[2] The fixed and coherent system which these territorial social divisions imply may well be a result of their having changed their functions when they stopped being principally local groups. We can imagine them as a stage in a process of growth and change, a stage in a process which became petrified by a radical change in their nature.

These groups were not just a succession of formally similar, ever more inclusive groups in the way some segmentary lineage systems are. They gradually changed nature according to their level in the segmentary structure and three such levels can be distinguished. The most inclusive

---

[1] G. P. Murdoch, *Social Structure*, 1949.

[2] The groupings Professor Condominas refers to as *fokon'olona* are the lowest level of segments in this system. I do not use the term myself because to do so runs counter to common usage. Indeed nowadays the word *fokon'olona* tends to be used by the Merina peasants to contrast groups of neighbours not related by kinship within groups of kinsmen and affines.

does not concern kinship groups at all—it is that of the "districts" of Imerina. Imerina was divided by Andrianampoinimerina into six districts, *toko*. These are Avaradrano, Vakinisisaony, Ambodirano, Vakinankaratra, Imamo, Valalafotsy, Marovatana and Vonizongo (see Map 2). These were territorial divisions and, to a certain extent, administrative districts. Today they are only significant as geographical terms for certain areas. They are relevant to the wider kinship system, however, because they are subdivided into smaller territorial segments which are the "demes" mentioned above. In this way the district of Avaradrano is divided into the demes of Tsimahafotsy, Mandiavato etc. This means that in the past the kinship groups and the territorial and ultimately the administrative organization were combined. These divisions of the districts form the core of the second analytical level of segmentation. Here a difficulty arises because some of these divisions immediately below the district level, such as the Mandiavato, are themselves divided into groups which are thought by the Merina to be homologous with other groups which are first divisions of the districts. For example, the Zanakandriambe and the Zafimbazaha are considered

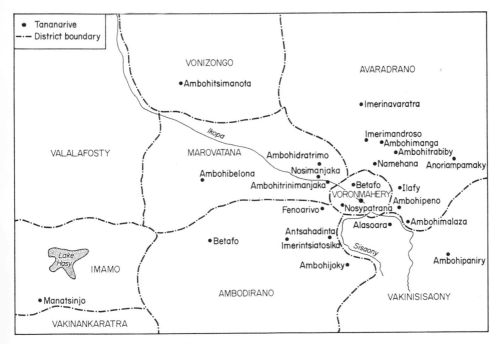

Map 2. The districts (*toko*) of Imerina after A. and G. Grandidier, *Ethnographie*, Vol. I.

Map 3. Provisional map showing some of the larger deme divisions of the district Avaradrano.

I	Tsimiamboholahy	VIII	Ambohidrabiby
II	Andriandranando	IX	Zanakandriambe
III	Andriantompokoindrindra	X	Zanakandrianato
IV	Andrianamboninolona	XI	Andriamamilaza
V	Zanadralambo	XII	Valonjatolahy
VI	Tsimahafotsy	XIII	Zanadravoromanga
VII	Zanadoria		

Note: Zazamarolahy and Andriamasinavalona are found in isolated villages in the territory of other demes.

to be the same kind of group, but the Zanakandriambe are a section of the Mandiavato who are in turn a section of the district of Avaradrano; but a group such as the Zafimbazaha is an immediate division of the district itself. (Of course for the present time locality does not mean co-residence but co-location of tombs. The Merina often talk as though this were much the same since, as we shall see, in a sense a man's *home* is more where he will be buried than where he lives.)

Discussing the Merina demes as though they were territorial divisions is the easiest way of identifying and classifying them. This is because the kinship character of these groups is unfuriatingly elusive. Nevertheless, it is the kinship element which is uppermost for the present-day Merina. I was told of several demes that its members were *iraytampo*—"one womb". This is an expression stressing the strongest feeling of physical kinship and of filiation since the mother-child link is thought particularly close. Equally revealing is the assumption that two people of the same deme *must* somehow be kinsmen. In many instances when I discussed with an informant someone he did not know, as soon as it became clear that they were both members of the same deme, the informant said, "We must be kinsmen".

In what way then are demes kinship groups? It is clear that in the past when demes were observable as local groups it was not sufficient to have been born in the territory of a particular deme to acquire membership. An extra qualification was needed, that of kinship. The particular mixture of territory and kinship is well expressed in the myth which relates how Andrianampoinimerina gave territory to each family. We need not take this story literally but it is characteristic of the association of kinship group and territory. "Andrianampoinimerina allocated land to the six districts; this area to the Avaradrano, this to the Vakinisisaony, this to the Marovatana etc. Then he divided the territory of the districts; this area to the Valalafotsy, this to the Mandiavato, this to the Tsimi-amboholahy. To the large families he gave much, to the smaller families he gave less". (Callet, 1878, p. 732.)

Not only are the demes considered to be families, they are also called after a founding ancestor. For example, Zafimbazaha means "the grandchildren of Andriambazaha". Andriantompokoindrindra is both the name of members of a deme and the name of the founder of that deme. This is sometimes elaborated so as to show the divisions of a large deme in a genealogical framework. Figure 1 shows the case of Zafinandriamamilazabe. This is, however, just a charter for the territorial division of the deme. With few exceptions, the members of the groups are completely incapable of demonstrating their relationships to eponymous ancestors, but their claim to such a relationship shows clearly enough that these groupings are visualized as kinship groupings.

If the belief in descent from an ancestor gives a name and an identity to the deme it is not by stressing an ascending line that membership is defined but by stressing lateral links to other well accepted members of the deme. Anthropologists' studies of genealogies have tended to

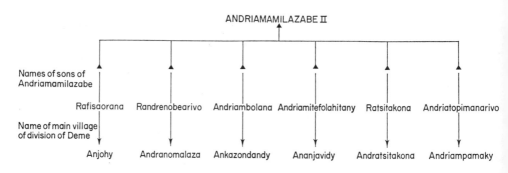

Fig. 1. Genealogy showing how the divisions of the deme Andriamamilaza are represented as being founded by sons of the deme founder, Andriamamilazabe II. Each of these sons is then associated with a territorial division. Some of the divisions are sufficiently distinct to also merit being described as demes.

concentrate on societies with unilineal descent but genealogies arc important also in many other types of society, though they differ in their nature. I was fortunate in discovering one geneology which a family had had produced on their own initiative and not at my request. It showed clearly the two main concerns of these genealogies: establishing a fully documented relationship to the deme founder through an ambilateral line and linking up a number of people who knew they were relatives.

In fact the kinship unity of the deme does not come from a concept of descent. It comes from the fact that ideally the deme is the group which contains all kinsmen, the group in which the Merina feels all the members must be relatives, and the group within which he should find a wife. Indeed it is rather because one should marry in the deme than because one is descended from its ancestor that all deme members are kinsmen. To further understand the nature of the deme we must therefore turn to an examination of traditional marriage rules.

Marriage

The first point about marriage in the traditional system is that in-marriage is expected within the deme. Discussing this for most demes, informants did not usually state it as a rule but simply said that in the past everybody had married deme neighbours. Furthermore, genealogies which I collected seemed to support this picture, and several 19th-century writers have noted the tendency towards in-marriage. For some demes a clear rule of endogamy was given as the ideal—a rule which in the past I was assured was strictly enforced. For example, I was told of such a rule for the Zafimandriamamilaza and the Zafimbazaha. Since demes are ranked (see p. 68) the demes of higher rank are particularly strict in their enforcement of endogamy, although in some cases in the past a man from a higher deme could take as a secondary wife a woman of lower rank. This practice cannot, however, be called hypergamy because the children of such a union belong to the lower rank of the mother.[1] In some other cases marriages between demes are allowed according to the rules when a special alliance exists between demes, e.g. Tsimahafotsy and Tsimiamboholahy, or when there is a tradition of common ancestry, e.g. the Zanahandriambe and Zanakadravoramanga. None the less, it is clear that the normal type of marriage is marriage within the deme. The reason for this is less because of any rule about marrying in or not marrying outside the deme but because of marriage preferences between specified kinsmen.

One would expect a preference for in-marriage merging into a rule of endogamy to divide people into exclusive groups at one level only. This is not the case in the Merina system. The reason becomes clearer if we compare Merina demes with another kind of endogamous group, the castes (*jati*) of North India. While both these groups are further divided their subdivisions are different. The subdivisions within the *jati* are *gotra*[2] which are exogamous unilineal descent groups. By contrast, the subdivisions of the deme are a kind of smaller deme also with a high degree of in-marriage. This explains the difficulty, mentioned above, relating to the fact that groups which are subdivisions of others belong to the same category as the groups they divide. In the case of the Merina

---

[1] For a fuller discussion of the rules of in-marriage and its relation to rank see p. 199ff.

On rules of marriage and rank of children for the higher groups see R. F. Callet, *Tantaran'ny Andriana*, p. 326, and A. and G. Grandidier, *Ethnographie*, Vol. II, p. 170.

[2] A. C. Mayer, *Caste and Kinship in Central India*, 1960.

deme, the sub-groups within it, whether more or less crystallized, are miniature demes with a high degree of in-marriage. This fact explains the difficulty one has in trying to fix a level for the deme in the segmentary system, and explains why subdivisions of a larger group are thought to be equivalent to groups parallel with the larger divisions.

The basis for the difference between the formal aspects of the Indian system and those of the Merina system is that, while the structure of the *jati* is maintained by emphasis on the *prohibition* of marriage outside, the Merina group depended on, and to a certain extent still does depend on,[1] the prescription of marriage with a close relative. Although it is not specifically *forbidden* to marry anyone within the deme, one *should* marry more specific persons.

Marriages should take place between kinsmen and the general rule is the closer the kinsman the better, but there are certain qualifications to this. The most "suitable" spouse for a man or woman is the child of his or her parents' cross-cousins. Marriage with certain relatives is incestuous: there are parent-child incest rules and any marriage cross-cutting the generations is disapproved of. Marriage between full and half siblings is incestuous. In addition, marriages between descendants of two sisters are forbidden. The latter prohibition is in theory extended to any number of generations, but in fact is disregarded after three.

Although there is universal agreement on the general principles there is a bewildering variety of opinion when we come to specific formulation of the rules. The most common statement is that the expected marriage in the traditional system is marriage between the grandchildren of a brother and a sister, *Zafim'olona mpianadahy*, that is, the children of cross-cousins. Certain people, however, claim that for *their* deme only great grandchildren of a brother and a sister marry. In some demes actual cross-cousins were expected to marry. In other cases the rule was not expressed at all in terms of which relative but in terms of the number of generations. I was thus told that the expected marriage was "at the third generation, "*taranaka faha-telo*", with the exception, of course, of descendants of two sisters. Certain general features were always present in this. Informants always claimed that for their deme only more remote relatives were expected to marry than was the case for other demes.

The relatives about which there was doubt as to whether they were expected to marry or forbidden to marry were always: (1) cross-cousins,

---

[1] See Chapter 6.

(2) patrilateral—parallel cousins, (3) children of patrilateral parallel cousins. It would be quite pointless for me here to attempt to list the rules for the various demes, because I could get no agreement. Many people were willing to discuss this matter and attribute certain rules to certain demes, but evidence from other people was almost always contradictory. Nevertheless, the differences which the informants attributed between demes and the difference of opinion amongst them always concerned the kinship relations already discussed.

The explanation of this apparently baffling diversity became quite clear from the statements of informants. It is the result of the paradox that is marriage in Imerina. All these marriages, as indeed all marriages between cognates, are in various degrees incestuous (*mamonsavy*). The Merina notion of incest is not a simple yes/no matter; marriages are more or less incestuous. Although I have no direct informants' statements to support this, it seems to me that all Merina notions of incest imply a belief in the exceptional strength of the mother–child link. The way of stressing kinship most emphatically is to say that two people are "of one womb". There is no corresponding expression to describe children as being descended from one man. Incest is the conceptual antithesis to kinship. I have often heard a man who failed in his kinship obligation described as someone who had committed incest (or witchcraft). In fact I feel fairly confident in saying that the importance of the concept of incest, for the Merina at least, and perhaps more generally, is to be explained in terms of defining and emphasizing its opposite—kinship. This is the only way to account for a concept of something which rarely occurs and, in the one case I came across, it did not lead to the often reported feelings of horror, but was rather overlooked. If incest is seen as the negation of kinship we can understand why all marriages between kinsmen are thought of by the Merina as tainted by incest. It also explains why marriages between the children of sisters are thought of as more incestuous than other marriages of cousins. The closest kinship link being that of mother and child, it follows that matrilateral parallel cousins are *more* kin than other cousins. The only aspect of the Merina belief in incest which is not accounted for by the above consideration is the fact that marriage between patrilateral parallel cousins is thought of as more incestuous than the marriage of cross-cousins. It must be remembered that the difference between these marriages is only slight.

Therefore two separate but opposing beliefs seem to exist in the Merina mind. One is that all marriages between kinsmen are inces-

tuous and the other that the closer the kinship link the better, and the
Merina themselves recognize the contradiction. It is explained by
stating that the rules encouraging ever closer endogamy are of quite a
different nature from the incest rule. This is quite simply and explicitly
put. The reason given unhesitatingly by all informants as to why there
are rules favouring marriage between close kinsmen is that these marriages help in keeping rice lands undivided. These preferred marriages,
that is marriages between kinsmen, are considered as an unpleasant
necessity. They are called *"lova tsy mifindra"* or "inheritance which does
not move away". Given the reliance on irrigated rice land and the rule
whereby women inherit as well as men from both their fathers and their
mothers, the only way of avoiding dispersal of land rights by endless
subdivision is by requiring marriage with close neighbours and kinsmen.
Since in the traditional system neighbours are kinsmen, this is one and
the same thing. The object of these marriages is clearly expressed by the
actors as indeed their term for such marriages shows. They are intended
to ensure that rights to land to not fall to outsiders. In theory this could
be achieved by some simple system of exchange, but the complexity of
the situation makes this impossible.

Children inherit from both parents individually and normally all
children inherit irrespective of their sex.[1] This applies to all land including rice fields, and to cattle, houses and household goods.[2] Inheritance by both sexes presents a particularly acute problem in the case of
scarce rice land,[3] since a couple can only cultivate what they have inherited from one side or the other, unless their parents all come from the
same village.

This has always been the case and it was once very common to marry
within the same village which, in the circumstances, usually meant
marrying kinsmen. When marriage does not occur in the same village

------

[1] Inheritance is regulated by the wish of the dead person. Any rule of inheritance is therefore
alterable. Usually it follows a set pattern. In the past the eldest child inherited slightly more
than the others. The youngest also inherited slightly more than the others but slightly less than
the eldest. Male heirs got slightly more than female heirs. However, all children of either sex
and irrespective of their birth order always got a substantial share. Nowadays, with only a few
exceptions, they all inherit equally. A. and G. Grandidier, *Ethnographie*, Vol. II, p. 317 and p.
330ff. G. Julien, *Institutions Politiques et Sociales de Madagascar*, 1909, p. 306.
[2] The only exceptions to this are certain books containing astrological information, proverbs,
and family history which are passed from head of family to head of family (see Bloch, 1968).
[3] Land other than rice land is not scarce and rights to it are hardly more than nominal and
therefore of little concern here.

some of the children go away and do not cultivate their land. In the past this meant mainly the women as marriage is traditionally virilocal. Women, therefore, left their land in trust to their brothers and this is what still happens today. (In fact women also leave their cattle with their brothers until they are sure they will not divorce.) Although the brothers cultivated it, it was the woman's own, and could never be sold[1] because the land was an assurance in case of divorce and widowhood, so that the woman could return to cultivate it (Callet, 1878, p. 248). There is another more general reason why such land is not sold. It is because there is a general rule that it is wrong to sell land which has become a relative's *fivelomana*, "means of subsistence". What happens to the produce is less clearcut. The rule was that the brother should send the amount of rice which would normally be due to the owner when the land is in *métayage* to his sister.[2] In fact, from my own observation of the present day, this does not always seem to be done. If the distance is very great and the amount of rice small the sister may not find it worth while to pay for the transport. In one particular case when this situation arose the sister told me she left the rice to her brother but that she expected as a result that the brother would be particularly generous to her children when they visited him and that he would give them clothes and hats, which in fact he did.

Other factors than distance and amount also enter into the decision of whether to send the product of the land or not. These are considerations like the relative wealth of the two households and the frequency of visits by the sister to her brother. In practice this relationship is unclear and may well be the cause of repressed tension.[3]

The situation which exists between a sister who has left her parental village and a brother who cultivates her land is passed on at death to their heirs. The children of the brother inherit from their father, both the land which fully belonged to him, and the trust which he had in his sister's land. The sister's children inherit the rights to their mother's land. This means that cross-cousins often stand in the relation of trustees or lenders to one another. In fact in the past, as well as now, it was not always just women who went away at marriage. Sometimes women

---

[1] A. and G. Grandidier, *Ethnographie*, Vol. II, p. 212.

[2] For conditions of *métayage*, see p. 192.

[3] I was told by a psychiatrist that many of the patients at the psychiatric hospital were obsessed by the notion that they had been cheated of their inheritance as a result of leaving their parental village.

stayed and men went away. This kind of trustee relationship is likely to occur between all first cousins, though less often than it does between cross-cousins. In the same way that the original trust is first transmitted to the next generation by two siblings, it can be transmitted by cross-cousins to their children, and so on, which means that fairly distant relatives may find themselves in this kind of relationship.

This trusteeship deserves greater scrutiny as it is an essential aspect of the relationship between cross-cousins, and between all kinsmen. The individual who has inherited a right to land in trust, though it is not really his property, is not likely to be willing to part with it. In fact, most probably he will think of the land as his own and deny the competing claim. He may not even know that such a claim exists. The greater the number of generations through which the land has been passed on in trust and been cultivated by his family, the more he will consider it as his own. The point of view of the cousin and his descendants who have a right to the land but do not exercise it is different. They no doubt still consider the land as their own, but they are well aware that there is little they can do about it. The more generations that have elapsed since the original giving in trust, the harder it will be to claim or sell the land. Also the plot will have become smaller. The restraint in not claiming the land is said to be because the land is a kinsman's *fivelomana*. A vague feeling remains that your kinsman owes you something. Repeatedly I was puzzled by statements by people claiming land as theirs when I knew that it really belonged to somebody else. It only later became evident that one could say that any land belonging to a kinsman could be said to "belong" to you and this was explained to me by a legally minded informant precisely in terms of a multitude of unenforced claims. This feeling is strong between cousins, especially cross-cousins. When the position is as vague as this, quite clearly the notion of trusteeship has become so modified that it is doubtful whether this is the right word to describe the relationship. It is not clear at what stage and after how many generations the relationship passes from one similar to that of owner of land and tenant to the much vaguer one just described. There is no rule about this as external factors relevant to the original trust still apply.

The preferred character of the marriage between the children of cross-cousins thus becomes easily understandable. The father of the boy or girl, as the case may be, feels that although he cannot enjoy his property his descendants will be able to do so as a result of such a marriage. At least his cousin's child will not marry a stranger to him, which would remove his inheritance still further by making the future trustees of his land his cousin's grandchildren—remote relatives. The same principle also applies for marriages of more distant kinsmen and in this way explains the more general preference for kinsmen, since not all marriages can be marriages between children of cross-cousins, if only because these relatives are not always available. In such cases other relatives, possibly more remote, are chosen. Given the system of inheritance and the fact that sometimes it is the men who go away and the women who stay, many other relatives may cultivate land which the Merina considers his own, especially since at each generation every individual inherits both from his father's and his mother's side. The network of trusts and rights of land rapidly becomes extremely complex, although most of these rights and trusts are half forgotten.

The actor knows that having common kinship usually means having claims to your kinsman's land and his having claims to yours. In fact, families can be thought of as webs of unenforced claims to land. As we have seen, the reasons why they are not enforced are complex. First, there is the concept that it is wrong to foreclose on a kinsman's *fivelomana*. Then, more cynically, it could be argued that because it is well known that in the incredibly complex genealogical framework of the Merina kinship groups which results from repeated in-marriage, when A has a claim to B's land, this most probably means that B has a claim to A's land. The tangle of genealogical links is illustrated by the present-day example given in Fig. 2 (p. 63) where only some of the possible links are shown between members of a particularly conservative local family. The general policy is therefore to leave well alone, but also to make sure that kinsmen do not marry out of the family and lose land from the common pool to outsiders. Marriages between kinsmen are felt necessary for practical reasons and they are therefore all classified under the heading of *lova tsy mifindra*.[1] That is, they are a practical necessity which goes against the more general feeling that all marriages between kinsmen are in some way incestuous and they give rise to a very obvious feeling of embarrassment, even anxiety, about the occurrence of this "preferred" form. This was very obvious to me in the many instances when an informant rather shamefacedly admitted that they practiced *lova tsy mifindra* marriage although they did not practice cross-cousin marriage

---

[1] A. and G. Grandidier, *Ethnographie*, Vol. II, p. 166, footnote 5.

like the "so and so's" but only marriage of children of cross-cousins. I was even told that in the past a sacrifice to remove incest was made before a *lova tsy mifindra* marriage took place.[1]

This contradiction is the explanation of the variation of formulation of marriage preferences between different informants. The rules are, so to speak, balanced between the negative aspect, incest, and the positive aspect, preference. Informants when talking about marriage in a general way tend to stress how they, in comparison to others, only allow *lova tsy mifindra* marriages between comparatively remote relatives as they feel that outsiders are naturally shocked by the incest element of such marriages. On the other hand they will urge as close a marriage as possible on their children stressing the importance of keeping the patrimony undivided.

In this way in the traditional system all marriages are thought of as occurring between related people for the purely practical purpose of not allowing inheritance to pass to strangers, irrespective of the fact of the existence or absence of a specific rule of endogamy. It is in this sense that the demes are endogamous and it follows therefore that most marriages in fact occur within a very much more restricted group than the deme. The significance of this for the system of groups in the traditional system must be examined, together with other factors, and this must be done in the light of the more general kinship group structure which was also the administrative structure of the Merina kingdom.

To fully understand the effect of in-marriage on the segmentary system we must look more closely at two concepts which I have up to now taken for granted. That is the concept of kinsman (*havana*) and the concept of family (*fianakaviana*). These concepts derive their form from the traditional system.

The Concept of *Havana*

The word *havana* is usually translated into English by the word "kinsman". The value this concept has for the Merina is central to the present argument, and is of prime importance to the actors themselves. In fact we shall have to return again to this topic and a consideration of the concept here can only be preliminary.

---

[1] The same situation is described for the Bara by J. Faublée, *La Cohésion des Sociétés Bara*, 1954. A similar situation is described for the Gonja in "Cross Cousin Marriage in North Ghana". E. and J. Goody, *Man*, 66, Vol. I, No 3, pp. 341 to 355. Interestingly enough it was also the case here that such marriages could not be dissolved.

A man describes as *havana* all his blood relatives. It implies a personal relationship between two people. Although the term does not include affines there is no conceptual opposition between affines and *havana*,[1] because in the ideal system a man's affines are also his *havana*, since he should marry *havana*.

The importance of the concept *havana* is that it is the concept to which the maximum moral value is attached. In sermons, in the moral songs of the minstrels who come on great occasions,[2] in any speech for any occasion, the duty of mutual love, help and cooperation between *havana* is endlessly stressed.

A kinsman in need has a theoretical right over all a man's property, though in fact this right is usually limited to food and shelter. As soon as a kinsman enters the house he will ask for a meal and behave as though the house was his own. His behaviour in this is often somewhat aggressive, asking for more, or complaining about the quality of what he is given, which is a kind of public demonstration of the relationship and the rights that go with it. Even for more important things a request from a *havana* can only be refused if the person to whom the request is made can show that he has not even enough for himself. A *havana* is above all someone who should be trusted completely. The importance of the concept is most clear when we note the great suspicion with which a person who is not a *havana* is viewed. Really, a person who is not in any sense a *havana* is a potential witch and Merina to this day are terrified of having to eat in his house since witches are poisoners. This manifests itself most strikingly in the reluctance the Merina shows in going to hospitals and the way in which this reluctance is overcome. Hospitals are clearly part of the threatening modern world, but a part which interferes most intimately with the ordinary Merina while most other manifestations of this world can be kept, to a certain extent, at a distance. Hospitals, therefore, are particularly associated with stories of heart thieves (Bloch, 1969). The only way that the Merina peasant will agree to go to one is if he is accompanied by large numbers of *havana*. This indeed presents a very great problem to the authorities in dealing with these extra people who insist on sleeping in hospital wards to protect their relatives from non-*havana*. The need for security with *havana* is also emphasized by those people who for some reason are forced to live away

---

[1] In fact some informants thought it could be used for affines (see Chapter 6).

[2] Mpihira gasy.

from all relatives. This is rare but I came across a number of school-teachers whose posting had isolated them in this way. It is significant that I met three schoolteachers who were involved in witchcraft accusations or who believed they were being bewitched and finally had to leave. Their fear becomes a major administrative problem for the government which finds it difficult to appoint people in areas where they have no relatives. In the village where I worked there lived a fully trained agricultural adviser who had left his well-paid post for a miserable farm because he was too afraid, so he told me, to stay without relatives. This is not new and Grandidier has already described how at the beginning of the century it was difficult for Merina to have relations with non-kinsmen.

Nothing illustrates better how the Merina concept of *havana* is seen as being the only possible kind of social relationship than the fact that the Malagasy radio, in order to imply a link, has to address its listeners as *"Havana"*. Although this use of the word is often ridiculed by the Merina themselves, the radio station was really faced with a difficult problem, since no element of rapport can be suggested with another term. In the ideological system, the only permanent moral relationship an individual has with another person is one of kinship and a non-kinsman is a dangerous uncontrollable person, a potential witch.

These examples show the sentimental value of the concept *havana*. They also clearly show its two sides. A *havana* is a person with whom there are genealogical links and he is at the same time a trusted neighbour. That is to say, that the people with whom one lives one's life are people with whom one has kinship links, which means that the links which spring from common residence and agricultural co-operation are not distinguished from the moral ties of kinship. This merging is of great interest because, as will be shown, since the two kinds of links are not in fact conterminous, the feeling that they should be is maintained by referring back to the picture of a past society where kinship, common residence, and cooperation are one and the same thing. If the rule of in-marriage within a local group is kept to, then all the people with whom continuous practical relations are maintained are kinsmen.

The Concept of *Fianakaviana*

Closely linked to the concept of *havana* and, likewise, having for its ideal model the system of the society of the ancestors, is the idea of *fianakaviana*, normally translated as "family".

The *fianakaviana* is the group which includes all Ego's *havana* and also all Ego's affines. It differs from the concept *havana* in that it conveys the idea of a group while *havana* conveys the idea of an interpersonal relationship. Very much like our own word "family" the word *fianakaviana* can apply to a variety of more or less inclusive groups focussed on the nuclear family. The extensiveness of the reference is determined by the context. I have thus heard the word used to refer to the family of parents and children, and to all kinsmen and affines of Ego living in a particular locality—a grouping which is referred to in the following chapters as "local family". However, unless it is clearly otherwise, the word normally means a much larger group of kinsmen and affines. For the sake of clarity I shall only use the Malagasy word *fianakaviana* in this book when I mean the word used in this, its most inclusive meaning. The Merina use the phrase *fianakaviana be* (the big *fianakaviana*) when they feel that some ambiguity might exist and they want to distinguish this meaning of the word.

In this sense ideally the *fianakaviana* would include all Ego's kinsmen and affines. In practice some non-kinship criterion is and, we may assume, has always been involved in limiting the group. Apart from very close relatives, it includes those relatives and affines with whom the right links existed and with whom one had some kind of social intercourse, whether economic, ritual, or of neighbourhood. It has often been defined for me by informants as the group of people that one invites to the more important ceremonies such as *famadihanas* (see Chapter 6) and marriages. The *fianakaviana* is not, however, a fixed group defined by exclusive criteria. When two strangers meet and are able to establish some kinship or affinal link, however remote, it is sufficient for them to recognize that they are of the same *fianakaviana*.[1]

This kind of bilateral grouping is well known to the anthropologist in societies with or without unilateral groups. These are Ego-centred groups which are not permanent elements in the social structure. They are different for every individual except full siblings. The *fianakavianas* do not really fit into the picture since, for the actors at least, they are considered discreet corporate groups continuing through time. The written genealogy of a Merina family which I have in my possession shows this. It was drawn up without my prompting by a member of the *fianakaviana*

---

[1] I have not called this group a kindred group as anthropologists differ in their views as to whether the term "kindred" can include affines or not.

who had reached a high position in the administration and who lived in Tananarive and it was shown to me by a number of people who were related. Although these people were not siblings, they considered that *all* their relatives were included in the genealogy. This was not only an Ego-centred category but an ancestor-centred category in that it purported to show descent either through the male or the female line of a number of people from a specific source. In other words this group is both a kindred group and what has sometimes been called a cognatic descent group. Professor Fox in a recent book (Fox, 1967) again stressed that we should always clearly distinguish between groups with an "Ego focus" and an "ancestor focus". For Merina concepts, however, the *fianakaviana* uses both foci. Of course, in operation the ancestor-focussed group (or rather tomb-focussed group) and the Ego-centred group are not identical, but they are closely linked.

The reason why the *fianakaviana* manages to combine some of the facets of an ancestor-focussed group and an ego-centred group is because of its high in-marriage. This is shown by what happens to a child of marriageable age. The parents look for a spouse from within the *fianakaviana*. This means that all marriages should occur within this group, with the effect that the members of a *fianakaviana* are related many times and in many ways to each other. Although today the rule is far from completely obeyed, the extent of intermarriage can be gauged from the example given in Fig. 2 which shows how a small group of inter-related people can be further linked by other kinship links. Since kinship is concentrated within this group any two members will have very similar *fianakaviana*, even though they are not full siblings. In the words of Grandidier who puts this matter concisely:

Les Merina se divisent non seulement en castes bien distinctes mais chacunes de ces castes comprend de nombreux clans (demes) ou groups de familles issues d'un ancêtre commun qui se subdivisent eux-memes . . . chaque famille (*fianakaviana*) a son individualite propre, et leurs membres ne se marient non seulement pas avec ceux d'un clan qu'ils considerent inferieur a eux, mais le plus souvent, afin que les propriétés ne sortent pas de la famille, ils se marient en famille . . .

Ethnographie, Vol. I, pp. 235–237

A *fianakaviana* was, in this way, a potential sub-group of a deme. The demes, as shown above, are often subdivided into smaller groups which I have classed also as demes. In some cases there may even be further levels. *Fianakavianas* may easily become such groups when the frequency of in-marriage increases so much that practically all marriages occur exclusively within them. They then become demes and form a group considered as constituting descendants of an eponymous ancestor (see Fig. 1). In this way the Ego-centred group acquires even more of the characteristics normally associated with a descent group.

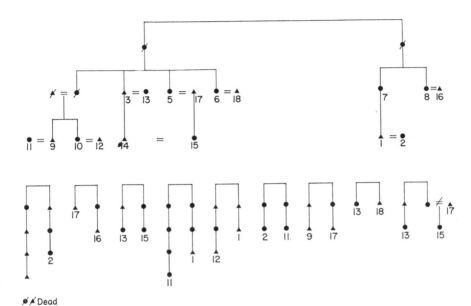

♂ ✗ Dead

Fig. 2. This diagram shows the multiplicity of kinship ties between individuals arising from in-marriage. The large genealogy shows the genealogical links among the important members (1 to 18) of a local family (see p. 97) represented in the simplest way. The smaller genealogies show other linkages and especially how affines are also kinsmen. These are not all the possible ways in which relationships between these people could be shown.

Note: Other genealogies in this book will only show the simplest possible genealogical links.

To return to our general classification of levels of segmentation, we saw that the first most inclusive of these was the district, followed by the demes, and we can now include the *fianakavianas* as the third level.[1] But there are certain difficulties in doing this. Firstly, *fianakavianas* have no distinct limits and are not normally conceptually contrasted with demes. Merina will say that all members of the deme are members of their

---

[1] A. and G. Grandidier, *Ethnographie*, Vol. I, p. 236.

fianakavianas. How far this identification of *fianakaviana* and deme is maintained in other contexts in which the word occurs varies with the size of the deme. Large demes may contain a number of more or less crystallized *fianakaviana.*

The second difficulty in considering the *fianakaviana* as a level of segmentation in the general political organization of Imerina is that it is not a fully corporate group. This difficulty is lessened if we take into account the element of locality and land ownership and its close link with prescribed marriages. As we have seen, normally very many marriages took place within a small group of neighbours. These neighbours were also kinsmen since it was believed that all neighbours were kinsmen and that a village was a group of particularly close kinsmen. In reality it was probably never completely so, but it enables an individual to think that belonging to a village or group of villages closely associated in the past is tantamount to belonging to a *fianakaviana*, which means that when dealing with the place of the *fianakaviana* in the traditional organization of Imerina we are not really dealing with a kinship grouping at all, but with villages. If one can go on informants' statements referring to the present, it seems that to a large extent the two units, *fianakaviana* and village, are conceptually merged and are seen as corresponding in membership. When the actor is involved in the political field the village (ancestral) aspect is uppermost; when dealing with activities not requiring a fully discrete group the *fianakaviana* is uppermost. Thus, even if the *fianakaviana* is not really conterminous with a village or a group of villages, the ideology of the family is transposed to the local unit.[1]

Although in most cases the correspondence between the *fianakaviana* and a territory is not really complete, it seems that, given time and certain ecological conditions, this correspondence might become more and more real. This would be possible if more and more marriages were to take place within the *fianakaviana* until all marriages were within a given area. It is clear that if this were to happen the *fianakaviana* would become a deme and that the process suggested is the process by which new demes were formed in a situation of expansion.[2]

This brings us back to the problem of distinguishing between what I have called demes and the concept "*fianakaviana*", which in practical

---

[1] See below p. 108ff.
[2] See Chapter 7.

terms is not difficult since the *fianakaviana* is a smaller unit of a deme, but we must discover what these formal differences are. Since the first is the embryo of the second, there are, as one might expect, various in-between stages. Thus the really significant factors, the localization in a specific territory of the deme and the frequency of in-marriage, cannot be used for discrimination, since it is not clear where we should draw the line. The only possible criterion of distinction between the deme and the *fianakaviana* is that while demes are named *fianakavianas* are not. The distinction between demes and *fianakavianas* as analytical concepts is obviously of only slight sociological significance, but this does not mean that the difference between them is of no importance. These two groupings differ along a continuum according to two important factors.

The first is that the demes were segments of the political organization of the kingdom while the *fianakavianas* were independent of the administrative organization.

As such the factor of locality must ultimately have validated membership for those for whom this might be in doubt, although much more clearly for the deme than for the *fianakaviana*.

Secondly, it must be borne in mind that for the reasons already mentioned these demes were *de facto* endogamous and so were corporate kinship groups. Some of these demes had a specific rule of endogamy while others contended themselves with the automative effects of *lova tsy mifindra* marriages. By and large we find that the demes of higher rank had a specific rule of endogamy while those of lower rank did not.

The important fact to notice here is that the Merina kinship system in its categorical form merges interpersonal kinship and kinship groups. Further, since these groups are associated with a territory, it means that the individual's most important relations are tied to a place. As will be discussed at length in the following chapters, the final tie of kinship to territory is operated by that most important symbol of Merina kinship, the tomb, which, of course, finally attaches the concepts of *fianakaviana* and of *havana* to a particular place in old Imerina, a particular place associated with a deme. Interestingly enough, this linking is evident even in the system of concepts, especially when we include the concept of bewitching (*mamonsavy*). The meaning of this word really covers what may be described as "unnatural" behaviour. To bewitch for the Merina is to cause harm secretly, by using either supernatural or natural means. Poisoning by putting a poisonous substance in somebody's food is not differentiated from the supposed effect of blowing with evil intention on the door of a sick person. There is no elaborate belief as there is for some African people in precisely what a witch does or what kind of person a witch is. In some way *mamonsavy* corresponds more closely to sorcery in the way Evans-Pritchard (1938) used the word. However, many other features of *mamonsavy* link it with what we normally call witchcraft. I do not want to concentrate here so much on the side of witchcraft as a manifestation of interpersonal tension as on beliefs about what witches do. In fact there is little connection between these two aspects. Witches in general are creatures of the dark. They can be either men or women but they are mainly women. They meet in covens or operate singly. They appear naked, wearing their clothes on their heads and are liable to seize passers-by, jump on their backs and ride them till they drop with exhaustion. They knock on doors at night, especially when they know that somebody is ill or dying, and dance around, and sometimes they attempt to steal the bodies of the dead. They are generally inverted creatures who do the opposite of what is right and proper and the belief in them in this way serves to define what is right and proper. As we might well expect in such a situation, witches are closely associated with tombs and their favourite haunts are on top of tombs, a place most feared and carefully avoided by good people on most occasions. Not only do witches visit the tombs at night, but they dance there naked, the greatest possible act of sacrilege. In this way witches can be said to be "anti-tomb". If the tomb stands for the good things of the traditional system, the belief in witchcraft is also part of the traditional system but seen as a mirror image of it. In fact it seems to me that in such a system, where actual witchcraft accusations are fairly rare but where talk of witchcraft and the activities of witches is most important, we could explain the belief as a kind of defining device for more positive views. I never heard children being taught in what way they should behave near tombs or how wrong it was to go naked. On the other hand this *wrong* behaviour by *wrong* creatures was continually described to them which had the logical effect of implying what the *right* behaviour of *right* people must be. I have no doubt that this is how the most significant values in many societies are defined.

When we come to consider the concept of witchcraft we note a relationship with kinship in that the Malagasy often think of certain relatives as possible witches and even have a proverb saying, "You should look for the witch among your own family (*fianakaviana*)". Nevertheless, this is not in any way central to beliefs about witchcraft and I only heard of one case when a relative suspected another of witchcraft.[1] The common anthropological theory that witchcraft accusations occur between morally bound people since no other outlet for aggression is possible does not easily fit in Imerina since most accusations of witchcraft are typically between unrelated people. Indeed it seems to me more at the level of the logical connection between concepts that the connection between witchcraft and kinship can be seen to exist. First of all, as we saw before, someone who is not a kinsman is seen as a potential witch, and is suspected of witchcraft. In my experience accusations seemed to occur only when people were thrown together and obliged to have the kind of relationships normally only expected of kinsmen. This is a point which underlies much of what follows. The second conceptual link between kinship and witchcraft is of another order altogether. The word *mamonsavy*, although understood by the actors as a unitary concept, covers a semantic field and includes the fear of incest. The Merina attitude is in a way similar to their attitude to witchcraft. Although it is an idea continually bandied about, the amount of talk about it bears no relation to the very rare occasions when *accusations* of incest are made. I only came across one story of someone being accused of incest and it seemed that the matter was rapidly forgotten. It seems that the talk about incest is another defining device for stressing the positive value of its psychological opposite—kinship. Again, like witchcraft, it is a socializing device for the non-sexual value of kinship. It is the same thing as witchcraft because like witchcraft it is the ultimate wrong while tombs and kinship are the ultimate right. This is further shown by the way people will sometimes say just to stress how wrong something is that it is "*mamonsavy*". The basis of Merina morality can perhaps be illusrated diagrammatically in the following way.

—	Witchcraft	Incest	—
	(*Mamonsavy*)	(*Mamonsavy*)	
+	Tomb	Kinship	+

The tomb is the symbol of kinship and the morally positive values of ancestral *Malagasy* society, while kinship is contrasted and thereby defined by the concept of *mamonsavy*, which in its witchcraft side mani-

---

1 When I use the word witchcraft here I am talking strictly of *mamonsavy*. There are other forms of supernatural aggression, e.g. *ambalavelona*.

fests itself in contempt for tombs and the dead and on its incest side implies the opposite of the behaviour between kinsmen derived from the mother-child link.

Rank

The distinction between demes with a specific rule of endogamy and those without leads us to a consideration of one final aspect of traditional Merina society, that is its division into what has been called three "castes". These are andriana, hova and andevo; terms translated in the literature as "noble", "commoner" and "slave".

As I am only dealing with the hova and andriana, I shall concentrate on them and only briefly discuss the position of the andevo.

Certain writers on Madagascar have assumed that once the "nobles" in some way ruled over the "commoners". This common misconception must be removed in order to understand what was involved in being an andriana or a hova. (Condominas, 1962, p. 119. Further information on the "castes" is given in Grandidier, 1915, Vol. I, p. 237ff., Callet, 1908, p. 303 *et passim*.

Various facts show that the difference between andriana and hova never carried with it a difference in the exercise of political power. Firstly, there were far too many andriana for them ever to have been an effective ruling class. In Imerina, at the time of Andrianampoinimerina, at least a third of the free population was andriana.[1] Quite clearly such a high proportion of the population could never have been leaders with political power. Secondly, Malagasy history is full of stories of whole demes living in quite considerable areas being made andriana or even losing the rank. To mention a few such examples, there are the Andriamamilaza who were made andriana, the Tsimahafotsy who were offered the possibility, and finally the group round Anbatomaina who lost their rank. This goes to show how unlike the European idea of nobles the andriana are. It is unthinkable that an English mediaeval king would have dreamt of enobling all the people in Norfolk.

Certain facts become apparent if we mark out on a map the villages traditionally inhabited by andriana. We find that whole districts, which are delimited more by geographical boundaries such as ridges and hills

---

[1] This is estimated by noting the proportion of villages traditionally inhabited by andriana to those traditionally inhabited by hova. For a similar estimate see A. and G. Grandidier, *Ethnographie*, Vol. I, Part I, p. 245.

than by social ones, were (apart from the slaves) inhabited exclusively by andriana[1] (see Map 3).

This is important as it shows that andriana groups are structurally homologous to hova groups. That is, like the hova they are divided into localized kinship groups with a high degree of in-marriage. Like most hova demes they claim descent from an eponymous ancestor but cannot in fact trace a genealogy back to him.[2] It is because of this that I have up to now discussed demes and their sub-groups irrespective of whether they were andriana or not.

Some of the customs which distinguished the andriana have survived to this day. They included the right to certain forms of greetings,[3] the right to speak first at public assemblies, sumptuary laws, the right to minor legal privileges such as the form of capital punishment etc.

These were ritual differences only and in themselves were not politically significant. It is not even as if ritual distinctions clearly marked off the andriana from the non-andriana. Similar privileges existed for distinguishing hova groups from each other and andriana groups from each other, and there were also a number of demes of uncertain status.

Apart from ritual differences, traces of division of labour existed. This, however, only applied to part-time activities. An example is that the andriana deme Andriantompokoindrindra were the only people who could work tin. That is not to say that there ever was any idea that in any sense the members of the Andriantompokoindrindra deme were by that fact tinkers, but that Andriantompokoindrindra were the only people who could take up this work. Here again the privilege of exercising a special craft was not a distinguishing feature of the andriana as opposed to the hova. Certain hova groups had their specialities as well;

---

[1] This does not apply to the highest categories of andriana. Their exceptional position will be discussed later. Professor Condominas sees this differently—"Alors que les hova sont repartis en *fokon 'olona* en clans,—la caste andriana est compartimentée en lignage . . ." 1960, p. 119. The distinction is here based on the assumption that the andriana can demonstrate their descent to their eponymous ancestors while the hova cannot. However, there seems to me to be no sharp difference in this matter between andriana and hova. The published histories of two andriana demes fail to link up the early genealogies connected with their founders and the present deme.

[2] R. Ramilison, *Ny Loharanon'ny Andriana Nanjaka* . . ., Andriantomara—Andriamamilaza, 1951–2. J. Ratsamimanana and L. Razafindrazaka, *Ny Andriantompokoindrinda*, 1909.

[3] R. F. Callet, op. cit., p. 370ff. W. E. Cousins, "The tribal divisions of the Hova Malagasy", *Antanarivo Annual*, Christmas, 1887.

for example, the Zanakdoria were the only people who had the right to weave the beautiful silk *lamba mena* for the dead.

One point of difference between the hova and the andriana is that the latter claimed some kind of genealogical relationship to the monarch[1] and this association with Merina royal history still gives them prestige today. The ranking of the andriana groups among themselves— Zanadralambo, Andriandranando, Andrianamboninolana, Andrian-tompokoindrindra, Andriamasinavalona and the tiny highest divisions, the Zazamarolahy and the Zanakandriana—is determined in terms of the nearness to the royal family of the deme ancestors.[2]

Andriana, therefore, is a term used to denote certain demes high up in a ranking hierarchy. This hierarchy was not linked to the distribution of power.[3] The Zazamarolahy and the Andriamasinavalona were an exception to this but they only represent a tiny proportion of the andriana and their power under the kings of Madagascar derived not from the fact that they were andriana but from the fact that they were Zazamarolahy and Andriamasinavalona. Their exceptional position can be ignored in a general discussion of the Merina ranking system.

Today the significance of ranking is diminishing. However, people of higher rank still attach value to the rank of their deme. Rank is only a corollary of deme membership. There are two things which still mark off the andriana. The first is that even today their tombs are inside their ancestral villages while those of the hova are outside them. Secondly, and more important, is the greeting used for andriana. Unlike the rest of the population andriana can be greeted by *"Tsara-va-tompoko?"* ("How are you, Sir?") which contrasts with other forms of greeting meaning much the same thing. The andriana consider that they should only be addressed in this way. What actually happens is that no non-andriana is ever addressed like this, and all andriana address each other in this way. However, in the critical relation between non-adriana and andriana only very rarely do non-adriana address andriana with this greeting. This is especially so now that the government has discouraged

----

[1] This claim was also made by some hova groups, e.g. the Zafimbazaha.

[2] Despite belief this cannot really be true since, if the rule were strictly applied, the Zanadral-ambo would come before the Andriandranando, but it is roughly right and is generally accepted as such.

[3] There never was any idea that political offices, apart from that of the sovereign, were in the past vested in any of these groups. In fact the most well-known officers of the Merina kings were hova.

the practice as anti-egalitarian. Only those non-andriana who are temporarily or permanently dependent on andrianas use the greeting, apart from a few town sophisticates who value the old order so much that they are willing to humble themselves for its sake.

If the difference between andriana and hova was never great, the difference between these two groups and the andevo (slaves) was fundamental. The andriana and hova are thought of as having always had slaves, but it was only from the reign of Radama I that the conquests of different races increased the number of slaves to very nearly half the population. Not all slaves belong to the darker race of Imerina originating from non-Merina peoples. There were "white" slaves and there were a few "black" demes such as the Manendy.[1]

The position of the slaves was the subject of much missionary writing and so we know a certain amount about their role, though their actual condition is difficult to guess.

The slaves lived in the houses of their masters until they started a family. They were then allowed to build a smaller hut near the dwelling of their masters. They were in the position in which children and other landless relatives in Merina society were, and like children they were called *ankizy*. They were expected to work in their master's fields and only worked for others when he instructed them to do so. They were under his jurisdiction and generally he was legally responsible for them, but he was forbidden to kill them, as was the case for a child. The fact that they had no legal standing meant that they were not involved in the major territorial and kinship organization of the state but were only legal extensions of their masters.[2]

Apart from the slaves who were not part of the social system of Imerina in their own right, we can conclude by saying that the whole of Imerina is divided into territories traditionally inhabited by demes and where only deme members are buried. These demes were ritually ranked and those of particularly high rank call themselves andriana. The division between andriana and hova is only part of a wider ranking system stratifying the andrianas among themselves. As I have said,

---

[1] A. and G. Grandidier, *Ethnographie* Vol. I, p. 246.
[2] H. F. Standing, *The Children of Madagascar*, 1887, p. 106ff. J. Sibree, *Madagascar, the Great African Island*, 1880, p. 180ff. W. Ellis, *History of Madagascar*, 1838, Vol. I, p. 92. W. E. Cousins, "The abolition of slavery", *Antanarivo Annual*, Christmas, 1896. It is interesting to note that in Madagascar slaves were buried near and in some cases in the tombs of their master. A. and G. Grandidier, *Ethnographie*, Vol. III, p. 49.

this ranking was in structural terms of only minor importance, but it is linked with the fact that certain demes had strict rules of endogamy while others were rather vaguer. Obviously in this system the higher demes had a greater interest in keeping purity of blood. The lower ones were satisfied to maintain their identity much more by relying on the fact of common locality. To this day the ranking system is still a source of slight but significant prestige.

Demes and *fianakavianas* in the traditional system depended for their existence on three factors: common ownership of land, in-marriage, and incorporation in the wider administrative system of the Merina kingdom. None of these things can really be said to exist nowadays, but the groupings still continue and the rank associated with them is still valued. Their members consider they retain the corporateness of the past, irrespective of the much more complex reality of the present. The question is how can they use this model of a past society as an ideal for the present. The answer lies in the fact that this traditional society, with its systems of interlocking groups, is fixed in a permanent way. It is built into the countryside of traditional Imerina in the form of tombs— massive buildings made of heavy blocks of stone.

It is believed that in the past a deme or a *fianakaviana* was associated with the area where most of its members lived, and because it had a territory it was incorporated in a wider system.[1] Now the old areas of the groups are not inhabited solely by the members of these groups. The situation has changed; membership is shown not by where the Merina lives but by where he will be buried. That is, when a Merina dies he ultimately goes to the tomb of those people he considers to be his ancestors, and the tomb is situated in a *fianakaviana* deme and district territory. Each village has a number of tombs, usually around half a dozen. In this way the association of people with group territories is maintained.

This topic will be discussed at length in Chapters 4 and 5. It means that the organization of the groups which have been discussed here is maintained by a huge model, which is no less than old Imerina composed as it is of territorial divisions in which the individual finds his place by means of his tomb.

----

[1] Clearly a certain number of individuals must always have lived away, and this must have increased gradually from the time of Andrianampoinimerina, but it is clear that the almost complete dislocation of these groups has only occurred in the last 40 years or so. The general contrast between the past and now is therefore much more than a simple matter of degree.

3

Social Organization of the Ambatomanoina District[1]

The Ambatomanoina District

Certain concepts associated with the traditional structure of Imerina have been described in the previous chapter. The present-day Merina are conscious both of the existence of these traditional social concepts and of the fact that they themselves have departed from them in terms of time and space. For them traditional social action represents an ideal, which is shared by all Merina and, as such, is a unifying factor. Wherever they are, and whatever their social position may be, they all accept the picture of the organization of old Imerina implied by these beliefs, and believe that it should in some way be the framework for their lives. In contrast to this uniformity of ideal, the societies in which they live today present, as they are aware, almost endless variety. They may live in Tananarive as professional men or factory workers, or in remote areas which they are slowly colonizing, or amongst other peoples as farmers, schoolteachers, pastors, etc. This means that our discussion of Merina social organization must shift its focus as it passes from the ideal organization to the actual organization. When describing the traditional ideal, useful comments can be made for Imerina as a whole. When dealing with everyday social relations, however, the wide variation in the conditions in which the Merina live means that we must restrict our examination to a much more limited area. I have neither enough knowledge nor enough space to take into account all the varieties of present-day Merina

---

[1] See Map 1.

social organization and will restrict my study to a part of present-day northern Imerina.

The passage from an all-embracing ideal system, which only comes to life on special ritual occasions, to the much more limited everyday practical organization of a small part of the province of Tananarive is not accidental. It is the passage the Merina peasant himself makes in reverse when he passes from the society in which he lives to the society of his *tanindrazana*. The present study is principally concerned with the interrelation of the two societies: the ideal society of the past and the practical society of the present, the interrelation of *Malagasy* times and the present-day *Malagasy-vazaha* opposition. This interrelation can only be made meaningful if we know something of these two societies. Thus, in the same way as I outlined certain relevant aspects of the traditional society, I shall now turn to a brief outline of the present-day society. It might seem at first that my main concern here—actions directed towards the *tanindrazana*—is independent of the actual situation. This is how the actor sees it. However, even those acts which seem a deliberate denial of the practical organization of the present, are moulded in a number of ways by that very organization. Also the categorization of social relations in the present organization, even in such practical matters as politics and agricultural organization, is also affected by the ideal of the past.

The particular district which I shall describe here lies beyond the northern frontier of traditional Imerina. It corresponds with the administrative area which is named after its biggest village, Ambatomanoina. I am especially concerned with some of the villages in that area that I know particularly well.

The total surface area of the Ambatomanoina "canton" is 331 square kilometres and the population is 6400, giving an average population density of 19·2 per square kilometre. The land consists mainly of grass-covered lateritic hills of poor agricultural value, but the few valleys in the area are very fertile. The climate is similar to the rest of the northern part of the plateau, though rather hotter because of its lower altitude. The natural vegetation is poor, dry grass on the hills, and rich marsh vegetation in the valleys. It is completely devoid of trees, apart from the high summit of Vohilena, a mountain which dominates the whole area. There, a small but dense tropical rain forest is found.

Even within this limited area great variation in social organization can be seen. The variation can be largely explained by the fact that this

is a district of colonization. The various kinds of groupings which exist
are often little more than stages in a development through which the
colonists and the villages in which they live go as time elapses after their
arrival. Therefore the best way of treating the social organization of the
Ambatomanoina district is to describe it as a process.

History

The early history of the Ambatomanoina district is unclear and the
many oral traditions relating to various hill forts are only now in the
process of being placed in a sound historical framework, though the
work of archaeologists is proving an aid to historians.[1] According to Vérin
(personal communication) it seems that the tradition that the area was
once occupied by people of a Sihanaka type culture is to some extent
justified, but that intermixed with them were Merina peoples living
mainly in the famous village parts of the region such as Ambohitsatakady.
However, there is as yet no record of early habitation in the area we are
considering. The inhabitants of the Ambatomanoina district never feel it
necessary to go back before the reign of Andrianampoinimerina in their
historical accounts of the area, and only very few people can trace a
connection with this particular locality which goes back as far as this.
This is not to say that there is no genetical connection between any of
the present inhabitants and the earlier inhabitants of the area, but, in
spite of much obsessive interest in the past, this connection was never
mentioned to me.[2]

As far as the people of Ambatomanoina are concerned the history
of the district began when Andrianampoinimerina sent out expeditions
to secure his northern frontiers from Sihanaka raids after he had
unified the kingdom. Accounts of these expeditions are given in the oral
traditions recorded by Callet, though they rarely refer to precisely the
area in question.[3] What happened, however, is fairly clear and accords
well with informants' statements. The military expeditions of Andrianampoinimerina and his successors became in time the garrisons of a
series of forts and in this way began the permanent populating of the

---

[1] C. Mautaux and P. Vérin, "Traditions et archeologie de la vallée de la Mananara (Merina
du Nord)", *Bulletin de Madagascar*, No 283, Dec. 1969.
[2] This would not be quite true of other nearby areas with otherwise similar histories such as
the area named Ambolibelena in the Anjoyndre district.
[3] R. F. Callet, *Tantaran'ny Andriana*. 1908, p. 606ff.

area. These first settlers, and indeed those who followed them, were the first *voanjo*, "seeds", of the area.[1] Seeds is exactly what they turned out to be. They drew kinsmen to them to cultivate the new lands and they in turn increased in numbers and were followed by yet other relatives so that their descendants are now numerous. This process, which I shall examine in more detail, is typical of what happened in the many areas colonized by the Merina in Madagascar. It even applies to a certain extent to traditional Imerina, where many of the inhabitants are living as *voanjo* away from their *tanindrazana*. That is not to say, however, that all areas of Merina colonization are similar. Different ecological conditions have meant different techniques of cultivation and different social organization. The area under examination, for example, is exceptional in that there rice is not transplanted into the fields but broadcast directly.

The peopling of the Ambatomanoina district has been going on for a century and a half, although most of the population studied had arrived only within the last fifty years. There have been various reasons for the movement of population into the area, and yet certain characteristics of the process of colonization can be observed.

The places chosen by individual colonists, with no previous ties to the area, are of two kinds. First, there are the early settlements placed by Andrianampoinimerina and his successors. These were primarily forts. Secondly, there are the administrative centres which have grown up since the coming of the French and which, in this particular case, are the main reason for the influx of population.

On the whole we know little about the forts. Some are famous in Malagasy history like Manohilahy and Vohilena, but there were many others which are not even mentioned in the *Tantaran'ny Andriana*. The remains of the fortifications can be seen everywhere crowning the hill-tops.[2] They were placed high up for strategic reasons and they dominate whole areas. Some of these strongholds seem originally to have been old Sihanaka forts which were invested by Merina soldiers. This was the case at Manohilahy and Ambohibeloma, where the fighting that led to their capture has become legendary. These hill-top forts were first inhabited by soldiers who came from various parts of Imerina, but especially from the district of Avaradrano. Judging from their descendants they were

---

[1] A. and G. Grandidier, *Ethnographie*, Vol. I, p. 249.
[2] Not all were Merina forts, see P. Vérin, op. cit.

mainly Tsimahafotsy, Zanadralambo, Tsimiamboholahy, Andrian-amboninolona and Mandiavato. There were also a number of Andria-masinavalona who were often in command of the soldiers. They were accompanied by royal slaves, Tsiarondahy, and later joined by Manendy, a "black" deme, whose main function from the point of view of the government was to look after the royal cattle put to graze in this area— once it had become secure from Sihanaka raids.[1] It is fairly clear that, as the population increased, cultivation, especially rice cultivation, became more important, since not enough supplies could be brought from Imerina. The valleys were roughly terraced and rice was sown. Later, cultivation led to the founding of new villages as the hill-tops were of difficult access and too remote from water and the rice fields. Only the relative pacification of the area made it possible to settle out-side the fortifications of the military posts. Nowadays the original forts are nearly all abandoned and some villages nearer the valleys are peopled by the descendants and relatives of these early colonists. The exact process by which people gradually left the fortified hill-tops and came to live in the valleys is not known, but it seems likely that it was similar to what is happening today to the administrative centres— villages to which, like the forts, people have not come through personal choice but to which they have been sent. The parallel between the old Merina forts and the administrative villages is clear when we consider that both have been the means whereby large numbers of people have been attracted to a new area. In both cases the people sent were few but, because the land was rich, they were soon followed by numerous relatives. While the original colonists were soldiers their present-day counterparts are post office workers, school teachers, servants of admini-strators, Protestant pastors and Catholic catechists.

This is not the only similarity to be found between the administrative villages and the earlier forts. Groups of people go out from the admini-strative villages, as they did from the forts, to find other, newer villages in the nearby countryside. I shall therefore refer to them as "radiant villages".

Radiant Villages

The traditional concept of a Merina village is a local unit where every-one is kin, and which is part of a larger area also united by kinship ties.

---

[1] R. F. Callet, *Tantaran'ny Andriana*, 1908, p. 266.

Since in a radiant village the people have been sent from different parts of the country they are most probably not kin. The village of Ambatomanoina is an example.

Ambatomanoina is, like many similar rural administrative centres, an example of ribbon development principally along one main street. The population of 532 consists predominantly of peasant cultivators, but its importance springs from the fact that it is a trading, educational, medical, administrative and religious centre. The houses are of the usual Malagasy type; a few in the centre are two-storied brick, built with corrugated iron roofs, first-floor balconies and windows and wooden shutters, but the majority are less grandiose than these, degenerating into simple impermanent one-roomed mud and bamboo structures with grass roofs. Most houses are between these two extremes. The village contains a "hospital", run principally by two partially trained nurses and a midwife, though in theory under the authority of a locally trained doctor who was rarely there during the particular year when I lived in the district. The hospital building contained little more than three dormitories and there was practically no equipment and only the most rudimentary store of a few medicines. Next to the hospital in importance came the administrative offices and the two churches. The administrative buildings contain barracks for three gendarmes who are responsible for keeping the peace over a very large area, and who were in occasional radio contact with the capital. There are also government officials who are principally concerned with tax collection. These are the "Chef de Canton" and his secretary and an agricultural adviser. Ambatomanoina also had a mayor, who had official duties, and a secretary to the town. Both these offices are held by part-time officials. There are two churches, a Protestant church run by a Malagasy pastor and a Roman Catholic church where full mass is said when the local Jesuit missionary is in the village. Associated with both churches are a number of part-time religious office holders. There are also two primary schools. One is a Catholic school run for large numbers of children by very young men with very little education themselves who are in the village on a temporary basis. The other school is a state school with fewer pupils. It is run by a qualified primary teacher and teaches basic reading and writing skills. Between them these two schools teach children from the whole of the administrative area of Ambatomanoina.

Apart from being an administrative centre, Ambatomanoina is also a trading centre. Ambatomanoina owes its importance to the fact that it lies at the end of the only practicable road towards the north.[1] This means that lorries and *"taxis-brousse"* can usually reach it. The *taxi-brousse* makes the journey to Tananarive at least twice a week, carrying people who have gathered in Ambatomanoina from a large surrounding area. The lorries are used mainly by Tananarive entrepreneurs who come to buy the available cash crops grown in the immediate vicinity of Ambatomanoina or have been collected from further afield by small-scale local entrepreneurs. This type of activity is the most significant economically but other forms of trading go on in Ambatomanoina. There are many shops ranging from the relatively well supplied shop of a Chinese trader, who also is involved in trading cash crops with the out-side world, to tiny shops which come into existence one day a week and have an ephemeral life. It is true to say that nearly everybody in Ambatomanoina tries to set up a shop, but for most this trading is more of a drain on resources than a source of income. Only three shops in Ambatomanoina seem to be well established and do profitable business. The whole topic of shopkeeping in Imerina needs a study to itself. But as far as we are concerned here the relevant point is that the notion of trading is intimately linked with radiant villages. The values linked to trading give a clue to the instrumental ideology with which the migrant Merina sees his relation with his neighbours in the new area. However, the number of traders in Ambatomanoina should not lead us to assume that trade is a mainstay of the village. No Ambatomanoina traders are full-time shopkeepers nor, with the exception of the Chinese trader and possibly one other, is most of the trade income derived from shopkeeping. In the majority of cases this income must be small indeed. Ambato-manoina is also a technological centre. During my stay a power rice husking station was set up by one of the Tananarive entrepreneurs and this was gaining in importance, less because of its ability to process rice, than because the owners, disposing of considerable capital, bought rice cheaply after harvest and then sold it at a high price in times of scarcity. Apart from this there were numerous craftsmen: blacksmiths, carpenters, brickmakers, watchmenders, a motor mechanic, barbers. Again, numbers are misleading because many more than those practising had the necessary skills and individuals continually set themselves up as crafts-men for a short period and then give up. Also, none of these people could be said to derive most of their incomes from their crafts.

---

[1] The road has recently been extended further north.

Finally, there is also a weekly market in Ambatomanoina, but this too is economically insignificant, although it may not always have been so. This is probably due to the increasing activity of traders from Tananarive with lorries who buy outside the market directly from producers, and small middlemen who operate outside the market-place. More important is the yearly "fair" when large numbers of itinerant traders set up stalls in Ambatomanoina and when inhabitants from far and wide come to buy consumer goods, especially cloth, hardware and agricultural implements.

Ambatomanoina then is a rural centre as well as a peasant village, but because traders, clerics, administrators and schoolteachers are also for much of their time cultivators, it is not divided into two categories of people. By contrast with the surrounding hamlets, however, the inhabitants of Ambatomanoina and of radiant villages generally aspire to other forms of income than simply deriving it from cultivation. Whether in fact they succeed to some degree in these occupations or not is another matter. They are, none the less, seen as a different kind of people; this is expressed by the contrast between the ambanivohitra and the ambohivohitra, literally the habitants of the higher part of the hill or village and those who live in the lower part of the village. This contrast refers back to the traditional Merina village fortress placed on the summit of some dominating height when to be in the main village literally meant to be high up, while living outside meant living below the village. Thus the inhabitants of Ambatomanoina live below the village, in spite of the fact that this is not so in geographical terms.

Ambatomanoina was essentially founded in 1920 by seven people sent to the area in the service of the government and other central organizations. These were a school teacher, two people connected with the church missions, a post office employee, a government official and two servants to look after the government house. They were sent as a nucleus to govern the dispersed descendants of the previous radiant villages. Very rapidly these people themselves proved to be focusses of attraction for their kinsmen and these kinsmen's kinsmen. Now the village of Ambatomanoina has a population of 532 and most people can trace a relationship to some official sent there. If we include the villages which have grown from Ambatomanoina we can estimate that the population amounts to over 700 people. A good proportion of these people are related to the original seven, as well as to some of their successors. The process of this expansion is fairly clear. The Merina kinship system allows at all levels a great amount of choice of place of residence. Children after a short period of marriage may choose to live with the parents of either the bride or groom. There are many ways whereby children may be fostered with relatives. Also, almost any relative may choose to come and live with a man who has a lot of land. The owner of the land will normally welcome the new addition as he will need his labour, while the newcomer will be willing to work because he can hope to obtain some land for himself.

Local Families

In this way a family can expand very rapidly. If a man has a lot of land the kinship system will draw people to him surprisingly fast. The first people who were sent to the radiant villages had a wonderful opportunity to lay claim to vast areas of land, since much land was unclaimed and it was necessary only to mark a boundary in order to establish a valid claim to such land. They were soon joined by kinsmen from their *tanindrazana*. More recently less land has been available and the situation has changed. Those who have recently come to the village have not normally been able to obtain free land, and this has meant one of three things. Either the newcomers have not stayed or they have married into families already settled, or they themselves have stayed but have not been followed by many of their kinsmen because they have been unable to get much land. In this way the families of the original settlers have become the most important element of the population of the radiant villages. Figure 3 shows an example of the development of this type of family. The original couple is marked by two circles. They were sent to the village to lead Roman Catholic worship in 1927. By now a large number of people explain their presence in the village by their relation to them, and these people are all marked on the genealogy. Together they form eight households. All the large kinship groupings in Ambatomanoina have similar histories in that they originate from one of the people sent to the area in the early stages of the village's history.

A group of people of this kind, who are all in some way genealogically related and who normally live in one village, form a significant unit in the social organization of the area where they live. I shall call this group a local family. We can therefore say that the local family is a group bound by genealogical links, although in some cases these links may be remote by Merina reckoning, but that it is ultimately defined by the coincidence of common kinship and common residence.

There are two kinds of local families in the Ambatomanoina district. The type already mentioned, that is, a group inside a larger village, and a local family which is in fact an independent hamlet. I shall return later to this second type. The size of the local family when it is part of a larger

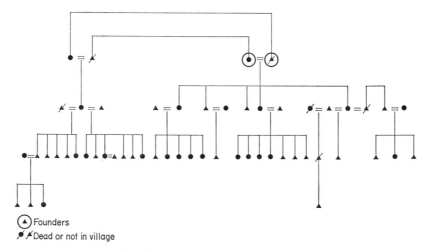

Fig. 3. Local family in radiant village.

village may vary from one household to around ten. For the peasant the local family is a *de facto* group in the sense that no moral rule determines its existence. The morally valued group is the whole family (*fianakaviana*),[1] most of which lives in other parts of Madagascar. The local family is for the actor that part of the *fianakaviana* which *happens* to live in the village, and so it has no name, but this does not mean that it has no sense of unity. In fact, it seems that, since this group is such an obvious group, it needs no such symbol of unity as a name or even ritual marks to distinguish it from other similar groups. Normally all the houses of the local family are grouped together in the village where they are situated and its members lead a life very similar to that of an independent hamlet inside a village. This is the group which, as will be explained below, forms the nucleus of the cooperating agricultural team. Its very strong sense of unity is particularly obvious in the behaviour of the children of such a group.

[1] See Chapter 4.

When asked where their houses are they answer that they have many houses, listing if need be all the houses of their local family and not distinguishing specially that of their parents. By this they mean that all these houses are ones which they can enter freely, in which they can take food, and perhaps sleep the night without asking. They are also the houses where the adults may chide them as if they were their parents. In contrast, if an adult from another house should chide a child he would be suspected of witchcraft.

It is unnecessary to discuss the kinship terminology at this point in full here but one aspect is relevant to the organization of Merina local families. Merina terminology is of the Hawaiian type. Therefore there are few terms and classification is pushed very far. This means that all relatives, however remote, can be addressed in terms also used for close relatives. A member of a local family is therefore able to refer to all the members of his family by the same terms as he would use to describe a group of very close kin. This is particularly significant for children and young people since I often discovered that they were convinced that the relationships within the local family were genealogically the closest ones that could be implied by the term of address they were using, although according to the adults this turned out not to be so. Thus, although the genealogical composition of the local family might be tenuous, it appears to the actors to be much closer than it actually is.

The local family recognizes a head. This head should in theory be the eldest living man or woman of the family. In fact the situation is more complicated. If a senior man is in a strong position within the group he will be recognized as head. The actual power of the head varies greatly according to circumstances. The most clear-cut case is when the head of the family is the legal owner of the land cultivated by its members. This is likely to happen when a man becomes a focus of colonization and people are drawn to him because of his land. In such a case the original colonist retains legal control of the land but allows it to be cultivated by his relatives rent free. With time the arrangement becomes more and more permanent, but the original owner always has the right to withdraw the land and this is quite clearly a powerful sanction. When the head of the family is also the owner of its land he therefore wields considerable authority. In many families, however, there is no one in this kind of dominant position and in such cases it is usually the eldest living man who is the head. If this is the situation the head has little or no authority and is more a chairman at family councils than a leader. These family councils are also typical aspects of local family life and take place very frequently. If there is a particularly important topic which has come up the family may be called to a formal meeting by its head, but such meetings may take place informally at any time either in the village or in the fields.

The family whose genealogy is given in Fig. 3 can be taken as an example of such a local family inside a radiant village, although it is rather larger than average. Since the radiant villages were originally formed by individuals who were not kin, it follows that these villages are made up of local families of varying size who are not kin among themselves. This has a direct effect on their wider political organization. In these villages the authority of the government is continually appealed to to settle disputes. The Merina government, the French after them, and finally the Malagasy government, have used a form of village council called after the word for community, *fokon'olona*. This council includes all the members of a local area and its existence in this form is thought of as a kind of substitute for the traditional state of affairs where the *fokon'olona* is a family council. This ideal manifests itself when, in a very loose way, the language of kinship is used for the *fokon'olona*, and the actual *fokon'olona* is seen as radically different from a family council. For the Merina this council, and the social unit it represents, consists of a group of neighbours as opposed to a group of kinsmen. This contrast will be illustrated in the discussion of funerals. The *fokon'olona*, in the sense of community, is what binds these non-kinship linked villages. The use of the council as an arm of the administration, however, has reduced in the radiant villages the strong feeling of community which they were reported to have had.[1]

As we have seen, radiant villages are the villages which pioneers in a new area join. They are also the villages people move away from to found new, smaller villages that are usually not far from the radiant villages and are offshoots of them. I shall call them satellite villages and there is an enormous variety of them. It is, however, apparent that all these villages are related in that the satellites from the radiant villages seem to follow a recognizable development. Consequently, their variety can be accounted for by the fact that they are merely at various stages of

---

[1] The topic of the *fokon'olona* is the subject of an immense literature which has been reviewed by G. Condominas. His conclusions are not entirely consistent with my findings. For a discussion of the nature of *fokon'olona* and how it articulates with the institution described here see Bloch, 1970.

development. Some of them are satellites of the earlier kind of radiant villages, the Merina forts; others of the more recent radiant villages, the administrative centres. Yet others are themselves satellites of satellite villages.

The reasons why people move out of the radiant villages are mainly of a practical nature. Often they leave the radiant villages because their houses are too far from the rice fields. This is an inevitable result of shortage of rice land. As radiant villages get bigger the land near the village suitable for making into rice fields gets used up, and latecomers are forced to cultivate farther and farther away. This is obviously very wasteful in labour because of the time taken in getting to the fields in the morning. The situation is made worse when agricultural equipment has to be carried there and produce carried back. The first step in moving out is to build a shelter, usually simply a grass roof on four posts, in the fields. It is then possible to get protection from the rain and cook a meal. The next stage is for a light wall of woven bamboo and daub to be added so that the family can sleep there at particularly busy times. Once this has been done a position is soon reached in which about half the year is spent in this house *an tsaha*, "in the fields", and the other half, during the dry season usually, in the more substantial house in the radiant village.

As soon as any length of time is spent in the fields a series of problems arises. Living alone arouses a whole set of fears, both natural and super-natural. It is dangerous to live alone, especially in such an isolated district as this. In the past marauders, cattle rustlers and brigands of all sorts abounded, and even now cattle thieves are very common. Going to live for any length of time in a particular place means taking your cattle with you and this, taken with the fact that cattle for the peasants in this area are the major store of wealth,[1] means running a great risk. Cattle rustling is considered by some people in Imerina, and even more by some peoples to the north, as a praiseworthy and manly operation and therefore completely different from other forms of stealing. It is done either by stealth or by an attack on a village by a band of raiders. In the latter case the village is surrounded, usually at night, and the assailants throw stones with string slings against the doors and shutters of the houses as a warning of what will happen to the inhabitants should they dare to come out. In the meantime the cattle are driven sufficiently far

---

[1] This is not the case in other parts of Imerina.

away. It is clear that with such a threat an isolated house is in a very poor position to defend itself. This means that as soon as a household settles away from the main village, it will try to gather other people around itself. This can be done in one of two ways.

Satellite Regrouped Villages

The first solution, the less favoured, is adopted by people who only control a small amount of land. If the family only possesses a small plot of land it is very likely that other people nearby will be in a similar position. That is, they will be living for part of the year in isolated field houses. If this is the case they may all join up to form a common settlement.

Villages which have been formed in this way are easily recognizable because, although the various elements join up sufficiently closely to be within calling distance of each other, they nevertheless seem to stay as far away as possible from each other. These villages are formed of many small nuclei of kinsmen, easily distinguishable from each other. Each small unit lives together on its own patch of ground cleared of weeds. The next group is usually quite a distance away and separated by rough grass (see Fig. 4). I shall call these villages "regrouped" as this describes the process by which they came into existence. The fact that the villagers are not members of one local family means that they live independently from each other and they have no head. They may push their separation as far as to call their village units by different names, as is the case for the village in Fig. 4. The fact which the Merina pick on to characterize this state of affairs is that people living in such a village do not share one cattle pen. Regrouped villages are similar in their structure to the radiant villages in that they are made up of several local families and that only links of neighbourhood bind them to one another. One family in such a village will probably not consider its co-villagers as socially closer than people of another nearby village. But the contrast between villages which share the same cattle pen and those which do not is not always a guide to the composition of the village, as there are villages where everyone is kin but where they do not all share the same cattle pen. When this happens, however, it is felt to be wrong.

The family groups within a small regrouped village are often somewhat different from the local families in the radiant villages. The reason for this is that as they are always very small, they may consider themselves as part of a local family in the larger radiant village which they have left. The members of such a segment will try, as far as is possible, to continue to behave to the other members of its local family still in the radiant village as though they still lived in the same village. This is very

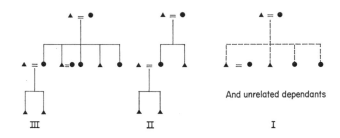

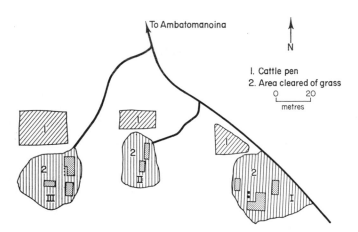

Fig. 4. Genealogy and plan of a satellite regrouped village (Belohataona—or Ankazo —near Ambatomanoina).

difficult as the required behaviour is associated with continual contact and, with time, the link between the segment of the local family in a regrouped satellite village and the main body of the radiant village tends to break. When this happens the kinship unit in the satellite village will itself become a local family.

Growth and fission take place in the regrouped satellite villages in a similar manner to the way they occur in the radiant villages. It is possible for newcomers to come and settle if they have any kind of tie with any of the villagers, and, because membership only involves neighbourhood links, it is said that an outsider cannot be excluded from a village of this type. But this is not so in satellite kinship villages, which will be discussed below.

With time these villages are likely to develop and begin to resemble radiant villages. In the same way as for radiant villages, growth leads to the foundation of new satellite villages. This again contrasts with kinship villages in that moving away is not thought a wrong action and is not necessarily associated with internal quarrels. If a local family moves away from such a village it is not the concern of the village as a whole.

Satellite Kinship Villages

Regrouped satellite villages are one of the communities which can be formed when farmers decide to move out of the radiant village. The other alternative is, in fact, preferred. It involves forming what I shall refer to as a satellite kinship village. The creation of such a village consists in attracting kinsmen or affines by giving them land to cultivate. It follows that founding such a village is something which can only be done by a person who has much more land than he can cultivate himself. In very much the same way as a local family grows in the radiant village, the founder of a kinship village becomes surrounded by a mixed bunch of relatives or affines. These are people who either have no land or not enough to cultivate in their home village, or people who want to escape from the authority of whoever had "given" them land before. There is a difference, however, in the formation of a local family in a radiant village and the formation of a satellite kinship village. In the case of a satellite village the founder is much more anxious to gather a group of kinsmen round him in a short time than were the early colonists in radiant villages. This means that he tries to attract kinsmen by offers of land to cultivate, and that if near relatives cannot be induced to come, more remote ones will be invited. The result of such a policy is that the kinship composition of these villages is usually genealogically more tenuous than that of a local family in a radiant village. The genealogy in Fig. 5 gives an example of this.

In spite of the sometimes remote character of the genealogical link which joins together the members of such a group, these villages are clearly more homogeneous than the regrouped satellite village. All the

Plate 2a. A satellite kinship village with its rice fields in the background. (This is the same village as shown in Fig. 5.)

Plate 2b. Boys harvesting (part of a harvesting party).

houses are close together on the same patch of cleared ground. There is normally only one cattle pen used by everybody (See Fig. 5 and Plate 2a). Such a village is clearly at the same time a local family in the sense in which the phrase has been used above.

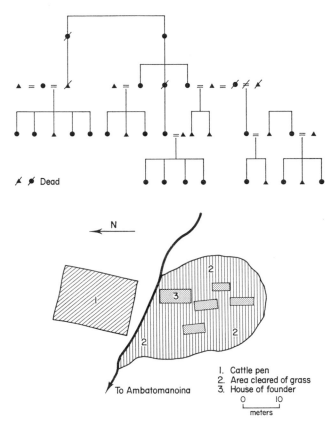

Fig. 5. Genealogy and plan of a satellite kinship village (Ambodomanga near Morafenokely).

Despite similarity with local families which form part of a larger village, and the looser genealogical ties, the local families which compose a village are particularly closely knit groups. The reason for this is to be found in the relation of the founder to the people he has induced to join him. The founder "gives" land for the others to cultivate. It is the kind of gift which a father may give to his children at marriage. It is not an outright gift in that the donor retains the right to withdraw it. This puts the founder in the position of the strong head of a family described above. In all the cases I came across the founder or his only heir was in fact the head of the local family. Because he is the head of a clear-cut unit his authority is particularly decisive. And social control within these villages is almost entirely outside the sphere of the central government. The position of the founder can in some cases be inherited by his heir if only one inherits his land. One example of this in the Ambatomanoina region was a satellite kinship village of one of the old fort radiant villages which had been in existence for over 80 years and had a population of 85 (Anosikely). This is, however, quite exceptional. Usually, as we shall see, these villages tend, with time, either to change character or, more frequently, to segment.

One does not become a member of a kinship village in the same way as one becomes a member of a radiant village or a regrouped village. After the initial foundation, it is quite out of the question for someone who is not a close kinsman of a member to join. The kinship villages do not segment in the same way as radiant or regrouped villages.

The strong authority of the founder is based ultimately on his control of land. He becomes quite naturally the head of the local family and may use his office to enforce his will in a way that is not possible for the head of a local family in a radiant village. At his death, however, a difficult situation arises. The land is divided equally between his sons and daughters, if, as is common, he has more than one heir. There is therefore no longer only one owner of the land in that particular village, but several, which means that no one wields as much power as the founder did. In this way the child of a founder does not have the tools with which to maintain the influence his father had. The office of head of the family is, unlike the land, not divisible among the heirs of the founder. This position will only pass to a person who combines seniority with ownership of at least some of the land which the village possesses. This usually means that it is passed on to the eldest son of the founder. He finds himself in a difficult position. He has the same office as his father but without the power which his father had. That is, the new head does not control all the land of the people he should lead. His siblings, who should obey him, have, in fact, as much control of land as he has. This dangerous situation is relevant to the present discussion in that it is the most common cause of segmentation of kinship villages.

A greatly simplified example of this process will show the pattern of this division. A village, which I shall call by the fictitious name of

Ambohiray,[1] was founded around 1910 and developed fairly rapidly. The founder owned all the land cultivated by his kinsmen, a very considerable area. In 1932 the founder died and his six children inherited. Of these, four were men and two women. The land cultivated by the other villagers was also divided between the children, and in this way these people passed from a situation in which they were all clients of the founder to a situation in which they were clients of one or other of his children. The eldest son became head of the local family and for a time the village stayed together. However, tensions developed, especially between two of the younger sons. Almost simultaneously, around 1935, the new head of the family died and the next son in order of seniority— who happened to be one of the quarrelling sons—inherited the headship. This proved too much for the other son and he went to live at the other end of the valley they had all inherited from the founder. With him went his dead brother's children and those who cultivated his land. In this way the original village split into two villages and a certain amount of bad feeling remained between the new heads of the two villages so formed.

This shows how, when kinship villages segment, they split right down the centre as one faction leaves and some bad feeling is inevitable. The resulting villages have a very similar structure to the parent one. In this way the satellites of satellite kinship villages are normally also kinship villages.

Finally, we may note that this brief description of the process of the formation of villages in the Anbatomanoina district ignores another aspect of the development process which is the tendency of regrouped and radiant villages to become kinship villages. This will be discussed in Chapter 7.

Agricultural Cooperation

The recruitment of people to villages has many aspects in common with the recruitment to groups cooperating in agricultural work. Both are activities of a practical nature where the relative importance of kinship and non-kinship criteria can be observed objectively.

In the Ambatomanoina district, as for the whole plateau of Madagascar, the staple crop is rice. Rice cultivation is by far the most important

---

[1] I give a fictitious name to this village as the information presented here was given to me in confidence.

activity both in the evaluation of the actors and because of the amount of work it requires, and this puts rice and the cooperation involved in its cultivation in a very special category. The rights and obligations relating to rice cultivation are extremely important and the denial of any of these rights would be tantamount to a refusal to have any kind of relationship with the people concerned. Rice is thought of as the source of life and all activities connected with its cultivation are of fundamental importance.[1] The organization involved is recognized as being of a practical nature but it is maintained by the strongest moral values.

In contrast there are many other crops which are generally cultivated, but to which little moral value is given to cooperating in their production. If a group of people is needed to help in their cultivation this group is defined in terms of the activity it would be performing if it were cultivating rice.

The other crops fall into various categories. First there is a series of secondary food crops, the most important of which are bananas, green vegetables, sweet potatoes, *voandzeia sub-terranea*, taro and manioc, which are all cultivated by individual elementary families. Secondly, there are cash crops—principally groundnuts and dried beans and to a lesser extent a surplus of rice, maize and manioc. More recently tomatoes and onions have been introduced in a few villages bordering the road. Cultivating these crops requires very little cooperation beyond the elementary family, but when it is necessary it is simply organized on an *ad hoc* basis. It is therefore sufficient to look at the organization of rice cultivation to see the pattern of cooperation.

Rice Cultivation

The technique of rice cultivation is different in the Ambatomanoina district from what it is in central Imerina. The main difference is that instead of first sowing the rice in seed beds and then transplanting it by hand into the rice field, the seed is broadcast directly on the main fields. This is to be seen as an adaptive response to the absence of scarcity of rice land which characterizes central Imerina. Because they have so much land the inhabitants of Ambatomanoina now broadcast rice seed instead of transplanting and are thereby able to cultivate a much larger area than would have been possible if they had practised a more inten-

---

[1] R. Linton, "Rice, a Malagasy tradition", *American Anthropologist*, Vol. 29, 1927, pp. 654–660.

sive type of cultivation. In 1965 and 1966, however, government agricultural advisers tried to introduce transplanting in the area and under government pressure a few transplanted rice fields were to be found.

The agricultural cycle really begins in September with ploughing and the repair of the irrigation and drainage channels.[1] This is usually done by a group of about three men. It is very heavy work and continues until the beginning of the rains in October. Little else is done during this period so, although the work is hard, there is very little need to hurry. In some cases no plough is available and the fields are dug with the long spearlike Malagasy spade. Sometimes the fields are merely trampled by cattle after they have been flooded. The next task is the most dramatic, and the most important from the point of view of cooperation. When the rains come the fields are flooded until all the ground is thoroughly waterlogged. Then, on a day fixed well in advance, a large group of people gather bringing with them their cattle. This usually means around 30 people and perhaps 50 to 100 head of cattle. They come, usually around 10 o'clock, after having done some other work, and wait by the rice field. After encouragement from the owner of the field, or perhaps from a more senior person who takes his place, the cattle are made to wade in the mud followed by the young men and boys of the party. The cattle are then driven round and round the fields, followed by yelling and sometimes singing youths who urge them along with switches from nearby bushes. As the cattle are driven hither and thither they break up the lumps of clay left by the ploughing, ultimately reducing the whole surface to the smooth, liquid mud which is required for sowing. The process usually takes a whole day. If the cattle show signs of flagging a young man jumps on the back of a bull prodding it so as to irritate it. The bull then jumps about wildly driving the rest of the herd on as it tries to throw its rider. This dangerous game is considered to be a demonstration of virile valour and is greatly enjoyed by all. While the young men are driving the cattle on, the older men repair the small dikes which separate the terraces with their spades, since these are continually broken down by the cattle. Those parts of the fields which have been trampled sufficiently are sown, usually by a senior man, but never by the owner. It requires considerable skill to broadcast evenly. As the

---

[1] Common ownership and upkeep of the channels for irrigation is not normally of the same crucial importance as has been described for Ceylon (Leach, 1961). This is due to the fact that once the rains start water is plentiful and that in the Ambatomanoina district irrigation ditches only serve one or a few owners. (The situation is different in old Imerina.)

sower moves rapidly through the fields he is followed by a shuttle service of young women who continually hand him rice in small baskets. The other women who are not helping in the fields stay in the house of the owner of the fields and prepare a big meal for when the work is finished. Although quite clearly very important work is done, such an occasion is considered as a very pleasant way of spending the day, which is understandable if we take into account the party spirit which pervades the whole proceedings. More important, the big meal that follows, at which a lot of meat is eaten, is much appreciated since it comes at a time when food and money are scarce. It is clear that most people consider themselves amply repaid in this way for the work they have done. After the rice has been sown little is done until harvest, apart from regulating the amount of water which enters the terraces. This task is performed by the owner. Harvesting is organized on much the same lines as sowing. It takes place mainly in June. The work is carried out with straight sickles by ten to fifteen men. It is again followed by a meal. Harvesting involves slightly fewer people and takes longer than trampling the mud. There is less labour available at that time than at sowing because rice sown early takes longer to ripen than rice which has been sown late. After cutting

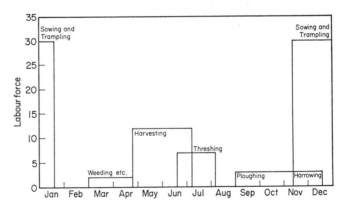

Fig. 6. Labour requirement for typical rice cultivation in the Ambatomanoina district.

the rice is stacked to dry for an unspecified length of time. The next major task is threshing. This is done by a much smaller group of between six and ten people. Both men and women take part. The threshing of one householder's harvest usually lasts several days. A threshing area is cleared and then covered with a floor of dried cow dung. The rice is then scattered on the ground and the cattle belonging to the owner of the rice are driven round and round over it, in much the same way as was done in the fields before sowing, but on a much reduced scale. The hooves of the cattle separate the rice from the straw. The straw is then removed with pointed sticks and the rice which is left on the threshing floor is swept up. It is then winnowed to remove dirt and finally stored.

The whole process of rice cultivation in terms of the number of people required for various tasks throughout the year is shown in diagrammatic form on page 94. The horizontal dimension represents time, the vertical dimension represents the number of people involved.

Categories of Agricultural Cooperators

We have seen how the various tasks involved in rice cultivation require a varying labour force. The question we must consider now is who cooperates with whom in these tasks. If we bear in mind the variety in the structure of villages and the fact that villages vary in size, it becomes clear that no simple answer can be given. However, some general principles hold true. The farmer is surrounded by a group of kinsmen with whom he has constant contact, his local family, and beyond this by neighbours who may or may not live in the same village. The size of the local family varies very much, although for those living in satellite kinship villages it is always relatively large. First of all it can be said that normally the following rule holds true. A man always relies first on his household and then, for tasks requiring a large number of people, on his local family, and finally on neighbours. Let us examine these three units in turn from the point of view of agricultural cooperation.

The *Mianakavy* Grouping

First there is the household. This includes people who normally live in one house, although if it includes a recently married child his or her family may be living provisionally in a closely associated house and count as part of the household. This group is referred to by the name of the head of the group followed by *mianakavy*. This refers to parents and children. The head of such a group is normally the owner of all its land and may be either a man or a woman. The structure of the *mianakavy* group in kinship terms can vary very much. It can be an elementary family or part of an elementary family; it can be an extended family or part of an extended family; it can be recruited along less close kinship lines by means of the extensive system of fostering.[1] If the kinship system allows for great variation in this group, its composition is none the less restricted by the fact that it is a group with an economic task to perform. This means that from a practical point of view there is an ideal composition for such a group. Although there is great variation in the amount of land owned by different individuals, there is much less variation in the amount actually cultivated. This is because if a person owns much more land that his household cultivates he will "give" it to relatives to cultivate in the way already described. Conversely, if a person has too little land he will look for a kinsman who will give him land. The economically ideal number for the household can be estimated if we consider the normal tasks which must be performed by it. There is often need for a ploughing or a digging team. Malagasy ploughs need two adult men to work them: one to guide the plough, another to drive the oxen. Merina digging also requires two men. This is because digging is done by two men spearing a large clump of earth from opposite sides and turning it over simultaneously. Apart from the two men employed in ploughing or digging, someone else—who may be a boy—has to look after the cattle. As for the women, one adult woman and one girl are usually necessary for the household tasks and agricultural work, but an extra woman is useful for mat-making and fishing.[2] Most *mianakavy* groups have this basis of two men, a responsible boy and one or two women and a girl. Usually there are also a number of young children. Most households, if they fall below this level of manpower, look for kinsmen to attract or children to foster, or if they are too numerous they divide sooner or later. This, however, is never seen as being due to economic reasons as the following example shows. The household of a man whom I shall call Ratovo consisted of himself, his two sons of 17 and 15, who were still at school, a married daughter and her husband and three grandchildren. As it stood it was well fitted to the agricultural tasks described above. The son-in-law was cultivating land given to him by his father-in-law. Nevertheless, father-in-law and son-in-law had been on bad terms, as far as I could gather, even since the daughter's marriage 11 years before. They had quarrelled repeatedly and many of

---

[1] A fuller examination of this topic leads to a consideration of the domestic aspect of kinship, which I hope to discuss in another publication.

[2] In the parts of Imerina where transplanting is carried out the work of women is of very much greater significance, which leads to serious modifications to the picture drawn here.

these quarrels were remembered in detail, but in the end they had made it up again. During the year 1965, the head of the household decided to end the fruitless schooling of his eldest son and to find him a wife, whom he duly married and brought back to the household. Shortly afterwards, father-in-law and son-in-law quarrelled again, and this time the father-in-law took back the land he had given to his son-in-law, thereby expelling him and his wife and children from the household. Clearly he had become able to do what he had long wanted to do because he had obtained another working man, his son who had finished his schooling, and another working woman, his new daughter-in-law. This example shows clearly what can happen in such a case. The split is explained not in economic terms but in terms of kinship or of quarrelling, although at a different level it is the economic effect which has regulated the size of the household.

This *mianakavy* group forms a work unit and there is no question of acknowledged exchange among its members. The fact that they all usually depend on their head for land means that he organizes what they do. For rice cultivation this group works alone when repairing the irrigation system, when ploughing and when transporting and storing the rice. It also works together for much of the cultivation of the other crops. When the cooperation of this group is requested by a non-member, it is the head only who is asked and it is understood that the others will come with him. If the head of the *mianakavy* group receives two such requests for the same day, he may divide the group.

The Local Family and "Artificial" Kinsmen

Beyond the household the farmer is surrounded by his local family which varies in size, and beyond the local family by his neighbours. The variation in size of the local family (there are even a few totally isolated households) means that it is not possible to say, as we were able to for the household, that any particular tasks are done by the local family. If the local family is too small for the needs of the task neighbours have to be called in.

The tasks which require more people than there are members of the household can be classed according to the number of people needed. We can divide the people with whom the farmer has relations according to the tasks in which they cooperate with him and see to what extent they correspond to such categories as local family and village.

From the point of view of agricultural cooperation the group immediately beyond the *mianakavy* group is the one called upon for such tasks as threshing and harvesting. It is felt that this group should correspond to the local family and the cooperation it involves is thought of as only compatible with close kinship. In fact the local family may be too small and neighbours may have to be included. This situation only occurs in radiant and regrouped villages. When neighbours do have to be called in for such tasks the relationship between neighbours in such a group will be most intimate. The clearest manifestation of this intimacy is that, although such neighbours are not kin, they refer to each other as if they were. This topic is discussed below, but here it must be noted that when a Merina family requires the help of non-kinsmen at this level of cooperation, the fiction of artificial kinship is so strong that the anthropologist may take a very long time to discover it (if he does at all).

Within this group, when one *mianakavy* group requires the cooperation of the others whether related or not, the head will go to the other households "inviting" them to come and work. The timetable for work is established informally within such a group so as to avoid clashing. The word "invite" is a translation of the word *manasa*, which can be used equally for an invitation to a wedding or any other pleasant occasion. This shows how little this is considered as a *quid pro quo* arrangement. No clear exchange system is evident, although one may assume that over a long period, and taking into account other goods and services, an exchange system does exist. In fact the idea of a simple exchange between people who are so closely related is considered immoral. When I suggested such a thing it was firmly denied and I was told that people only worked for each other because of their love for one another. The suggestion that self-interest entered into this was clearly defamatory. The reason is that agricultural cooperation is thought of as the very essence of being kinsmen (*mpihavana*). Cooperation is thought of less as an economic service than as a demonstration of a moral link.[1]

These general principles apply in the same way but to a lesser degree to the links within two further circles of cooperators which I wish to distinguish between.

Beyond the circle which conceptually corresponds to the local family

---

[1] It is interesting to note here that in the area where transplanting is practised and where labour is for some periods of the year very short, the situation is radically different. A strict and meticulous exchange arrangement is made and there is much less talk of kinship love, except for very close kin.

is a wider circle called upon for tasks requiring larger numbers of people, the main one being trampling the earth in the rice fields. People are "invited" in the same way as described above and accept in order to show, as they never tire of pointing out, their reciprocal kinship love (*fakatiavana*). Most of them are not kinsmen in any way as few local families are big enough to allow for this. This is well known, but again the relationship is kept in the idiom of kinship. Here, however, a fairly easily discernible pattern of exchange can be seen, although it is also denied.

Still beyond this group is an even wider group which can be said to include most people with whom a person comes into contact. These are people who theoretically could be invited to help with the trampling but never are. There is no sharp break between people in the category discussed above and this one. A man always tries to keep as many people as possible in the former category as the fact that they gather at least once a year to his call is a demonstration of his influence. But it is obviously impracticable to ask too many people and one has to be content with the fact that one says that these people could be called upon if necessary. The point of saying that such and such a person could be called upon to work for you is tantamount to saying that he is a kind of kinsman. This is because agricultural cooperation is typical of the behaviour of kinsmen. To understand this extension of the notion of kinsman, *havana*, in this way, it is necessary to examine again the meaning of the word no longer in its ideal context, but in its present-day context.

Havana Mpifankatia

In the traditional system a man is thought of as living exclusively with kinsmen and all regular local social relations should be exclusively with kinsmen. Especially important is that the notion of kinship implies economic and political cooperation for the Merina even though this may be of a somewhat unspecified nature. Nowadays, it is still felt very strongly that a person cannot be trusted if he is not a kinsman. No obligation is felt to be binding unless the parties are kin. Contractual relations are not seriously considered and have no place in the traditional system. They are thus felt to be unsafe, especially over a length of time. Some aspects of this have already been touched on.[1] The reason for this view is

---

[1] See pp. 59–60.

obviously linked to the already mentioned fact that the Merina possess
no intermediate category which conveys the idea of cooperation without
that of kinship (categories such as "neighbours" or "friends" which are
so significant in certain parts of Africa).[1] The situation in the Ambatomanoina district, however, is that everyone has to rely to a certain extent
on non-kinsmen as neighbours, as helpers in the fields, and as partici-
pators in the same political system. It is very difficult to make these
people one has as neighbours and helpers more reliable, since traditionally one should have such rights and duties only between kinsmen.
The peasant solves this problem either by forming kinship links through
marriage in spite of the obstacles,[2] or by pretending that those people
who in the traditional system would be kinsmen are in fact kinsmen.
This kind of relationship is referred to as *havana mpifankatia*.[3]

   This really means a kinsman "because he is loved". In this way the
notion of *havana* is extended to non-genealogical kinsmen. All the people
in the various spheres of cooperation distinguished above are normally
referred to as *havana*. In the early stages of field-work informants often
told me that other people in their villages were their kinsmen, but later
on I found they were no such thing, and that this was common knowledge. The point is that it is not right to have co-villagers who are not
kinsmen, and the avowal that some people in a village are not kinsmen
is tantamount to saying that these people are not wanted in the village
and that the other villagers have no lasting obligations to them. Repeatedly, when walking with villagers along a path we met people who
might cooperate with them in agricultural work. I was informed that
they were kinsmen, only to be told when they were out of earshot that
they were not "truly".[4]

   The explanation of this phenomenon is that traditionally the two
sides of the category *havana*, practical cooperation and genealogical
relations, are merged. The movement of population is given as the ex-
explanation of the fact that for practical reasons these two aspects have
become separated and that the individual finds himself with two sets of
kinsmen, cooperative *havana* and the genealogical *havana*. I have called

---

[1] J. Beattie, *Bunyoro—an African Kingdom*, 1960, p. 61. J. S. Fontaine, *City Politics*, 1970, Chapter 12.
[2] See Chapter 6.
[3] This is not literary Malagasy and is an expression only heard in the countryside, especially in this area. However, other equivalent phrases are used elsewhere.
[4] *Tena*—a literal translation of this word is "really".

the first kind of *havana* "artificial kinsmen" because this is how the actor sees them. This reality means that, although people will say they trust each other and are kinsmen, the fact that they are not gives this situation an ambiguous element which makes the individual maintain his link with his real *havana*.

The relationship of being *havana mpifankatia* is continually being acted out by what may be called a minute ritual. A distinguishing feature between a *havana* and a stranger is that, while the latter waits to be offered food as a favour, the kinsman has a right to his kinsmen's food and may *demand* food. This is manifested especially in the way *havana mpifankatia* behave when they pass each other's houses. They should shout "*Inona masaka?*", which literally means "What is cooked?" or "Is there anything worth eating here?". This is often accompanied by even more aggressive behaviour such as snatching food, or a statement such as "There is nothing good here anyway". This would be extremely offensive from a stranger. The right to *demand* food is also evident in the continual asking for *paraky*, that is, specially prepared tobacco for chewing. Most Merina men and women carry a little tobacco with them and this represents a fairly significant expense and is far from valueless. However, whenever *havana mpifankatia* are together they continually demand *paraky* from each other. This is grudgingly given, but given it is, until there is none left and that has to be demonstrated by showing the empty box, which may be so awkward that some people keep two boxes, one continually empty for display and the other for their own use.

This behaviour has much of the elements of a joking relationship including its ambiguity. It is a public demonstration between people of their being kinsmen and it shows the right to demand food. Interestingly, this behaviour is much more marked between remote kinsmen and *havana mpifakantia* than between really close kinsmen. The reason is obvious; in the latter case there is no need to stress a well-established relationship.

The notion of *havana mpifankatia* is also closely linked with the notion of *fokon'olona*. A word which is used when referring to the administrative village council. It is also employed in a rough sense to mean the local community when it refers to all the people in the locality who have permanent relationships together. Professor Condominas has stressed the kinship ideology of such a group,[1] which is present in the sense that all

---

[1] G. Condominas, *Fokon'olona et Collectivités Rurales en Imerina*, 1960, p. 192. Also Bloch (1971).

communities should be kinship communities. This means that kinship sentiments are often used to describe relations within the *fokon'olona* because the *fokon'olona* is the *fianakaviana* made up of the *havana mpifakatia*. However, by that very fact it is also realized that it is not the real *fianakaviana*. And this is shown in the way the invitations to a ceremony are always classed under the two headings: *fianakaviana* and *fokon'olona*. The *fianakaviana* side of this contrast will be considered in the next chapter.

PART II

The Link with the *Tanindrazana*

4

Tomb and *Tanindrazana*

In Chapter 2 I described the most clearly formulated equipment of rules and concepts which the Merina peasant possesses for ordering social life, and in Chapter 3 a typical situation in which Merina peasants find themselves was discussed. There are two reasons why this equipment is most difficult to use. The first is that the society implied by these rules and concepts is different from the society which faces the peasant in his everyday life. The second is that the traditional system is based on an anchoring of people to specific valued localities but that the majority of Merina peasants do not live in these localities. The problem is therefore either living a life which ignores the traditional moral and social system and which is consequently unpredictable and dangerous, or living a life governed by the traditional system which means not taking full advantage of the economic and political opportunities of the present. The Merina solution is neither of these alternatives. It consists in maintaining one's place in the traditional system ritually and occasionally, in order to be free, to carry out unhindered one's everyday activities. In this chapter I show how the Merina peasant manages to participate in the society of the ancestors while living in a totally different society. This he does by building up a continuing sacred existence in his ancestral village, which manifests itself in certain limited contexts, while governing his everyday life in a profane way. This chapter and the next discuss how this continuing "sacred" existence is established by examining how the link with ancestral villages is maintained by such people as the inhabitants of Ambatomanoina, who live away from their *tanindrazana*.[1]

---

[1] A. and G. Grandidier noted the importance of the *tanindrazana* in *Ethnographie*, Vol. II, p. 42ff.

The *Tanindrazana*

One of the more obvious results of the feeling of not being morally attached to the *tanindrazana* is that the Merina feels that he is not attached in the same way to the place where he lives. This manifests itself in the fact that if a man is living anywhere else than in the actual land of his ancestors he always says he is a *vahiny*, a word which can be translated as either a "guest" or a "stranger". This is the case irrespective of the number of generations which may separate him from the time when his antecedents lived in a particular area. Thus, nearly everybody of free descent living in the Ambatomanoina area says he is a *vahiny*, in spite of the fact that his family may have been living there four or five generations and have forged a whole network of practical social links with other people in the area.

The status of *vahiny* deprives the actor of certain rights. This is clear in the difference in attitude to local recruitment in the new area and that in the *tanindrazana*. In contrast to his status of *vahiny* in the new area a man is *tompo-tany* in his *tanindrazana*. Literally this means an owner of the land, or a master of the land. These implied rights are largely a question of sentiment, since legally a man has the same rights wherever he lives, but the belief that he does not can have practical effects as the following example shows. During the period of my field work in the Ambatomanoina area a very unpopular man settled in the village. This man was suspected of being a cattle thief and furthermore was a leper. The people who most strongly objected to his presence brought the matter up at a meeting of the village council. The general opinion of the council which emerged was that, although nobody really wanted the leper and his family in the village, the fact that everybody was a *vahiny* and not a *tompo-tany* meant that they had no right to exclude anybody. An elder put forward an opinion at this meeting which was widely repeated that, since they were all *vahiny*, they had no right to exclude anybody who was in the same position as they were themselves. The notion of being a *vahiny* is an example of the turning away in certain contexts from the practical organization towards the *tanindrazana*. This can also be seen in the behaviour of two Merina who meet for the first time. They always find a way of asking each other, either directly or indirectly, "Where is your *tanindrazana*?" The very frequency of this question emphasizes the importance of the *tanindrazana*.

The point to notice is that at an early stage in a social relationship when two people are, so to speak, placing each other socially, the ques-

Plate 3a. Andrainarivo which is an ancestral village (*tanindrazana*) in the canton of
Fieferana.

1 Moat   3 Tombs
2 Church   4 Houses belonging to *originaires*

(Most of the residents live outside the moat in small houses not shown in the photograph.)

[*Facing* p.106

Plate 3b. A Merina tomb (rather above average). (Photograph by courtesy of P. Vérin, Centre d'Art et d'Archeologie, University of Tananarive.)

tion which is asked is not where someone lives, but where his ancestors lived. The answer to "Where is your *tanindrazana*?" is the name of a locality in central Imerina since the ancestors of all Merina come from that area. We should not assume, however, that because the question is directed to the past, this question is asked because the enquirer is more interested in the forebears of a man than in the man himself. Quite clearly, when a man asks another where his *tanindrazana* is, he wants to know something about that man's position now. This amounts to saying that something can be discovered about a man's place in society by knowing the name of the village of his ancestors.

First of all the name of a man's *tanindrazana* is indicative of his rank. Since the *tanindrazana* is in the traditional area of Imerina it is, like all other localities in this area, associated with a social group. To ask a man the name of his *tanindrazana* is a way of finding out in the first place to what deme his ancestors belonged, and therefore to what deme he belongs. As we noted in the second chapter, the various demes were ranked in a system which was associated with closeness to the monarch. Even today there is a certain amount of prestige in being associated with a deme high up in this ranking order and therefore it is of interest to know to which deme a person belongs. This can be discovered in two ways. The first is to ask directly, but this is considered ill-mannered. The second is to ask the name of a man's *tanindrazana*, which is itself a sufficient indication of his rank, because which villages are associated with which deme is common knowledge. An experienced Merina carries in his head a sociological map of old Imerina. It is by associating a person with a locality in that critical area that rank is established. In this way, if a person says that his *tanindrazana* is the village of Ilafy,[1] it follows that he is a Tsimiamboholahy, or if he says that his *tanindrazana* is Ambatofisaorana he is an Andriamasinavalona.[2]

Quite obviously a system which distinguishes differences in rank and group is also one which links together people of similar rank and group. Since people of the same deme are linked to the same or associated group of *tanindrazana*, it is possible to place a person in the traditional system by knowing his ancestral village. Knowing a man's *tanindrazana* enables another to discover whether he is lower or higher up in the ranking hierarchy or, most important of all, whether he is in the same group.

---

[1] See Map 2.

[2] This socio-geographic system does not take the descendants of slaves into account.

Referring to a *tanindrazana* is therefore a way of using the traditional territorial organization as a tool for classifying the people with whom one comes into contact.

One of the main reasons for finding out people's *tanindrazana* is to discover other members of one's own deme, but what this means is less straightforward than might appear. To know other members of one's deme is important because being a member of the same deme is a sign of something else, namely kinship. There is no strong feeling of loyalty among deme members simply because they are deme members, but because it is assumed that deme membership implies kinship, and kinship demands the strongest loyalty. In practical terms this means that once a man has found someone of the same deme as himself through asking where the other's *tanindrazana* is, he will then try to establish a genealogical link with him. It will then be in terms of being a grandfather's brother's son, or whatever the case may be, that the relationship will be recognized. In other words, belonging to the same group of *tanindrazana* means kinship. We must therefore examine in detail the relationship between what the Merina see as "membership" or "ownership" of the *tanindrazana* and kinship.

Tanindrazana and Kinship

In the traditional system the individual is seen as belonging to an exclusive descending group within which all marriages should have occurred. This I called a deme. Then, inside this group there were less distinct units which had a partly localized character and within which all marriages normally occurred; these I called *fianakaviana*.

The present-day group which corresponds to the traditional *fianakaviana* is now more important than the deme. It is this group which is conceptually associated with the *tanindrazana*. However, before examining the relation of the traditional *fianakaviana* to the present-day category to which it corresponds, and the relation of this to the *tanindrazana*, I shall give a name to the various levels for which the word *fianakaviana* is used. Very much like our own word "family", the Malagasy word *fianakaviana* is a word of unspecified extension. Its greatest extension is sometimes referred to as *fianakaviana be* (a big family), but normally it is not clear who is included in the category. It is important to distinguish the traditional *fianakaviana be*, which was partly a division of the deme or the deme in another context, and partly an Ego-centred category, from its present meaning of solely an Ego-centred category which I shall call "dispersed family". Traditionally, the *fianakaviana* was a group of kinsmen and affines nearly all of whom lived in a restricted area consisting of a number of associated villages. Most marriages took place within this group.

In the present situation the *fianakaviana* is different from what it is believed it once was. This has meant two things: first, a man's dispersed family no longer has a local aspect but is found not only all over Imerina but sometimes all over Madagascar, and secondly, what was a near discrete group has become a web of relationship only definable for individuals. This has been a direct result of the weakening of the system of preferred marriages (see Chapter 5).

The present-day dispersed family is therefore an Ego-centred group within which marriages still occur fairly frequently. It is a group of people who can normally demonstrate links of kinship and affinity to Ego without having to go back for more than four generations. Anybody who stands in this relation to Ego is a member of Ego's dispersed family.

It is basically a moral group and not simply the group of kinsmen with whom one has some common economic or political interest. It contrasts sharply with the pseudo-kinship groups which are merely neighbourhood groups (see p. 101). It is the group one invites to such kinship occasions as marriages, circumcisions, and *famadihanas*. (A detailed description of the *famadihanas* will be given in the next chapter.) Finally, it is the group within which information about the activities of its members is circulated.

If the dispersed family is not specifically a political or economic group this does not mean that it cannot be used for political or economic ends. Continually peasants who need the help of officials look to members of their dispersed family to find a kinsman who might help, and an official who wants to buy rice cheaply does the same. This is not to say that these ties cease to be recognized when they are of no more practical use or even when they are a practical disadvantage. In the Ambatomanoina area there were large quantities of papyrus reeds which are used in mat-making. One household in particular was continually being visited by members of their dispersed family who came to collect the papyrus, and whenever this occurred the visitors stayed a few nights and ate meals in the house of their relatives. The latter complained to me about the inconvenience, but they never considered refusing this hospitality, an act which would have been a denial of kinship. It is precisely because family ties are not just expressions of practical consideration that so much importance is attached to them. Practical ties are automatically broken when they stop being useful, but the type of kinship ties we are discussing here are maintained because of their moral value. In contrast to practical ties the moral ones continue in changing circumstances. This means that these ties exist and are thought binding even when the people concerned have no contact. It is their apparent permanence which is so highly valued and this is expressed in the strength of the moral sentiments they arouse. Not only do they mean that a man is surrounded by dependable kinsmen, but also the notion of family, through its link with the *tanin-drazana*, means that he feels these permanent kinship relations are a part of a wider system in which all social relations take on this permanent and fixed aspect. When extended in this way the system is conceptualized in terms of a much greater permanence because the family, via the *tanindrazana*, places the individual in the ideal society of the ancestors.

The link between the dispersed family and the *tanindrazana* seems obvious to the Merina. Informants explained this link to me in historical terms. In the past all members of the *fianakaviana* lived in the *tanindrazana* area. Then they dispersed in small groups to various parts of Madagascar. The present-day dispersed family consists of those people who left the *tanindrazana* and their descendants. This appears to mean that, although the *fianakaviana* is now dispersed, all its members share the same *tanin-drazana*. This is perhaps an acceptable interpretation of the facts for the first generation who leave the *tanindrazana*. But even here a difficulty arises, since the *fianakaviana* was probably never localized in one village only but in a number. This is just ignored in general statements and it must be assumed that the particular village is taken to represent the traditional' 'land of our kinsmen" rather than being simply "the place where our *fianakaviana* lived." Even at this stage therefore, the link between *tanindrazana* and *fianakaviana* is less simple than it is made to appear. For the succeeding generations the situation changes even further. This is because if an exclusive association with the *tanindrazana* area is to be maintained, all marriages, or nearly all, must take place within the dispersed family. If this is not done, members of the dispersed family will, in a short time, have kinship ties with people who have different *tanindrazanas* not associated with theirs, and so it will not be true any more to say that common kinship means, *ipso facto*, sharing a common *tanindrazana*. But this is precisely what has happened. Many marriages now occur completely outside the dispersed family (see Chapter 6) and it is true to say that an individual's dispersed family, even though it includes many people who have the same *tanindrazana* as himself or one closely associated with it, also includes many with different *tanindrazana*.

This inevitable result, however, seems not generally to be taken into account by the Merina. Whenever people told me about their *tanindrazana* and their dispersed family they told me that everybody who "owned" their *tanindrazana* was a member or that the dispersed family had its *tanindrazana*.

Two problems arise. Firstly, there is the question of the relation between membership of the dispersed family and membership of the *tanindrazana*. Secondly, we must know how a Merina decides which *tanindrazana* he belongs to. The solution to both problems becomes apparent upon consideration of the Merina tombs. Each of the villages in old Imerina, the *tanindrazanas*, contains a certain number of tombs. Thus the village of Andrainarivo near Fieferana contains nine and the nearby village of Ambohizanaka seven. The demonstration of belonging to a *tanindrazana* is based above all on one fact. A person is ultimately buried in one of the many tombs of his *tanindrazana*. In other words a Merina finds his place in a complex segmentary system by where he is going to be buried, since association with a village in old Imerina is an indication of membership of a whole set of groups including district, larger deme, and smaller deme.

On casual enquiry a Merina will say that recruitment to tomb and ultimately to *tanindrazana* is perfectly straightforward. He will be buried with his close kinsmen or family in the place where his *razana* have been buried before and their *razana* before them. An informant asked in a general way suggests no element of choice nor does he indicate that non-kinship factors enter into the association with the *tanindrazana*. We know this cannot be so for the Merina have no rule of unilineal descent. The *fianakaviana* is not fully endoganous, and ownership of a *tanindrazana* cannot ultimately be multiple (one cannot be buried in more than one place). Therefore choice of membership has to occur. The way it is effected and how and why it is disguised becomes apparent in part when we understand what is meant here by *razana*, since it is the idea of *razana* which is used to denote the relationship with the ancestral village.

Tombs

In the preceding chapters the word *razana* has been translated as "ancestor". This is the most common translation of the word.[1] It is used in this sense in the phrase *fomban-drazana,* "the custom of the ancestors", where "ancestor" means some past, long dead, unspecified forebear. If in most instances it is perfectly satisfactory to translate *razana* in this way, there are cases where this is not possible. The word also means "dead person" or "corpse" when the corpse is related to the speaker. It is clear that the word "ancestor" does not really fully convey the meaning of the Malagasy word, since there is nothing strange in a parent referring to his or her dead child as a *razana.* Consequently, the notion of *tanindrazana* can only be grasped when we bear in mind the full lexicological referent of the word *razana,* which covers both ancestor and related dead.

We have seen how the *tanindrazana* is the place where a man believes his ancestors, *razana,* lived. It is, however, also the place where the dead are *now* and where one will oneself be buried. The importance of the double aspect of the word *razana* now becomes clear. It enables the actor to consider *razana* meaning "ancestor", and *razana* meaning "the dead" as one and the same thing. This means that by placing his relatives in the tomb when they are dead and wishing to go there himself, he closely associates himself with the lost society of the ancestors who lived in *Malagasy* times. He thus makes the land of his ancestors (*tanindrazana*) the land of his dead relatives (*tanindrazana*).

Tombs in the *tanindrazana* are the most solid and best built structures which the Merina undertake, and the land on which they stand is inalienable[2] (see Fig. 7 and Plate 3b). They all consist of a partly underground chamber usually approximately 20 feet square. The walls are of stone and cement and the top is normally capped by a huge stone slab covered by concrete. The chamber is reached by an underground staircase. The door to the chamber is a massive stone slab. Usually only the top four or five feet of the tomb emerge above ground and this part may be highly decorated[3] (see Fig. 7 and Plate 3b). Some tombs are brightly painted and topped with more or less elaborate stone arcades, etc.

---

[1] In the dictionary by Abinal and Malzac it is translated into French as *ancêtre* and *aieux.* *Dictionnaire Malgache-Francais,* 1963 ed.

[2] G. W. Parker, "On systems of land tenure in Madagascar", *Journal of the Anthropological Institute,* Vol. XII, 1883, pp. 277–280.

[3] The tombs of Imerina are so striking that more has been written about them than about anything else in Madagascar. See R. Decary, *La Mort et les Coutumes Funéraires à Madagascar,* 1962, A. Grandidier, "Des rites funéraires chez les Malgaches", *Revue d'Ethnographie,* 1886, p. 213.

Others are plainer as this is sometimes thought better taste. Because of continuing changes of style and intense competition, there is great variation.

As might be expected, tombs of this kind are very expensive. In the past they were built by the family itself, but now they are built by specialists. An average tomb costs 350 000 FMG (£500), but some cost

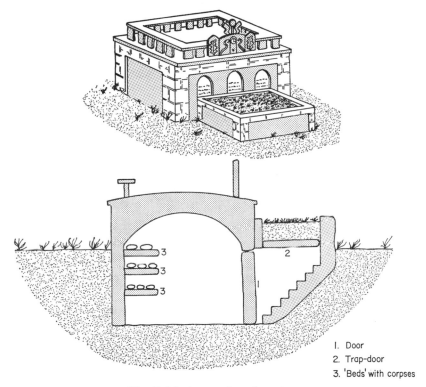

1. Door
2. Trap-door
3. 'Beds' with corpses

Fig. 7. Merina tomb and section.

more than twice as much. The expenses involved in building a tomb are far and away the greatest enterprise a Merina ever undertakes. A comparison with the price of houses in the village where he lives shows this. They tend to vary from 5000 FMG to, in exceptional cases, 100 000 FMG.

The very great expenses involved in building a tomb can be explained in a number of ways. Informants often told me that it was normal to spend more money on a tomb than a house since they would stay very much longer in the tomb. If we take this answer seriously it must be seen in the light of notions about the after-life which will be briefly discussed below. Another reason which is, I believe, significant is connected with jealousy. Jealousy is thought to be a major cause of witchcraft (*mamonsavy*). The fear of witchcraft was often given to me as a reason why people did not repair their houses and wore ragged clothes when they could afford better ones. On the other hand, expenses connected with the tomb are never thought likely to lead to jealousy and ultimately witchcraft. The only explanation I can find for this is that because the tomb, through its association with the *razana*, is good, it cannot possibly lead to witchcraft which is the very essence of evil. This means that competition for prestige through conspicuous consumption can only be indulged in safely when it is concerned with tombs and the *tanindrazana*.

These factors undoubtedly play a part, but I would link the expenses are involved with a much more fundamental desire which is often made explicit, viz. the desire to make a tomb which will last as long as possible. These squat buildings, constructed with huge boulders, are very durable, which is obvious from the many abandoned villages where the houses have disappeared but the tombs are still standing. They are the symbols of the association of their builders with the village where they are situated. They are in this way a denial of the fluidity of Merina society and indeed of all the societies of the living, and an assertion of an unchanging order where men are organized along clear-cut lines. In other words, they are the demonstration of what the Merina feels his society was and ought to be. By making a tomb the solidity of which gives it a durability which far exceeds everything else, the Merina affirms his allegiance to a particular social unit and an idealized way of life.

Anthropologists are familiar with social and kinship groupings which are thought of as permanent, continuing irrespective of generations. Clearly we are dealing with a phenomenon of this kind here. It would seem that any group which is identified with such a thing as a Merina tomb would have this quality of permanence. There are, however, two difficulties in considering the people associated with the tomb as a permanent corporate descent group, and the tomb as the symbol of such a group.[1]

First, we do not find any clearly defined group, like a lineage, for which the tomb can be a symbol. Secondly, it is difficult to say that a tomb is a symbol of something else, when the tomb itself is the most

----

[1] M. Fortes, "The structure of unilineal descent groups", *American Anthropologist*, Vol. 55, 1953, and "Totem and taboo", Proceedings of the Royal Anthropological Institute for 1966.

valuable possession of the people concerned. We shall see that these two problems are one and the same.

If it is clear from the great expense involved in building them that tombs are property; it is as such that we must examine them. (Ownership in the case of a tomb is having the right to be buried in it.) Three questions are important for understanding the nature of this property. We must know which people group together to build a new tomb, who maintains it, and lastly, how a tomb or a share in it are inherited.

Taking this last point first, we see that a Merina tomb, like any other property in Imerina, can be passed on to all children whether male or female, either by men or women. Also, in the same way as for other property, after a husband and wife have had a number of children their previously separated property becomes merged. In terms of tomb ownership this means that a woman, after she has borne her husband three children, has a right to be buried in her husband's tomb (see Table 1).

TABLE 1

Choice of tombs

These figures are obtained from information on where people were actually buried, pooled with information of where people said they would be buried

Tomb	Men	Women	Total
Father's	39 (50%)	17 (20%)	56 (70%)
Mother's	21 (27%)	22 (26%)	43 (53%)
Both	8 (10%)	7 (8%)	15 (18%)
Grandparent*	4 (5%)	9 (11%)	13 (16%)
Spouse	4 (5%)	21 (25%)	25 (30%)
Others*	2 (3%)	9 (11%)	11 (14%)
Total	78 (100%)	85 (100%)	

*These cases arise largely as a result of fostering, which is more usual for women than for men.

The right of a man to be buried in his wife's tomb is less clear. Certain families accept this right, others deny it, and in many cases this leads to tension.

It is clear, therefore, that most people have a choice of tomb. A man may go either into his father's or his mother's tomb and sometimes into the tomb his wife intends to be buried in. A woman may be buried in the tomb of her father, the tomb of her mother, or in her husband's tomb. This choice is even wider than it might appear at first sight, since it is possible in some cases to be buried in a grandparent's tomb, even though Ego's parent was not buried there. This is as far as the dictates of kinship take us and, as will be obvious, they only limit the possibilities but do not define which tomb should be chosen.

In spite of the choice offered by the system a decision must be made during life if only for practical reasons. Merina tombs, in spite of their massiveness, need regular upkeep, especially to improve their appearance. The large amount of concrete of which some parts consist is continually disintegrating, probably due to the poor quality of the cement and lack of sufficient technical knowledge. Quite apart from the repairs, there is also the occasional, but much more expensive, need to build a new tomb when the old one is full. It is built next to the old one and when it is ready some of the dead from the old one are taken into the new one, to stress the continuity between the two. The ceremony[1] this involves makes the expenses of building a new tomb even more onerous. Everyone who intends to be buried in the tomb will contribute, if not equally, as near to equally as the group considers reasonable from its knowledge of their respective financial circumstances. It is because of the large expense involved in owning a tomb that a choice must be made fairly early as to which tomb an individual wants to be buried in. Nobody wants to pay for the upkeep of more than one tomb.

What then are the factors affecting that choice? In theory, other things being equal, the father's tomb rather than the mother's should be chosen because of the slight leaning to patrilingy manifested in a great variety of instances. Informants told me that the mother's side is somehow weaker than the father's. This is put graphically in a proverb: "The mother is the moon but the father is the sun". This is a comparison which for the Merina implies an idea of weaker and stronger rather than opposites. The point is again made clear by the determination with which informants, who admit that there is a preference for the father's tomb, emphatically stress that if it is so desired it is always possible to go into the mother's tomb.[2]

---

[1] See Chapter 5.

[2] I must mention one exception to this. A well informed member of a family in the Marovatana assured me that for his family at least a strict rule of patrilineal recruitment to the tomb was enforced. I was not able to check up how far this had been observed, nor whether this was a local variation or in some way due to the great influence of the particular family under the Merina kings. On this point and in nearly the whole of this and the following chapter, my information is different and in some respects radically different from that obtained by Condominas (1960).

It is not, however, in terms of this patrilineal preference that the actual choice is really made. When pushed further many informants explained their choice in terms of affection for their mother or father or spouse. One informant told me that he would be buried in his mother's tomb because "milk comes from the mother, not the father", another that she would not be buried with her husband because he was a drunken lout, etc.

Although no general rules emerge from such preferences, they are underpinned by more regular factors. The point is that deciding to be buried in a particular tomb means joining an association the purpose of which is the upkeep of the tomb. This association meets when it is decided that repairs and improvements to the tomb should be made. It seems that if this group is to take decisions efficiently it must also be a closely knit group in everyday affairs, because, as it must act unanimously, it must reach decisions by means of informal pressures between its members. Clearly only if the members have a lot of practical interests in common and are able to recognize a common head, will such pressure be effective. This explains the fact that, although the composition of the tomb group varies, it is often formed round a local family, as defined in the previous chapter, and is usually headed by the head of that family.

Critical to understanding the structure of the tomb management group is the position of its head, as it is often in terms of a relation to him that a particular tomb group is chosen. This is a clearly recognized office and no activities can take place at the tomb without the approval of the head. Although he may not be the original initiator of repairs or rebuilding, the invitation to a meeting to discuss the matter must come from him. This means that the person who wants to build a new tomb or repair one must have the agreement of the head of the tomb group in order to get the matter discussed at all. In theory, this office should automatically fall on the oldest man of the group. It is sanctioned by the fact that, with the approval of the tomb family, the head can exclude some member of the tomb from being buried there. This is greatly feared. It occurs in cases when a repair or ceremony has been decided on and a member of the group refuses to participate. This, however, can only be applied against individual black sheep as normally if an important person in the family refuses to participate in the expenses he can block the whole proceeding. Thus only a head who can wield actual power over the members will be successful in reaching decisions. In this way seniority only is not a sufficient qualification for headship and seniority as a criterion of office is often tempered by other qualifications.

Three categories of people are commonly found to be effective heads of tomb groups: heads of local families, government employees (*fonction-naires*) and rich men. The different position of these three types affects differently who will and will not belong to their tomb group and so we must examine them in turn.

When the head of the tomb group is the head of the local family which forms the core of the group, he has the authority which comes from his position in the village where he lives. As we have seen, this varies, but often his authority is backed by ultimate control of the land of the other members of the local family. In cases where the head of the local family is not the owner of the land he is more in the position of a chairman and may be accepted just because of his seniority or because of sentiments of kinship piety. With such a head it seems much more difficult for the tomb management group to reach a decision. Often members of the tomb group who are impatient with its apparent impotence to get anything done may decide to break away and build a new tomb for themselves.

Powerful men, especially men in the employ of the government (*fonctionnaires*) often become heads of tomb groups. The hold they have on others is that the less fortunate members of their family know that they may well have to rely on their help when they get into difficulties with the administration.

Rich men too may obtain the office as their relatives will always be anxious to emphasize kinship links with them, as they know that if they are in financial difficulties their rich kinsmen will then be under an obligation to help them.

Tomb groups also include many people who are not directly dependent on the tomb group head. These people are faced with the problem that they must attach themselves to one tomb group or another, as they are probably too poor to make a tomb for themselves and their immediate dependents. They must therefore make a choice and attach themselves to one group. Once the choice is made it becomes difficult to reverse it because at each repair the members contribute financially and so nobody will willingly forgo being buried in the tomb to which he has contributed. Similarly, few people will accept a newcomer if he has not participated in the upkeep of the tomb.

In fact, for most people the choice of membership is not made in terms of a direct relationship with the head of the tomb group. This is because the choice has to be made shortly after marriage since this is the time when a man or a woman will be expected to start making contributions to the upkeep of the tomb. The individual will have a choice in terms of the tomb of his parents or parents-in-law who are still alive. When this is so the individual is not concerned with the head of the tomb family since his relation to him will be entirely through his parent or parent-in-law. The choice which presents itself is whether the individual concerned wants to participate in a joint venture of the greatest importance with his father's relatives, his mother's relatives, or his spouse's relatives.

In practical terms this normally means that a man chooses the tomb of the senior person he is most closely associated with, which usually means the person with whom he lives. Thus if Ego has been brought up by his mother and not his father, as a result of divorce or widowhood, he will normally be buried in his mother's rather than his father's tomb.[1] On the other hand, if Ego lives with his father's family, he will be buried in his father's tomb. In the same way, if Ego has been brought up by a grandparent he will normally be buried in that grandparent's tomb, irrespective of whether a parent of his has been buried there. A woman who dies in a place where she is with her husband's kin will probably be buried in his tomb.[2] A man who dies in such a position is also likely to want to be buried in his wife's tomb, especially if, as is probable, he has not participated in the upkeep of either of his parental tombs.[3]

Finally, it should be remembered that some people are not buried in any monumental tomb at all. This happens when they have been excluded by their family[4] or, more commonly, when they have failed to contribute to the upkeep of a tomb. They are always left in their temporary grave, often near the entrance of a particular tomb, such graves were often pointed out to me as the graves of *vahiny*. They are referred to as *fasana mandrosoa* or "entrance graves".

There is yet another way in which considering the tomb as property helps us to understand the nature of the group associated with it. That is

---

[1] Ideally, in the case of divorce, children should return to their fathers at the age of 14 or 15. This does not in fact happen (see p. 193).

[2] When an affine is buried in the family tomb he or she may not always remain there. See Chapter 5, p. 161.

[3] See p. 191.

[4] See p. 199.

for understanding the process of segmentation. As we have seen, for the tomb group to work smoothly, it must be tightly knit and preferably formed around the core of a local family. However close the tomb group may originally have been, the passage of generations means that the composition of the group becomes less close, and a section of the group may find that they have no further practical links with the other people with whom they share a tomb. This usually means that the head of the group has no more practical control over this section. Furthermore, he cannot threaten them with expulsion from the tomb if they refuse to participate in expenses, as they can block any decision involving such expenses. However, as neither party can achieve much positive action in such a situation the group which has lost its links will save money to build itself a new tomb which will finally mark its segmentation from the original tomb group.

When this happens the segment builds a new tomb, usually in the same *tanindrazana*. When the tomb is finished they will ceremonially take their ancestors from the old tomb to the new one.[1] This is normally possible because a segmentation of this sort occurs when kinship links between the segment and the rest of the family become remote. This means that the segment's immediate ancestors are not closely related to the other members of the tomb group, and can therefore be removed without difficulty from the old tomb.[2]

We can summarize this discussion of membership of the tomb group by saying that the tomb group consists of closely related people who own the tomb in common. A particular tomb can be chosen by reason of sufficiently close kinship to a member of the tomb group whether living or dead, but ultimately the choice is not governed exclusively by kinship. Many factors, political and economic, enter into the reckoning.

This conclusion is something of a paradox. The facts just presented are fairly evident. How is it then that informants only talk of kinship when explaining tomb recruitment and *tanindrazana* recruitment and deny, sometimes indignantly, that economic and political factors are relevant?

The answer seems to lie in the fact that to the actor what we can see as two analytical levels are merged. On the one hand there is the actual management group of the tomb which consists of the people who will be buried in the tomb, and on the other the people who may, according to the kinship rules, be buried in the tomb. At this second level is a bilateral

[1] See Chapter 5.
[2] See Chapter 5.

web of relatives which is not a group at all since it does nothing and owns nothing in common. It is comprised of Ego's own kinsmen and is a category different for each individual. I shall refer to it as the tomb family, although it is really an inner group within the *fianakaviana* or dispersed family.

In empirical terms this means that informants, when asked generally, tell you that all close bilateral kinsmen share the same tomb. The kinship category and the owners of a tomb are not separated and the fact that some of Ego's close kinsmen are members of other tomb groups is simply ignored. Furthermore, it is to the notion of the bilateral category of close kinsmen that moral value is given, while the actual tomb management group is not a subject of personal allegiance. The strong and continually stressed attachment to the tomb and the *tanindrazana* is thought of merely as an attachment to kinsmen. Many statements from informants show this but none better than the way a break of kinship obligation is referred to as "forgetting the *tanindrazana*".

The link to the *tanindrazana* is seen as something unchanging whatever the economic and political circumstances, since it is a link to a fixed order handed down from the ancestors. The fact of the practically based tomb management group is simply ignored. But it can only be ignored because the thing which links a man to the traditional order of society is a *tomb* and because of the double aspects of the word *razana*. This becomes clear if we view the relationship of those who are, or will be, buried in the tomb (the tomb group and the dead) and the tomb family as a process.

This point of view is forced on us by the nature of the choice involving tombs. It is not a choice which has relevance for the time when it is made but for the future, that is, the time of death. When a choice to join a particular tomb is made there is no question of excluding any kinsmen at this stage. That is, there is no question of cutting out members of Ego's tomb family. Even at the time of death the position remains unchanged, since at the funeral or the *famadihana all* kinsmen should participate, whether or not they will be buried in the same *tanindrazana*. The choice only really starts to effectively exclude some relatives when the funeral and the first *famadihana* are over and the kinship individuality of the dead has little relevance any more, since the dead person is not by that time an effective link between the living.[1] When this happens the

---

[1] See Chapter 5.

dead relative becomes merged with the tomb building. He has stopped being a *razana* (related corpse) and is only a *razana* (ancestor). In fact, there is more interest in the tomb itself than in the long dead. Thus time transforms a bilateral web into discrete groups which can fit into a segmentary territorial system. The focus is shifted from an actual person, whether alive or recently dead, to a non-individuated ancestor, and then to a thing—the tomb. The *razana* (related corpse) has kinship links and these are kept open as potential channels of cooperation for moral reasons. When a person who has died has been changed to a *razana* (ancestor) the position has changed since he is nothing but a symbol of the continuity of the group. The only kinsmen of the *razana* (ancestor) which are relevant are the living members of the tomb family—the others are forgotten. It becomes possible to consider the group of anonymous dead as the closest family group of the ancestors of the living tomb family. The importance of this is that, seen from the point of view of the living, the preceding generations in the tomb appear as a purely kinship-based group, since the individuality of those concerned has disappeared. Thus, if the kinsmen have been a continuing discrete group, it is easy to see their living representatives as a discrete group too, especially since membership of one's tomb family places one in the social framework of the society of the ancestors.

Tombs and Descent

The similarities between the situation I am dealing with and a system with unilineal descent groups are obvious. An individual in both systems feels himself, because of moral kinship considerations, to be the living representative of a group which has gone on from generation to generation, and which is part of a fixed all-embracing social order. In both systems this is a fact which directs his allegiance and his emotions.

In Imerina, however, it is not through membership of any group that these emotions are aroused. They are connected with the category of tomb family, which is not a corporate group.

The corporate group which actually does something and owns something (the tomb group) is not endowed with moral value. To the actors it is a purely practical organization for doing such things as buying cement. There is no place for the tomb group in the system of traditional morality. The ideology of descent is centred on things—tombs and other ancestral property—and the link of individuals to these things is felt to be simply kinship which is defined in vague terms so as not to bring out the ambiguity of its nature. This system is a well-known alternative to a unilineal rule of descent and Levi-Strauss has put this alternative succinctly. Of such a system he says:

Il devient impossible de définir l'appertenance au groupe directement au moyen de généalogies empiriques. D'ou la nécessité d'une règle de filiation non équivoque telle que la filiation unilaterale, d'un nom ou tout au moins d'une marque différentielle transmise par filiation et qui remplace la connaissance de liens réels.[1]

Only an analysis from an external point of view stresses how other factors, irrelevant to kinship, enter into the relationship of individuals to these things. To the Merina, tombs stand for kinship and moral obligations, irrespective of politics and economics.[2]

In seeing how a tomb is chosen we have seen how a *tanindrazana* is chosen, since this is determined by the place of the tomb. How far does this help us in understanding the relation implied by the Merina between the *tanindrazana* and the dispersed family? The core of the dispersed family, the tomb family, is linked to the *tanindrazana* by the fact that the tomb is in the *tanindrazana*, but do all the other tomb families associated with all the tombs in the same *tanindrazana* form the external fringe of Ego's dispersed family, a significant grouping for the individual members of any particular tomb family?

Some sort of filiative link is believed to exist between the dead in the various tombs in one village, but this is very vague and also applies to all tombs in a deme territory. It is also true to say that it seems that the frequency of intermarriage inside a village in the traditional system was high, but it does not seem as if the *fianakaviana* was ever limited to the village. In other words, even in the traditional system the correspondence of village and *fianakaviana* was only partial. In the present situation the correspondence of the people sharing one *tanindrazana* and a dispersed family is even vaguer. It is only at a symbolic level that the *tanindrazana* is linked with the dispersed family. In practical terms the individual

---

[1] C. Levi-Strauss, *Le Totémisme Aujourd'hui*, 1963, p. 16.

[2] Apparently much of the difficulty in deciding whether certain forms of Malayo-Polynesian social organization can be called descent groups springs from the fact that these groups have associated with them the ideology of descent but on analysis reveal themselves to be determined by non-kinship criteria (H. W. Scheffler, *Choiseul Island Social Structure*, 1965). In this case the difficulty seems to me to be non-existent, since the ideology of descent is associated with a thing and a concept (*fianakaviana*) not a group. The group bounded by economics and politics does not have this ideology of descent.

does not know and is not concerned with the group of people sharing a *tanindrazana*. Thus the importance of membership to the *tanindrazana* is not important *per se*. The *tanindrazana* is only important as the place where Ego's tomb is. It is the attachment to the tomb which causes the attachment to the *tanindrazana*. This leaves us with the question of why in many circumstances do the Merina talk of their *tanindrazana* when it is really the tomb which is important to them.

The answer is very simple. Unlike the *tanindrazana* the tomb has no name and so, when it is a question of placing an individual in relation to others in the wider system, it is to the *tanindrazana* that reference must be made. While it is the tomb which is important to the individual from a personal and familial aspect, it is the name of the place of the tomb, a name the full significance of which is widely known, which is relevant in the comparative classification of members of society. This is what Levi-Strauss has called "systematic activity".[1] Tomb and *tanindrazana* are two aspects of the same thing in different contexts. The *tanindrazana* is associated with the *fianakaviana* simply because the core of the *fianakaviana* is anchored in the *tanindrazana* by the tomb.

Eschatology

The relationship of people to the tombs implies their having notions of what happens to the dead inside the tomb. These notions are less important than might be assumed. The reason is that the great interest in death is principally focussed on the tomb as a building. Talk of tombs is almost unavoidable. During field work I continually noticed small children discussing amongst themselves their respective tombs. Adults always take the opportunity of broaching the subject. In contrast there was very little talk of what happened to the dead.[2]

The very lack of interest of the Merina in the after-life may account for the many inconsistencies in their eschatological beliefs. First of all, there is a general belief in ghosts, *angatra*. These are the ghosts of the unknown dead which are continually joined by the more recently dead. This category of supernatural beings is very weakly conceptualized. Its main manifestation is frightening people by making strange noises,

---

[1] C. Levi-Strauss, *La Pensée Sauvage*, 1963.
[2] This subject is fully discussed for the Betsileo by H. Dubois in *Monographie des Betsiléo*, 1938, p. 720. Merina beliefs are very similar but less elaborate.

especially in maize fields, but also near tombs. At one end of the scale the *angatra* merge with various nature spirits (*lolo*) which manifest themselves in the form of butterflies and moths. These need not concern us here. At the other end it is associated with our next category, the *ambiroa*. The *ambiroa* is thought of as the continuation of the individual's personality after death. Its equivalent during life only develops from the age of four or five onwards. It continues after life as a supernatural being of a somewhat mischievous nature. It is also associated with the tomb but most of the time it is thought to wander around the hills, come in and out of the house, and in some way be continually present. For the period following the death of a near relative there is much awareness of his *ambiroa* as associated with him personally. With time, however, he becomes merged with all the other anonymous *ambiroa*. During the period when he is still remembered as an individual he may appear in dreams to his near kin, often to give them advice or to ask a favour. The length of time when the dead are so remembered varies very much. It is related more to the position of those who might remember him than to any clear beliefs. Although the *ambiroa* does appear to the living it would be misleading to suggest that there is ancestor worship among the Merina.[1] There is no regular ceremony involving worship. Very occasionally an important offering will be made to the *ambiroa* of the dead in the tomb, which does suggest that the dead have some kind of power over the living. I only came across one fully documented case of this ceremony. It occurred when a young man wanted to marry someone outside his endogamous group. He apparently had a meeting of his dispersed family arranged and an offering of rum and honey was made at the tomb. This made it possible for their children to be buried in the tomb as the approval of all was given. Although this kind of ritual is very rare, I was told it was practised from time to time. This is a major ceremony, but minor offerings are also very commonly made at the tomb in the hope of securing specific benefits. Sweets, and small portions of

---

[1] I am only discussing the position as I found it during field work. It is possible that ancestor worship was more significant in the past, but it was always of less significance than royal cults and worship of *sampy*. By ancestor worship here I mean the kind of religious practice so defined by M. Fortes in "Some reflections on ancestor worship in Africa", *African Systems of Thought* (Eds. M. Fortes and G. Dicterlen), 1965. At no time during my field work was it suggested that any break with the *tanindrazana* or the tombs would be punished by the dead. Such suggestions on my part were emphatically denied. Those practices suggesting ancestor worship and described by Ellis in *History of Madagascar*, Vol. I, 1838, pp. 232 and 434, seem to have disappeared. Moreover, Ellis makes it clear that they were unimportant.

rum and honey are given by individuals without any ceremony or with just a short prayer. The multitude of different kinds of these small observances falls into the same category as other similar offerings which are given at almost any place with supernatural association. In addition to tombs, such offerings are made at particular stones associated with *lolo* or *vazimba*,[1] i.e. at streams, at certain mounds of earth thought of as *vazimba* tombs, or on the side of a path. It seems to me important not to overemphasize such offerings, whether they are made at tombs or in other places, as they are not taken very seriously by the Merina themselves and require almost no significant expense.

Although in the case of both the major ceremonies mentioned above, and the less important ones which take place at the tomb, the appeal is to the *ambiroa* of the ancestors, it is interesting to note that apparently no appeal is made to any ancestor in particular, but to all of them. This is also the case whenever a blessing is asked of them.[2] The *ambiroa* are an impersonal group. As they manifest themselves in these beliefs they have really lost all humanity. The group of unnamed *ambiroa* has merged with the actual tomb building. This conceptual transformation is the subject matter of the next chapter, but we can note here one of its many manifestations. In some families a small bottle of water is placed with a certain amount of ceremony on the tomb and left there for a year or so. It absorbs the power of all the dead in the tomb and ultimately the water is sprinkled in the houses of the tomb family. It is the *ambiroa* of the dead which gives the water virtue, but it is only the tomb as a building which is stressed and forms the link with the living.

The *ambiroa* is sometimes referred to as the *avelona*. This word is rarely used and most informants seemed to agree that the *avelona* was the same thing as the *ambiroa*. Some stated that after death what had been the *ambiroa* is then called *avelona*. One informant thought the *avelona* was a third soul.

Apart from the *ambiroa* the Merina believe in a second "soul", the *fanahy*. This is again one of the elements of the individual which separates after death. During life people are said to have either a good *fanahy* or a bad one, yet the *fanahy* is a much vaguer concept than the *ambiroa*, and, apart from this moral content, does not really mark off one person

---

[1] These are supernatural beings associated with people whom the Merina traditionally expelled from Imerina.

[2] For a fuller discussion of this see Chapter 5.

from the next. After death the *fanahy* was traditionally thought to go to Ambondrombe, a mountain in southern Imerina. Since the coming of Christianity, however, this has changed. The early missionaries assumed that the word *fanahy* meant soul and they taught that the *fanahy* either goes to heaven or hell as the case may be. This has, in fact, been accepted.

Ancestral Lands

Nothing attaches a man to his *tanindrazana* more strongly than does his tomb. It is the tomb which makes the *tanindrazana*, since *tanindrazana* taken in one way means the land where the dead are put. But there are other ancestral properties which link a man to his *tanindrazana* and we should discuss these before going any further.

If a man's ancestors lived in a particular village he will normally inherit some land in that village. If the heirs still live there, it is the land on which they will have to rely for a living. If they live away, it is only an extra. In both cases certain ideals are associated with this land. The relation of the ideal to the actual management of the land in the two different situations varies greatly. Here I am only considering cases where the owner of the land relies principally for his livelihood on other sources than land in his *tanindrazana*.

The land owned and inherited in the *tanindrazana* is also rather mis-leadingly called *tanindrazana*. Here again the association with the *razana* gives it a moral value. The contrast with land obtained in the new areas of expansion makes this clear. The ancestral land is a trust from the *razana* and is thought to have always belonged by right to the tomb family. New land has been obtained by government grants, and has been bought or claimed because it has been terraced. It is known that it has not always belonged to the family. The full significance of this is that to the Merina this second type of land is not rightly theirs. The argument runs as follows. All land originally belonged to the *razana* and was divided in such a way that each social group owned a certain area of land. This land should be the land of the successors of the *razana* of the group in question. If a *vahiny* owns this land he is breaking the order of the *razana*. In other words he is acting wrongly. Land cultivated by a *vahiny* is therefore not rightly his, irrespective of government laws. This notion is extended further to mean that because it is thought that there is always an association between a particular area of land and a social group, this means that the people who own land outside their *tanin-drazana* feel that it is not rightly theirs.[1] The contrast between "rightly" and "wrongly" owned land leads to certain actions. When the owner of land dies the system of inheritance is different in the *tanindrazana* and in the new area. In the new area it is accepted that the property will be legally divided at the death of its owner among his heirs. That is, the division will be recorded in the government land register. This is legal proof of ownership. The possibility that some of this land will ultimately go to strangers to the locality and be sold is clearly recognized. In the *tanindrazana* the land should not be legally divided. It should be divided only for the purpose of cultivation by the heirs, but this is not thought of as final. Because of the system of preferred marriages, and because of the notion of the continuity of the tomb group, it is believed that as the generations pass the actual individual rights to the ancestral land change but remain vested in the same group. It would, therefore, be wrong to make a final division of this land as this would be a denial of the continuity of the tomb group and its permanent association with this particular plot of land. Consequently the rule that such land should not be divided is a strongly felt moral norm. Divisions do occur and rights are alienated but this is always felt to be very wrong,[2] which brings me to another distinction between these two types of land. While land in the new area is continually bought and sold and this is quite acceptable,[3] land in the old area should never be sold. How this system actually worked out in the past is difficult to say, but now the problem is very complex. The rule that the land inherited from the ancestors should not be alienated was linked up with the whole social organization of old Imerina. It was a rule associated with the distribution of important resources. The same rule when applied to the present has taken on a

---

[1] This was made clear to me by the way I was told in the Ambatomanoina area by colonists that they had taken away this land from a group of people called the Marofotsy. In fact it is certain that no group of this name ever lived there. The word "Marofotsy" is in this area confused in such a way that it refers to the descendants of slaves. These "Marofotsy" came to the area either shortly before or at the same time as the "white" colonists. However, because the slaves built new tombs in the area (since they had no big tombs in old Imerina) the land is thought to be specifically theirs.

[2] Problems of this kind cannot be dealt with here as they really only occur when the land is still an important source of livelihood. When considering ancestral land as a link with the *tanindrazana* the problems of practical organization are not relevant.

[3] It is likely that with the passage of generations this new land becomes treated more and more as ancestral land.

completely different significance. For most people land in the *tanin-drazana* is no longer a significant economic asset. Owning land in the *tanindrazana* is now a symbol of a man's tie with his ancestral village. From a practical point of view it is usually quite uneconomical to own land in a village where one cannot cultivate it.

As a result there is now in all the old villages a large proportion of land belonging to the people who are often referred to by the French word "*originaire*". The *originaires* of a village are the people who will be buried in the village but do not live there. This land which they own is for the most part put in *métayage*.[1] This is an arrangement whereby the landlord gets from a third to an eighth of the crop, according to the value of the land, and whereby he supplies seeds, tools, etc. If not in *métayage* this land may be rented for a fixed annual due either in money or, more usually, in kind. If no one is found who is willing to take the land on these terms, it is either cultivated for a nominal rent or left uncultivated. In one village where I worked near Tananarive,[2] 65 per cent of the cultivated land belonged to *originaires* who did not have any close relatives in the village.[3] The figure is for a village where land was particularly valuable and people were willing to work land that was not their own. In other areas where land is less productive it is hardly worth their while to do so when part of the produce must be given to the owner. One such area is the district north of Ambatomena. There large areas of land are left uncultivated, because the owners cannot find people to cultivate it. In spite of this, they do not want to part with the land as it is a tie with the *tanindrazana*. I recorded one such case of a family living north of Ambatomanoina in a very fertile area who owned extensive land in their *tanindrazana* near Ambatomena. They tried very hard to find someone to cultivate the land for them but failed. The rice fields were slowly returning to marshes but when someone offered to buy the

---

[1] This topic is discussed by J. Dez in "Les baux ruraux coutumiers à Madagascar", *Etudes de Droit Africain et Malgache*, Ed. J. Poirier, 1965, pp. 72–94.

[2] Andrainarive, Canton Fieferana (see Map 2).

[3] This figure is calculated by taking into account the proportion of days the women of the village said they worked for outsiders when transplanting against the days they worked for themselves. However, land, which in this context they said belonged to them, may have belonged to relatives who allowed them to cultivate it without a rent. There is no way of establishing clearly the ownership of land in such villages as the villagers do not declare *de facto* divisions of land to the government and in fact deny that such divisions exist, as to do so would be to deny the communally owned nature of the land in the *tanindrazana*.

land they refused even to consider the offer because "the land of the ancestors should not be sold".[1]

One further case illustrates the strength of the attachment to this kind of land. A family originally from Ilafy, a famous village very close to the capital, left in 1922 to start a plantation in the far north of the island. They did this because they found their position in the old village slipping after the freeing of slaves. They left the land to be cultivated for a purely nominal rent by one of the families of the ex-slaves. The distance made it impossible for them to actually receive any produce and there was no money to be obtained at the time. Now only the grandchildren of the family of lessors are still alive, yet they continue to maintain the contract with the lessee in spite of the fact that, because of the proximity of the land to Tananarive, its value has become very great indeed. The notion of still owning land in the *tanindrazana* is more highly valued than the money which could be obtained.

Ancestral Houses

Not only is it important to have land in the *tanindrazana*, one should also, if possible, have a house. However, although everybody has a tomb in the *tanindrazana* and nearly everybody has a claim to a bit of land, only a few have a house. Nowadays, the people who succeed in achieving this ideal are often *originaires* who have made money in Tananarive and who then have a house built in the *tanindrazana*. Some well-off peasants also sometimes achieve this ambition. These houses are often palatial by Malagasy standards which means they look rather incongruous in the obviously poor countryside of Imerina. They are used occasionally for holidays or family ceremonies such as burials, marriages, etc, which are held in the *tanindrazana*.

The building of such a house in often a joint venture of a close family group often corresponding to the tomb group or perhaps only to a seg-ment of it. In the new area it is very common to find people living in

---

[1] The situation is further complicated by a series of new laws which state that a man who has cultivated land for a certain number of years without paying for it becomes the legal owner. The fear that this may happen makes the owners unwilling to let people cultivate for no rent. I know of one example when the ancestral land was actually sold. This was in the case of a family which, by attempting to start a small business, had run into very serious debt. They sold most of the estate but still kept two small fields of hardly any value in order to still own some land in their *tanindrazana*.

miserable huts of woven bamboo and daub, planning to build a "big house" in their *tanindrazana*. A big house in this context is one of two or three storeys built in part at least of baked bricks with glazed windows, a tin roof and a verandah. Such a house can cost from 200000 FMG upwards. Again, as with the tomb, conspicuous spending on houses in the *tanindrazana* can be indulged in, in a way that is not possible where one lives, because expenses made at the *tanindrazana* are *good* expenses and therefore cannot be a cause of envy and witchcraft.

Like all other ancestral property a share which is inherited in such a house should not be alienated. This means that a lot of these houses now belong to very many heirs. Unlike the tomb, however, there seems to be no system allowing for segmentation, and quarrels about the management of such a house are very common. This means that repairs cannot be done and many of these massive buildings start to decay as soon as they are finished, which gives an added derelict appearance to some of the villages near Tananarive. Indeed, villages of old Imerina have a very strange appearance to European eyes. There are a number of massive houses in construction, but the ones which are finished are all shut up and often in decay. The peasants tend to live near these pompous structures in pitiful dwellings. This is because they are rarely the *tompotany* of the villages where they live.[1]

Ancestral Churches

Apart from the houses of the *originaires* and the tombs, the villages of central Imerina also obtain their characteristic appearance from their churches. Almost every tiny village in the traditional area has at least one large church, usually Protestant. Often there are two, one Catholic and one Protestant.[2] Unlike the tombs, family houses and ancestral land, which are the concern of fairly small groups, the churches are the concern of all those connected with the parish. The parish normally comprises one village and its hamlets. Here again the parish is not limited to those who live in it but also includes those who consider it as their *tanindrazana*. This means that a Merina who lives away from his *tanindrazana* belongs to two congregations, the congregation in the village

---

1 See Plate 3a.
2 What follows applies principally to the Protestant churches. It is also applicable to the Anglicans. The position of the Catholic churches is also similar but there are significant differences.

where he lives, and the congregation in the village where he will be buried. From the point of view of the parish this means that the congregation is made up of two sections, the people who live in the parish and the people who have tombs in the parish.

This arrangement might seem particularly strange in a Christian context but, taking into account what has gone before, it is perfectly natural. The white Merina feels he belongs permanently to his *tanindrazana*, while the place where he lives now is considered as a temporary abode. The moral community for him consists of the people who share a *tanindrazana*; they are the permanent corporation through time. It seems normal that people who feel themselves to belong to some most significant grouping in society should join together to manage their church and to worship in it.

One of the most obvious effects of this system is that most members of the congregation of these villages do not live near the church. Indeed, there are examples of impressive churches being maintained in places where the village has almost completely been abandoned, the money for the upkeep of the church and the salary of the pastor coming almost entirely from dispersed *originaires*.[1]

Not only do the parishioners see themselves as belonging to the parish of their *tanindrazana*, it is also perfectly clear that this is what is accepted by the pastor. The parishioners always prefer to obtain a pastor belonging to their deme and indeed many pastors want to be placed in their *tanindrazana*. Even if he is an outsider he feels it is his duty to serve the *originaires* as much as the resident parishioners. This was brought home to me particularly clearly when a newly established pastor in Andrainarivo felt it his duty to visit not only all his resident parishioners but also all the *originaires*. This involved a series of trips to various places within a reasonable distance.

One of the reasons why the pastors attach so much importance to the *originaires* is that they are the main source of money for the upkeep of the churches. Normally the resident parishioners are very poor. Among the *originaires* there will be many who have gone to jobs in the professions, in the administration, or who have taken up farming in more productive areas. These are the people on whom these churches must rely. In the village of Andrainarivo almost exactly nine-tenths of the income of the church taken during a period of two months came from *originaires*.

[1] Anjohy (S. P. Ambatomena).

From the budgets which I was given by white Merina it appeared that all gave more to the church of their *tanindrazana* than to the church in the village where they lived.

Quite clearly distance makes it impossible for the *originaires* to participate fully in the life of the church. How far they do so depends on a variety of factors. First of all there are practical considerations. These involve such things as the distance between the place of abode and the church, and the amount of money available for the fare. Then there are more personal factors like the individual piety of those concerned and their affection for their *tanindrazana*. The number of generations that have elapsed since the family left the village does not seem to be relevant, but whether or not the family has followed in the traditional system of marriages is an important factor.

The most assiduous of the *originaires* try to go to their ancestral church on the first Sunday of each month for the monthly communion service. In Andrainarivo, out of an estimated total of 150 *originaires*, those taking communion on any particular Sunday varied from seven to fifteen. The total number of individual *originaires* I saw taking communion there on ordinary Sundays was 27.[1] Certain church feast days were of importance as they drew particularly large congregations of *originaires*. Particularly notable among these was All Saints' Day. On that day nearly all Westernized Merina families try to go to their *tanindrazana* to place natural or artificial flowers on the family tomb. This of course means that many of the *originaires* go to the *tanindrazana* on that day and meet each other. These meetings are significant as they enable news to circulate, and they are often the occasion for starting informal discussions on such topics as the repair of tombs, *famadihanas* and all matters of concern to the tomb group or the dispersed family. It is interesting to note that the respect shown to the particular dead and the group of dead in the tomb on the occasion of All Saints' Day is often paralleled only by the Merina with the *famadihana* ceremony.[2] Many consider it a more respectable form of ceremony than the *famadihana*. In this respect it should be noted that All Saints' Day is also of great importance to the French. The people who come to the tomb on All Saints' Day normally attend a service at the church. On All Saints' Day in 1964 there were 32 *originaires* present at the service.

Other more obvious religious feasts also bring in *originaires*, especially

---

[1] During a period of four months.
[2] See Chapter 5.

Christmas and Easter. Christmas 1964 was particularly well attended as the Christmas service was supplemented by short plays and singing, performed both by the children of the villagers and of the *originaires*. It was then perhaps that the distinctiveness of the two groups in the congregation emerged most clearly. First the children of the village performed a short nativity play. Then the children of the *originaires* took over and, in little groups, according to the places where they lived, sang carols which they had practised at home. On this occasion 57 *originaires* were present —a larger number than for any other ceremony.

Apart from the regular Church feasts, family celebrations also may take place in the *tanindrazana*, but this depends in part on the family in question having access to a house in the *tanindrazana*.

Baptism is often performed in the *tanindrazana* and the ceremony is followed by a meal served in the house. The Church ceremony of marriage is performed in some cases in the *tanindrazana*, but this is more common for Tananarivians than for peasants. The Protestant peasants tend to avoid the full religious ceremony. In some cases, when it is not possible to perform the marriage in the *tanindrazana*, the pastor of the *tanindrazana* may well be invited to the village of the groom to perform the ceremony there. In this way the link with the *tanindrazana* is kept without having to face the difficulty of organizing a feast from a distance.

Finally, funerals involving burials in the tomb and *famadihana* naturally involve ceremonies at the *tanindrazana*. These are so important that they will be considered separately in the next chapter.

The position of the church of the *tanindrazana* is particularly interesting for a number of reasons. First it is an institution which unites the various tomb families. It is the only concern which the members of a *tanindrazana* have in common. The religious ceremonies which are performed in the church give the *originaires* a common ritual organization. The church also supplies a paid official concerned with officiating for the *tanindrazana*. As mentioned earlier, when a family of *originaires* cannot have a *rite de passage* in the *tanindrazana* they do the next best thing: they call in the pastor of the *tanindrazana* to officiate for them. In all these functions it seems that the Church has replaced pre-Christian village and deme cults which only survive occasionally.

Perhaps the most striking way in which the Church unites the members of the *tanindrazana* is by organizing meetings of the *originaires* once a year at the church. These are fête-like occasions when a general service accompanies speeches concerning such things as the needs of the church and the upkeep of the *tanindrazana*. The stated purpose of these assemblies is to unite the *originaires* and to help with the upkeep of the church. Sometimes the history of the *tanindrazana* is recounted on such occasions.[1]

I have up to now considered only the non-theological aspects of the Church in the *tanindrazana*. However, it is of great importance to the actors that these are Christian churches. This means that they offer a perfectly respectable association with the *tanindrazana* for even the most Westernized Merina. Indeed, a pagan cult of the *tanindrazana*, or even a form of ancestor worship, would be unacceptable to many. The ambiguous value of the *tanindrazana*—a link with the past, and at the same time a link with Western standards—is of great significance. It explains how, even in the radically changed situation of Tananarive, the Merina can still join with relatives from more remote areas in joint projects. The *tanindrazana*, and the things associated with it, are all independent of the rapid social change now taking place. They are the half unconscious denial of such change.

We have now considered the main institutions which link a man to his *tanindrazana*. There are many others, some of which I shall mention briefly here.

One fairly recent development has been the creation of formal associations of *originaires*, and there are many of these in Tananarive. I only know two of these associations at first hand, but they all seem to be fairly similar. They have two main kinds of activity. Firstly they concern themselves with the village. They ensure financial support for the church. Other institutions are also supported, such as community projects and schools. In one case a village was asked to pay a contribution towards a school to be built in the neighbourhood. It turned out that the expense was far too great and the villagers appealed to the *originaire* association which supplied almost two-thirds of the money. The local branch of the Red Cross may also be supported by *originaires*.[2] The association may lobby influential politicians in order to obtain help for the village.

Apart from activities principally concerned with the *tanindrazana*

---

[1] It is difficult to estimate how common these meetings are. I know of an example of such meetings in the historic village of Ambatofisaorana. The school fête at the Anglican mission of Ambatoranana has some aspects of this. (H. Hudson—personal communication.)

[2] The Red Cross in Imerina is almost a compulsory institution to which all women must belong. Its main function is the distribution of *Nivaquine*, an antimalarial drug, to children. Other activities include the distribution of sweets, old clothes, etc.

itself, the associations are also social clubs of a kind. This aspect is restricted to Tananarive and need not concern us here. Lastly the associations are an important means whereby information relating to members
of the *tanindrazana* can be circulated.

In this chapter I have examined the importance of the *tanindrazana*
for the Merina peasants and have also tried to describe how the *tanindrazana* is associated with social groups. We have seen how to the Merina
the *tanindrazana* is the valued locality while the land where he lives is
not thought of in the same way. The reasons why the Merina should
want to attach themselves to a different place than the one in which
they live and carry out their main activities now become clear. Although
a mere list of advantages does not convey or ultimately explain the
nature of the emotion involved in the attachment to the tomb, it helps
us to understand why this link is maintained. These advantages are, in
order of increasing importance, the demonstration of rank, attachment
to a fixed social order and attachment to kinsmen.

Maintaining the link with the *tanindrazana* is a demonstration of rank
in two ways. Firstly, to have a *tanindrazana* in old Imerina shows free
descent. The slaves only had perishable tombs in old Imerina and, many
of them have built new permanent tombs in the new area and not in the
old where their inferior status is remembered. This aspect should not,
however, be overestimated since there are many other ways in which
"free" descent can be demonstrated. Most important of these is the fact
that physical appearance is usually sufficient indication of slave descent.
Secondly, the association with a tomb in a particular *tanindrazana* is a demonstration of deme membership and the demes are associated with rank. As
might be expected, the higher demes are the most eager to maintain the
link with the *tanindrazana*. This, however, is not a sufficient explanation
of the desire to attach oneself to a particular *tanindrazana*, since people
with very low deme status also attach great importance to this link.

The link to the *tanindrazana* is also a link to a fixed, apparently unchanging social order; a social order associated with the romance of the
past Merina kingdom, a past which in this particular case was a time
when the Merina were politically dominant and independent. The
Merina feels he belongs in a more significant way to his *tanindrazana* than
he does to the place where he lives. In this way he feels assured of a place
in a traditional, good order where all "free" Merina were a ruling race.
This is not simply a question of hankering after lost power; it is hanker-

ing after an order where relations are fixed and where anxiety about the behaviour of others is therefore non-existent. The strength of this feeling is understandable when we consider the bewildering social revolutions of the last 100 years in Imerina, and especially in the last 50—a time of violent social change when, repeatedly, acquired status, power and wealth were continually redistributed and the only permanent, reliable relations and roles were those associated with the defunct traditional order. In fact, the link with the *tanindrazana* constitutes the element of continuity in a changing situation.

Finally, the link with the *tanindrazana* is a link with real kinsmen. The link with an apparently unchanging moral order has two aspects. One is concerned with classifying oneself and others by reference to a critical area (old Imerina); the other is the association through the *tanindrazana*, or rather through the tomb, with kinsmen.

5

Funeral and *Famadihana*

In the last two chapters we saw how the peasant is part of a practical organization adapted to the economy and ecology of the place where he lives, but how, on the other hand, he identifies himself through his tomb and his tomb group with a quite different organization which is believed to have been that of the past. We saw how "real" kinship links and their transformation enabled the peasant to mediate between the practical and the ideal organization. This mediation was achieved by associating the living man with the anonymous dead within the tomb. My purpose in this chapter is to examine the *rites de passage* by which the passage of the living to the dead is ritualized. This is a universal function of funerary *rites de passage* but in this case these rites have an added significance in that they act out the relation between the ideal unchanging society and the flux of the actual society.[1]

There are two kinds of funerary *rites de passage* in Imerina. The funeral, which occurs very soon after death, and the ceremony called *famadihana*, which occurs at least two years afterwards. The funeral is the concern of the society in which a man lives, the *famadihana* is the concern of the dispersed family. This contrast is partly forced on the actors by the necessity of the situation. Merina funerals must be carried out within the three days following death but, since the exact day of death cannot be forecast and since preparations for the funeral must under no circumstances be initiated before the actual death (to do this would be tantamount to witchcraft), it follows that there is no time to gather together the dispersed family for the funeral. The local family has therefore to

---

[1] A. van Gennep, *Les Rites de Passage*, 1909.

rely on the cooperation of neighbours for the participation traditionally required at funerals. Indeed, for the Merina, death is the time when the solidarity of the local community, *fokon'olona*, should be most manifest. Of the great mass of writing which praises the community spirit of the *fokon'olona* all emphasize what happens when a death occurs.[1] The description of the funeral which follows will also show clearly this spirit of mutual help.

The funeral is a less important ceremony than the *famadihana*, but it has several rituals in common with it. These will be discussed more fully when the *famadihana* is dealt with. The smaller size of the funeral as a ceremony is due to two factors. First, there is very little time to gather much money; second, the short notice means that only the local family and neighbours can be present, while the larger dispersed family cannot be gathered in time. A funeral can be fairly expensive, but it is always much cheaper than a *famadihana*. My estimates for those funerals I witnessed varied from approximately 5000 FMG to 30000 FMG. In all these cases, however, a large amount, if not all, the expenditure was recovered from monetary gifts and presents of measures of rice from neighbours. These presents came in part from mourning gifts, and in part from an organized village levy. For example, in the village where I worked a *dinampokon'olona*, "act of the fokon'olona", required that 5 francs and a measure of rice (approximately 275 grammes) per adult should be given at every death to the bereaved family.

Funerals

The funeral usually occurs on the day after death. Three possible courses can be followed. The corpse can be buried in the big ancestral tombs, it can be buried temporarily in the earth or, more rarely, in another tomb.[2] Burial in the tomb is preferred but for a number of reasons it occurs less often than temporary burial.[3]

The reasons why people are buried temporarily are several. First of all, no children below the age of four or five can "enter" the tomb by themselves. They are called *Zazarano*, "children of water". They are said not to be strong enough to open the heavy stone door of the tomb and

---

[1] The Nationalist Journal *Fokon'olona*, edited by Ch. Razafindraibe, which advocates a revaluation of the *fokon'olona* provides many good examples of this kind of writing.

[2] See p. 161.

[3] This would not be true of people living in Tananarive or its immediate vicinity.

are brought into the tomb only when it is opened for an adult. Secondly, the tomb may not be opened twice within a year which means that, in the case of rapidly succeeding deaths, the second corpse cannot be buried directly in the tomb. Thirdly, people who die of certain highly contagious diseases, like plague, cannot be buried in the tomb until the flesh has disintegrated.

Much more important than such prohibitions is the question of practicability. A funeral in the family tomb is more expensive than one in a temporary grave. This is because more *lamba mena*[1] must be given when the body is placed in the family tomb as it is a definitive placing of the dead in the proper place. Since a funeral outside the tomb is a temporary matter, a poor funeral of this kind can be made good at a later date. If not much money is available—and this is the normal state of affairs—a temporary burial will be carried out.

When the family in which the death occurs lives a certain distance from its *tanindrazana*, there are also problems of transport and communications to consider. The body must be brought back to the tomb and the person in charge of the tomb, the head of the tomb group, must be contacted. The transport of the body on a *taxi-brousse* (converted delivery van) is again a major expense. In a certain number of cases the problems of communication may be completely insurmountable in the time available. In remote areas the distance to be covered, perhaps largely on foot, makes it impossible to bring the corpse back in time for burial.

For these reasons Merina living away from their *tanindrazana* tend to be first buried in temporary graves. It is difficult to give figures for this since the accessibility of the village where the death occurs is a major factor, as well as the wealth of the bereaved family. All these variables mean that only a very large number of cases would give a true idea of the frequency of temporary burial. For the Ambatomanoina area the proportion was almost half and half. This figure, however, is based on only very few cases.[2]

Generally it is true to say that temporary burial is typical of the *voanjo*. The very idea of a temporary burial from which one will later be

---

[1] These are silk shrouds. They are described more fully on page 145.
[2] Of the people who live near or in Tananarive a higher proportion are directly buried in the family tomb, since these people are usually in much closer contact with their *tanindrazana*. The position in Tananarive is different in a number of ways as other factors resulting from urban life affect all the concepts discussed here.

taken to the *tanindrazana* reflects admirably the position of the *voanjo*, since it is necessary to practice temporary burial because one is *away* from the *tanindrazana*, and *separated* from all one's kinsmen.

When a death occurs within a family the house is immediately prepared as it would be for any ceremony. The main room is tidied up or cleared completely and the clean papyrus mats, which are always kept ready for ceremonies, are spread on the floor. Then the north-east corner of the room, the most valued corner,[1] is curtained off with mats so as to form a small enclosure where the body will be placed after it has been prepared and wrapped in a plain cotton cloth. All this is done by members of the household before any indication of the death is given to the outside world. Afterwards the close local kin, especially the women and children, go inside and sit around the enclosure where the body has been placed and mourn. The women undo their elaborate plaits and allow their hair to fall loosely about their shoulders as a sign of sorrow. Only when these preparations are complete is the death announced to the other co-villagers, usually be means of a village crier. This is when the most dramatic demonstration of local solidarity occurs. As soon as the announcement is made the women of the neighbouring houses go to fill a pitcher of water from their big storage pots to the east of the hearth and carry it to the bereaved house. Then they bring the firewood which they had probably prepared for themselves for their evening meal and, abandoning whatever they were doing, go and prepare the funeral meal in the house of the dead man. They roast and pound coffee, husk, winnow and cook rice, and light fires. If the family of the person who has died is rich enough the neighbouring men go out to capture a bull. They chase and tease it until it is exhausted, and then kill and prepare it for the funeral meal. What is particularly striking in all this is the way in which the preparations are taken over, without even a question being asked, by neighbours who have been given no previous notice. The bereaved family has hardly any decisions to take and seems to be carried by the tide of their neighbours' help. This is characteristic of the whole proceeding.

Once the preparations are under way there is usually a short period when the neighbours retire to prepare and eat their supper. Later on, usually around eight or nine in the evening, they gather again. Some of the men have perhaps already fortified themselves for the night with

---

[1] J.-C. Hebert, "La cosmographie ancienne Malgache suivie de l'enumeration des points cardinaux et l'importance du Nord-Est", *Taloha*, I, 1965.

liquor. When they have all gathered there may be a short prayer and hymn singing led by any senior man or by a pastor if there is one present. Once this is over everybody settles for the night. The local family sit inside the house around the corpse and mourn. The women neighbours carry on with the preparation of the meal. The men sit all around the house but especially on the side where the windows and doors are, namely the west. There they pass the night playing dominoes or *fandroana*,[1] or betting, or whiling away the time as best they can. From time to time they sing and generally have as good a time as possible. Admittedly the songs are often Church hymns, but they are sung in a boisterous way which contrasts with the way they are sung in church. Hymns are the accompaniment of all social gatherings.

The scene presented during the night is therefore of the corpse in the north-east corner of the house behind its screen of mats, immediately surrounded by mourning and often weeping relatives, who are themselves surrounded by what, as the night goes on, becomes very like a party. Late in the evening the meal which has been prepared is at last served and eaten by all present.

The meat given on such occasions is called *hena ratsy*, or "bad meat". A name which also applies to the remainder of this meat which is taken home by those present. It is the subject of two taboos. It is forbidden to pregnant women, and also it should not be salted in case it is thought too good.[2]

As the night proceeds the neighbours are blessed and thanked at regular intervals by the head of the bereaved family.

The express purpose of this large gathering of apparently unconcerned people is the fear of witches (*mpamosavy*), for witches, it is believed, steal corpses, rejoice in death and try to frighten or otherwise harm mourners.[3] It is therefore the purpose of this outer ring of neighbours to protect the inner ring of kinsmen against the *mpamosavy*.

More subjectively, this protecting crowd gives the mourners the feeling of being surrounded by trustworthy people, *havana mpifankatia*, which is especially welcome at a time of uncertainty and danger. It is interesting to note that this practice marks off very clearly kinsmen from neigh-

---

[1] A traditional game somewhat similar to draughts.

[2] This topic has been much discussed by L. Molet in *Le Bain Royal à Madagascar*, 1956. I have found no evidence to support this author's theory relating to *hena ratsy*. Also on this subject, R. Decary, *La Mort et les Coutumes Funéraires à Madagascar*, 1962, pp. 31–32.

[3] M. Danielli, "The witches of Madagascar", in *Folk-Lore*, No. 58, June 1947.

bours, but in spite of this the fiction that neighbours are kinsmen is stressed most emphatically of all on this occasion. The blessings and thanks addressed to the neighbours are to "*Ry Havako*", "my kinsmen". This is sometimes pushed even further and the neighbours are called "*tena iray tampo*", "really children of one womb". This is a pretence and is known as such. It is another example of the notion of artificial kinship already described.

By morning the neighbours disperse once again and prepare for more formal visits of condolence. Representatives from all the nearby households go to the house where the body is lying. They are received by the immediate family who are, as before, sitting or leaning around the funeral screen. The women are still showing recognizable outward signs of mourning, with their hair undone and their *lambas*[1] tucked under their arms. They utter from time to time expressions of grief of a traditional kind. The visitors file in quietly and for a moment sit in silence; then, in a low respectful tone and missing out the usual greetings, they explain the purpose of their visit and give a small amount of money towards the expenses. This money is called "the fringes of the *lamba mena*". The sum normally varies from 5 to 50 FMG. In certain cases the group of neighbours supplies the entire sum to be spent on the funeral. This contribution is the most explicit obligation which goes with membership of the *fokon'olona*. It is a great sin to allow a member of the village to be buried without at least one *lamba mena* and, if the local family of the dead cannot supply it, the *fokon'olona* must. There is no question of asking the dispersed kinsmen as there is no time.

On the morning of the burial the body is placed in a rough coffin which has also been made spontaneously by the neighbours. Later it is possible that the body will be taken to a church, Catholic or Protestant as the case may be, where a funeral service will be held. From this point the ceremony is somewhat different according to whether the body is to be buried in the family tomb or temporarily in the earth. In the Ambatomanoina area this means that the body will either be taken, usually by *taxi-brousse*, to its *tanindrazana* or will be buried in the earth in the village where the death occurred. When the body is taken back to the ancestral tomb it is first loaded on to a *taxi-brousse* and as many neighbours as can possibly afford it accompany the local family. On arrival the party may be joined by relatives, if any live in the *tanindrazana*,

---

[1] See Chapter 1.

and by other inhabitants of the village. After a short meal they go in procession to the tomb. First of all a number of speeches are made, the most notable being by the head of the local family. This is a formal address which includes reference to God, the ancestors and the President of the Republic, but the main body of the speech is a eulogy on the dead man.[1] After this it is possible that if many children and relatives have given shrouds for the dead man they will be displayed and the names and villages of the donors will be announced.[2] This is now becoming rarer at funerals because usually only one or two silk shrouds are given. It is possible that there will also be a short graveside sermon and hymn-singing, sometimes led by a pastor. The general atmosphere of a funeral is one of sadness and mourning, and it is usually a quiet occasion. Once the ceremonies are over the body is placed in the most honoured position in the tomb, i.e. the upper shelf on the northern side.[3] After the body has been placed it is customary for the other members of the family to descend into the tomb and see where the dead man has been put.

The ceremony for a temporary burial is similar. The corpse is taken out of the village in a procession to a place on a hill-side, where the grave is dug by neighbours using old worn out spades. The bottom of the grave is covered with charcoal as this is said to keep the corpse dry. Then the rough wooden coffin is lowered into place. The coffin itself is carefully sealed with clay, and heavy stones are placed on top of it. Then the grave is filled and the place marked. The job of covering over the coffin as well as of digging the grave is, as we have noted, done with old spades. This is because traditionally the spades, together with the pole on which the coffin was slung, should be thrown away and abandoned. The spades are still duly thrown away but as the men leave they surreptitiously pick them up again. I was told that spades were too expensive to be thrown away completely. The return from the grave is a formal affair. Unlike in the procession going to the tomb, men and

----

[1] Such a speech is given and discussed by R. Decary, in *La Mort et les Coutumes Funéraires à Madagascar*, 1962, pp. 26–28. The funeral speeches I heard were similar to this though usually shorter and containing biblical references as well as proverbs.

[2] For a detailed description of this practice and others touched on here see the discussion of the *Famadihana*.

[3] K. Falck, "L'ancien village au Vakinankaratra", *Historisk-Antikvarisk Rekke*, University of Bergen, 1958. Also see p. 232. There is, however, another possibility—the corpse may be placed in the centre of the tomb on the earth. This is a kind of temporary burial within the tomb. A *famadihana* will later be necessary to place the skeleton in its proper place.

women return separately. The women are led by the chief woman mourner, usually a senior woman in the bereaved household. When the party of women returns a short rite of decontamination takes place. A small fire is lit on the threshold and those returning from the graveside have to step over it. A ritual with a similar purpose occurs the next day. All the people living in the house of the dead man go out and wash themselves, their clothes and all clothing and blankets in the house, in a nearby stream. This again is said to remove contamination with death.[1]

This short description of the funeral has shown how it is a ceremony which is the concern of neighbours, of the *fokon'olona*. Nevertheless, it is not just as neighbourhood cooperation that this help is conceptualized. It is spoken of as "help between kinsmen". Clearly, the notion that neighbours should be kinsmen is relevant here. The neighbours are acting in lieu of kinsmen, they are acting as *havana mpifankatia* and during the whole proceeding they all stress this by addressing one another as "kinsmen". At the same time it is general knowledge that they are not really kinsmen and the important ceremony is deferred until the real kinsmen can be there. This is the *famadihana,* which, in contrast to the funeral, always takes place in the *tanindrazana*.

Famadihanas

The word *famadihana* is the relative substantive of the verb *mamadika* which means "to turn over". In common speech the phrase *mamadika drazana*, "turning over the dead", is often used.[2] Turning over is used metaphorically in this context since at no stage is the turning over of the dead body a significant part of the ceremony. To say that the word *famadihana* refers to one ceremony is misleading. There are a number of easily distinguishable ceremonies which go under this name, but all these ceremonies share a common basis. They all involve firstly the exhumation of the body of a near relative after the flesh has completely decayed, secondly, wrapping the corpse in very fine, highly-coloured, decorated silk sheets called *lamba mena*, and thirdly, rewrapping the corpse and placing it in the family tomb.

---

[1] For numerous examples of similar practices see J. Rudd, *Taboo*, 1960.

[2] Note 3, p. 516, of the French translation of the *Tantaran'ny Andriana* by G. S. Chapus and E. Ratsimba states that the proper translation of the phrase is "transferring the dead" not "turning over the dead". Although "transferring the dead" does better convey what is involved, it does not seem to me to be a valid translation of the word *mamadika*. See *vadika* in *Dictionnaire Malgache-Francais*, 1888 and subsequent editions.

Lamba mena literally means "red cloth", although the shrouds are not necessarily red, but this idea distinguishes them from the more common plain white *lamba* worn by the living. The *lamba mena* are composed of stripes of many bright colours. They may be decorated at either end with silver or lead beads. The adjective "red" refers to their importance rather than their appearance. The use of colours in this way, for their symbolic value, is common throughout Madagascar. Some *lamba mena* are white as some groups, such as certain *Andrianamboninolona*, have an ancestral prohibition against the use of colours. In these cases the fringes are left unknotted to distinguish them from the ordinary *lamba*.

In spite of the basic similarity between all *famadihanas* certain different kinds are clearly distinguishable. Firstly, there are the ceremonies where the corpse is taken out of a temporary burial place and then taken to be buried in its ancestral tomb. This kind of *famadihana* is probably the most common and I shall call it the "return *famadihana*". Secondly, there are the ceremonies where the corpse, or a number of corpses, are taken out of the ancestral tomb and returned to it. Thirdly, there are ceremonies where the corpses may be taken out of an old tomb and placed in a new one. Finally, there are ceremonies where the corpses may be moved from one tomb to another, but this is very rare.

These ceremonies immediately bring to mind other ceremonies from other parts of the world. The most obvious of these are the second funerals which have long arrested the attention of anthropologists. The differences between most second funerals and *famadihanas* is clear. In the words of Sidney Hartland: "Among a very large number of peoples who practice earth burial in one form or another, the ceremonies are not completed until the bones have been taken up, cleaned and put in a place of final deposit. . . ."[1] Apart from the very obvious aspects which the *famadihana* has in common with these ceremonies, two fundamental differences must be noted. The *famadihana* is not an essential part of the funeral if the body is originally buried in the tomb. *Famadihanas* need not be, and indeed are not, performed for everyone. In no sense, therefore, can it be said that the funeral is not completed without a *famadihana*. Furthermore, it is quite common for one particular corpse

---

[1] "Death . . ." in Hastings's *Encyclopedia of Religion and Ethics*, 1911. On secondary burial there is of course the work of R. Hertz, "Contribution à une étude sur la représentation collective de la mort", *Anée Sociologique*, 1907. I shall discuss this work later. Other recent discussions of secondary burials include: T. Harrison, "Borneo death", *Bijtragen tot de Taal-landen Volkerkunde*, 1962; W. Stöhr, "Des todesritual der Dayak", *Ethnologica*, New Series I, 1959.

to be exhumed a number of times. This again is not the case for most second funerals.

Another comparison which springs to mind is between certain aspects of ancestor worship ceremonies, such as sacrifices etc. Again this is somewhat misleading since the *famadihana* is not a regular ceremony dealing with "the active participation of the dead in mundane affairs".[1]

Famadihanas are the most important ceremonies in which the Merina peasant participates and this very importance marks off *famadihanas* from other ceremonies linked with the passage through life. Their place is made clearer if we contrast them again with funerals.

Famadihanas can take place only a certain length of time after death. This period is usually of at least two years, but may be considerably longer. The law only allows *famadihanas* to take place during the months from July to September inclusive. This is, in fact, the period of least agricultural work and also the period when the peasants are likely to have most money. The first contrast with funerals is therefore that the ceremony can occur on a day chosen by the participants. This has two effects. Firstly, it is possible to save up for a *famadihana*. Indeed, once it has been decided to hold one it is delayed until enough money has been accumulated. This means that it is possible to spend much more money and have a much bigger ceremony than is usually possible for the funeral.[2] Secondly, it is possible to gather the dispersed family of the dead on the arranged day.

The relative importance of the ceremony is a generally acknowledged fact. Of the eight such ceremonies I attended the smallest involved 165

---

[1] J. Goody, *Death, Property and the Ancestors*, 1962, p. 379. The Betsileo are the people most closely associated with the Merina and it is interesting to note that H. Dubois, in his monumental work, *Monographie des Betsiléo*, also stresses that it is the funerary rites which are important, and not the minor sacrifices which occur at the tombs (Chapter 4). It is tempting to see the *famadihana* as an ancient ancestor worship ceremony transformed by Christianity. However, it seems that the *famadihana* had comparatively less importance in the past and never had any connection with the propitiation of ancestors.[a] Other ceremonies which have now practically disappeared may have been much more concerned with this, but it is difficult to assess their significance now. See the chapter on *Fatidra* by W. E. Cousins in *Fomba Malagasy*, 1963 edition (edited by H. Randzavola), and A. and G. Grandidier, *Ethnographie*, Vol. III.

[a] R. F. Callet, *Tantaran'ny Andriana*, Footnote 311, Vol. I, of French translation (Chapus and Ratsimba).

[2] A similar point is made by D. Miles in his criticisms of Hertz's theories on secondary burial in "Socio-economic aspects of secondary burial", *Oceania*, Vol XXXV, No. 3, 1965. In this case, however, it is impossible to explain *famadihanas* as being simply caused by shortage of money at death.

people and the largest, as far as I could judge, at least 500. Even this was not apparently a very large *famadihana*.

These ceremonies involve very great expense. The cost is always difficult to estimate as there is also a large-scale consumption of already owned goods such as cattle and rice. The expenses involved for the *famadihana* I attended varied greatly. This, and the fact that I was able to observe only a few, gives very little value to the figures obtained. However, the lowest figure was around 123 000 FMG and the highest 270 000 FMG.[1] The average was 169 000 FMG. For all these ceremonies the people directly involved had to sell cattle and, if they did not possess enough cattle, land. The expenses involved at a *famadihana* are second only to those of building a new tomb. They come under various headings. First of all food for the guests, which includes mainly rice, meat, sugar, salt and coffee. Many guests may be given meat to take home. Food is the biggest expense. Secondly, there is the expense involved in buying *lamba mena*. These may cost up to 3000 FMG each. Thirdly, there are expenses in getting the numerous government permits necessary for holding the ceremony, killing the cattle, etc. Fourthly, there are expenses involved in preparing the tomb. This may well involve major repairs like recementing the top, repainting, or even renewing the whole structure. Finally, there are a large number of other minor expenses which involve such things as transport, feeding helpers etc.

As I have noted, a second concomitant of the fact that a *famadihana* is planned in advance is that a different group of people is involved than is the case for a funeral. For the funeral the responsibility for the ceremony both in terms of money and organization rests on the neighbours. For the *famadihana* it rests clearly on the kinsmen of the dead. Throughout the ceremony the dispersed family of the dead is the group immediately involved. For the purpose of the ceremony this special position is recognized by the fact that the dispersed family are referred to by the phrase *zana'drazana*, which distinguishes them from mere neighbours. *Zana'drazana* means "the children of the dead", "children" here being used in the widest sense meaning relatives of some kind. At the climax of the ceremony it is the *zana'drazana* who stand near the tomb while the neighbours form an outer circle. The relation of the *zana'drazana* to the dead is shown in Fig. 9.

---

[1] This includes not only the goods bought for the occasion but all the goods consumed valued at their selling price.

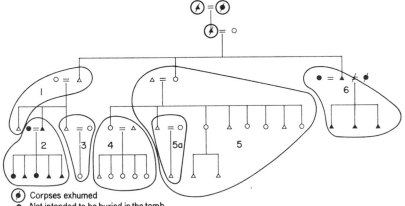

Corpses exhumed
Not intended to be buried in the tomb
Intended to be buried in the tomb

Household	Proportional contribution
1	1/5
4	1/5 (a rich family)
5	1/5
6	1/5
2	1/10
3	0 (just married)
5a	1/10 (living for part of the year in Tananarive).

Fig. 8. Division of expenses among the households of the *tompon'jama*. (*Famadihana* at Talata Volon'ondry, 1966.)

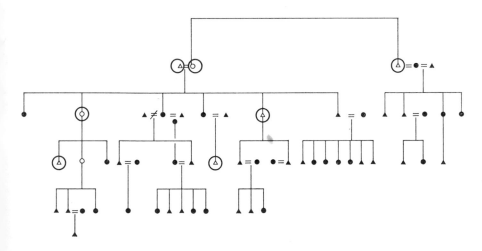

○ △ Dead
● ▲ Living

Fig. 9. Relationship of *zanadrazana* to the corpses exhumed. (*Famadihana* at Miakadaza, August 1965.)

Within the circle of *zana'drazana* is a smaller group of people who are directly responsible for the ceremony. They are the dead's closest kin, usually his own siblings and children. These are the initiators of the ceremony and they meet together to decide whether to hold the ceremony and how and when it will be carried out. The group of initiators are referred to as the *tompon'jama*, the "owners of the feast". They have a head who obtains his office by virtue of his genealogical position and he is responsible for coordinating the initiators. The role of the initiators of a *famadihana* is to organize the ceremony and make the money available. They, of course, receive contributions from more remote kinsmen as they also do from all those who attend the feast. These are voluntary gifts to the initiators and are shared out among them after the ceremony in the proportion in which the initiators have contributed.[1] Figure 8 shows the relation of the *tompon'jama* to the dead and how the expenses are divided among them. It is clear from this instance that the allocation of expenses is in terms of genealogical attachment to the dead. Thus if a man who had three children is to be exhumed, each of the children will contribute a third of the expenses irrespective of sex. If, however, one of the children is dead but is survived by two of *his* children, then they will each contribute one sixth.

The *tompon'jama* must be clearly distinguished from the tomb group. It is clear that participation in a *famadihana* is a demonstration of kinship links to the dead and is not a demonstration of attachment to a permanent group. We have already seen in the last chapter how on the one hand an individual's close kinsmen, and on the other his tomb group, are different (in other words, how an individual's dispersed family and the owners of his tomb are different). At all the *famadihanas* I attended many *zana'drazana* did not intend to be buried either in the *tanindrazana* or the tomb of the dead person, and this was even true for the *tompon'-jama*, as Fig. 8 shows.[2]

Any description of a *famadihana* runs up against the difficulties involved in the fact that there are not one but several forms. Furthermore, each form varies in different instances. This is indeed character-

---

[1] In some cases gifts which have come early, whether of rice or money, are incorporated in the pool for the *famadihana*.

[2] There is one exception to this. When a new tomb is built some of the dead are brought from the old one. These are usually ancestors which link together the tomb group of the new tomb. The *tompon'jama* corresponds in such a case to the tomb group and it is possible that some relatives of the dead who do not intend to be buried in the tomb will join the initiators.

Plate 4a. *Famadihana*. The crowd gathers as the tomb is opened.

Plate 4b. *Famadihana*. Wrapping a corpse in a new *lamba mena*: the corpse is inside the old decayed *lamba mena*.

istic of all Merina institutions and reflects the absorption of many peoples into Merina society and the variable influence of Tananarive.

This variation cannot be dealt with here. The basic ritual of all *famadihanas* is the same. For the purposes of description we need only distinguish between return *famadihanas*, when the first part of the ceremony occurs at a place of temporary burial, and those *famadihanas* where the whole ceremony occurs at the tomb. The ceremonies I shall describe are ones where the principal actors are villagers and not Tananarivians. Minor variations are ignored.[1]

Since even the difference between return *famadihanas* and others is only partial, I shall describe in full a *famadihana* which occurs entirely at the tomb and then note briefly the different characteristics of return *famadihanas*.

Although a *famadihana* is often planned about a year before it is to take place, the actual preparations usually start a month before the ceremony when an astrologer is consulted to determine the right day. Once this is fixed, or at least when the astrologer has given an idea of the approximate date, the local families of the *tompon'jama* gather on days which they arrange among themselves. They start to cut and gather the great quantity of firewood which will be needed. Sometimes they repair their houses. Once these early preliminaries are finished the family go to their astrologer to ask for definite instructions on the conduct of the *famadihana*. They want to know the times and days when the various stages of the ceremony must be performed, and also the colour of the coats of the cattle to be slaughtered and the exact time when the first bull should be killed. They must know also the colour of the *lamba mena* to be given to the dead. As to the ceremony itself, every detail has to be specified and a complete programme is made, setting out such things as how the tomb is to be approached, where the party will stop on the way, etc. All this will be indicated, although in many cases the astrologer will himself lead and direct the proceedings on the day. The astrologer discovers all this according to various means of divination. In all cases he requires quite a stiff fee, around 5000 FMG. This is on top of the regular payments made to him during the year.[2]

---

[1] This description differs in many respects from the one given by R. Decary in *Moeurs et Coutumes des Malgaches*, 1951.

[2] A full discussion of the place of astrology in Merina thought and society is impossible here but it can be noted, as a generalization, that the help of an astrologer is required for all enterprises thought to involve danger. It is noticeable that at no time is the knowledge of the astrologer thought more necessary than at a *famadihana*. Each family has its astrologer who is paid regularly as well as for extra or exceptional occasions (see Bloch, 1968).

A week or so before the day those who are to be invited are visited by the head of the *famadihana* and asked to come, or, in some cases when the family are more sophisticated, a letter is sent. Two days before the appointed time the whole dispersed family of the dead gathers, bringing with them new clothes and jewellery, and preparations start in earnest. They gather together the cattle which are to be killed and the *lamba mena* which are to be given. The village in which the ceremony is to take place bustles with activity, carried on in high spirits. Some men chop wood, others prepare the temporary house which will receive the guests. This is a rough building, the walls of which are made up of blades of an aloe-like plant,[1] bound together by bamboos. The roof is normally made up of banana fronds. Inside, planks, branches and bamboos are lashed together to make tables and benches. The women are usually occupied in husking rice and roasting coffee as well as preparing snacks for all the helpers. Later in the day the men prepare to kill the first bull. Before this is done a rope is tied to one of its back legs and to its horns. Five or six young men then hang on to the ends. The men tease the animal and make it charge them while they rush out of the way. Sometimes they jump on its back and attempt to hold on while it tries to throw them. This kind of highly dangerous game is always engaged in before killing bulls for a ceremony. When the animal is completely exhausted it is tied up, and then the head of the family asks a blessing from God, the dead, the holy earth, the spirits of land and water, etc. After the speech asking for the blessing has been made, the head of the *famadihana* family ritually sprinkles the bull with water in which an *ariary tsy vaky*, a silver coin which has not been broken,[2] has been placed. He then asperges himself and the attendants and finally the water is passed around and everyone takes a drink. This, like all Merina blessings, is said to give those who are blessed many children, a long life and great wealth. The bull is then killed, though the actual killing is not ceremonial.

Killing cattle for a ceremony is for the Merina always a dangerous occasion and I have often been told of stories where the wrong cattle were killed or cattle were killed at the wrong time and, as a consequence, people participating in the ceremony had died immediately afterwards.[3]

---

[1] *Fincrea longaeva.*

[2] In the past the Merina used to cut up Maria Theresa Thalers to obtain smaller coinage. Now a coin which has not been cut up is a symbol of purity.

[3] It does, in fact, seem that a surprising number of people do die at ceremonies. Probably this is due to excess tiredness and over-indulgence.

This was attributed to the lack of knowledge of the astrologer who had given a wrong decision on the day for the *famadihana* and the kind of bull to be killed. This fear reflects the general anxiety at such ceremonies. The astrologer may be wrong on a number of points and any mistake is said to have fatal results. The informants did not suggest that this was due to any supernatural agents. The causation is much vaguer. It seems that killing such a large living thing as a bull is dangerous as its death might be contagious.[1] Once death, in any form, has been introduced, only the greatest precautions can control it. After the first bull is dead the others are killed without any ceremony, but each is teased in the same way, as a chance to do this is never missed.

This preparatory period usually lasts until the morning of the day before the ceremony, when cattle are still being killed and prepared. Then the cooking is started out in the open in big iron pots and disused petrol drums. This is carried out exclusively by men and contrasts with everyday cooking, which is done indoors by women. The food is the usual food for feasts: rice, stewed beef and very sweet coffee.

The day preceding the actual ceremony is said to be the day of the dispersed family, while the day of the ceremony is said to be the day of the *fokon'olona* because only then are people who are not related expected to arrive. In fact this is not so clear-cut, but the distinction is characteristic of *famadihanas* since they are the time when the real kinsmen of the dead, the *zana'drazana*, are clearly marked off from the others in all activities.

As the evening draws on more and more guests arrive. As soon as they appear they are welcomed by a mixed band of flutes and drums and some of the *zana'drazana* who go out to meet them, dancing to the music. As they arrive, the guests may join in a short dance or perhaps just follow the band and those who have come to welcome them. They are led to the house of the head of the ceremony or another suitable spot where the leader of the party of guests which has just arrived sits down and listens to a short speech of welcome and thanks. He answers with a fairly similar speech, also of thanks, saying that the guests have come to rejoice with them because their kinsman has come home or because they have a new tomb, or whatever the case may be. He then goes on to say that as a blessing he gives a small contribution of money which he

---

[1] The idea of "cantagious magic" in the sense Frazer used the term is ubiquitous in Madagascar. (see J. Rudd, *Taboo*, 1960).

points out is tiny, but is a mark of *mpifakatiavana*, their love as kinsmen for each other. These contributions are carefully noted down in a book with the name of the donor. The book will later be used as a guide for how much the recipient will give the donor when he is invited to his *famadihana*.[1] After being thanked for their contribution the guests are given a meal.

Whether the first half of the ceremony takes place at the tomb or away from it, it is always preceded by an observance on the evening before. The *zana'drazana* go to the burial place and stand on the tomb or grave and, looking towards the north-east, "call" the dead. In fact, they address the spirits *(Ambiroa)*[2] of those whose bodies they will exhume. The senior person present calls the spirits, addressing the hills with the traditional far-carrying "cough".[3] He calls their names inviting them to rejoin their bodies, for tomorrow their kinsmen will come and take their bodies home. They should be present because they will be made happy. After this small offerings are made to encourage the *ambiroa* to be present. These are usually rum and honey. Then the tomb or grave is left until the time of the main ceremony.

The *zana'drazana* then return to the village and rejoin the other guests. Throughout the evening and the night dancing and singing, sometimes accompanied by bands, sometimes by a simple double-headed drum, continues in the temporary house. Much the same thing goes on the next morning, when more and more guests arrive and another meal is eaten. The *zana'drazana* then dress in their best clothes and jewellery.

Around midday the *zana'drazana* gather and are blessed by an elder of the family who wishes them various benefits and asperges them in the traditional manner. He also anoints the back of the neck or the head of those who will be immediately concerned with medicine supplied by the family astrologer. This protects them from danger which is generally associated with the dead and death.

Once this has been done the *zana'drazana*, carrying the *lamba mena*, spades and other things which will be necessary, gather, dancing, in the temporary house. This dance is different in spirit from the preceding ones. It is both excited and tense—excited in that dancing is always a sign of joy and high spirits and tense in that the *zana'drazana*, and especially the close relatives, children, parents or spouses of the dead, are obviously

---

[1] He either gives as much or, if a great length of time has elapsed, more.
[2] See p. 126.
[3] This is a short scream called "cough" in Malagasy.

frightened and deeply moved in apprehension of what is going to happen. This feeling persists throughout the main part of the ceremony.

The behaviour from then on only becomes clear if we bear in mind the fact that the ritual in a *famadihana* is very frightening to the Merina. Normally the dead and everything associated with them are studiously avoided. People who are alone always try not to have to go near tombs and there are endless stories of ghosts and how frightening they are. Coming into contact with the dead is always frightening, and the *famadihana* is in this sense a breaking of one of the basic precepts of society, which is respect and avoidance of the dead. Even pointing at a tomb may cause the offending finger to fall off. Not only does it involve coming into contact with the dead, but also with the skeletons of those with whom there once were the closest emotional ties. The desire of the close relatives to weep or run away is clearly apparent throughout the first part of the ceremony. The others on the contrary continually exhort the main participants not to weep, not to be afraid, to be happy and dance, as the dead are happy. The exhortations during this part of the ceremony show how the close relatives are being *forced* by the others to do a terrible, frightening thing. The women give themselves courage by dancing frenziedly on the way to the tomb—and this is acknowledged by the participants themselves. The men drink rum to achieve the same effect.

At the time decided by the astrologer the *zana'drazana*, followed by the others, set forth, dancing as they go and from time to time making high-pitched sounds which is the recognized way of calling the dead.

The journey to the tomb is usually under the direction of the astrologer who picks a roundabout route so that the tomb can be approached from the direction he has chosen. The party halts frequently on the way at places chosen by the astrologer. Everyone sits down and the *zana'drazana* dance frenziedly almost to the point of exhaustion. All the while the procession is preceded by a man carrying a Malagasy flag which is felt to be an essential part of the proceedings. The astrologer arranges the halts and their duration so that the procession arrives at the desired time, which is always around half past two. On arrival at the tomb, the leader of the procession digs a small hole near the north-east corner of the tomb in which he places the flag. The young men of the party start to dig out the trap-doors leading to the stairs which ultimately lead to the door of the tomb. Before actually digging, the young men usually rub a protective lotion on their heads supplied by the astrologer. In the earth that they remove they find certain charms—usually bits of wood and odd-shaped pieces of metal—which they pick out carefully so that they can be replaced later when the hole is filled in again. There is also always a locked padlock buried in the earth which, as it was explained to me, is a way of stopping ghosts from coming out. As soon as the trap-doors have been cleared they are opened (see Fig. 7). The men who have been digging rush away, which is one more illustration of the very real terror with which the whole operation of opening the grave is viewed.

The women are recommended during the whole proceeding to dance harder and harder. This has the effect of a drug and they become exhausted in the heat of the afternoon sun.

When the trap-doors are opened, the massive stone door of the tomb is revealed. The head of the *famadihana* family throws a stone down the stone staircase which leads to it. Immediately after, he rushes down and opens the door. He enters the tomb and in the doorway asks for the blessing of the dead in a formal prayer. He then sprinkles the skeletons with medicine and rum as a token offering. The medicine is said to be both a protection for the living and a gift to the dead. The first person in is followed by other members of the family and, with a certain amount of Dutch courage, they choose which skeleton or skeletons they will honour by taking out.

Once the corpses are identified, they are wrapped up in linen cloths, since the old *lamba mena* are most probably decayed by the decomposition of the body and the damp. Safely wrapped, the bodies are taken out of the tomb and immediately each bundle is again wrapped in a fine papyrus mat, usually specially prepared for the purpose.

Once these bodies have been taken out, they are placed in the custody of the women closely related to the dead. They hoist the body on their shoulders and start to dance with it in an anxious manner, going backwards and forwards.

The touching of the bodies by the women is the turning point of the ceremony. The bodies are touched by the people who are expected to have the strongest emotional links with the dead. They are touched by as close kinsmen of the dead as possible: parents, children and sisters. The reason why it is important that *women* should touch them is that women are the recognized vessels of kinship emotions. They, it is supposed, have the strongest tie to their kinsmen, and their emotional attachment is what is thought to keep the kinship links strong.

Here, however, an important distinction must be made. The very obvious emotion and fear aroused by the dead is really only very marked for the recently dead who have not been touched before—those for whom the *famadihana* is principally being held. The others are extras and much less attention is paid to them. This first contact with the recently dead is—obviously to the observer—a time when terror and revulsion are strong. The younger women have to be forced to touch the skeletons. Once actual contact has been made, the fear visibly diminishes and this continues till the end of the ceremony. In the end the fear is replaced by joyous excitement which often turns to Bacchanalian high spirits and by this time the recently dead are treated in much the same way as the long dead.

While this has been happening the crowd divides itself very clearly: the neighbours and more remote friends sit or stand at a certain distance, while the actual *zana'drazana* and the tomb family remain near the corpses and the tomb, many of them standing on the tomb.[1]

After a time the skeletons are laid on the laps of the women who sit on the ground, and then a short funeral-like service may be carried out by the local pastor or, in the case of Catholics and Anglicans, by a catechist. Once this is over the oldest man of the famly makes a speech recalling the life of the person or persons whom they are principally honouring, describing all their achievements in a traditional manner. After this, he will start to pick out the *lamba mena* which are to be given to the dead from the pile on the tomb. There are often many *lamba mena* for each corpse, as usually all the children or all the siblings are under an obligation to bring one. Other relatives may also do so. This means that in some cases 10 or 12 *lamba mena* are wrapped around one skeleton.

The number of dead honoured at a *famadihana* varies and they are not all given the same treatment. This is most clearly seen by the number of *lamba mena* given.

Most *famadihana* are principally for one man or woman. The person specifically honoured is always someone who has not been touched since their funeral. This usually means that they have died fairly recently and are personally remembered by a number of people present—parents, children, etc. It is the exhumation of these people which arouses the greatest emotion. It is they who receive the greatest number of *lamba*

---

[1] This would normally be an act of extreme disrespect—something which only witches would do.

mena. Quite explicitly it is for them that the ceremony is performed. These are the people who are given the most honoured treatment.

After them there is a second category. These are the bodies which are taken out of the tomb, like those of the first category, and danced with. They are not, however, the people for whom the ceremony is specifically held and they normally receive from 1 to 3 *lamba mena*. A *famadihana* may already have been performed for them. If it has not it usually means that they have very few, if any, close relatives or that those they have do not have much money. These people may have been dead a considerable time—20 to 30 years.

A third category includes those who are given a *lamba mena* each but whose bodies are not taken out of the tomb. Their corpses are wrapped surreptitiously by relatives who go quickly into the tomb while the main ceremony is taking place. This is done to avoid the tax normally levied by the government for each body exhumed by people who either do not wish the treatment afforded to the second category or who cannot afford to pay for it.

Finally there is a fourth category which is different from the first three in that the dead are not remembered personally. All skeletons visible in the tomb are wrapped irrespective of who they are and in this way the tomb is generally tidied up. These are mainly the skeletons of people who may have died a considerable time ago. They may be wrapped up in bundles of two, three or more in relatively cheap or small *lamba mena*. The differential treatment reflects the way the Merina considers the dead of his family. Those who have been dead a long time are not much taken into account.[1] Their names and personalities are forgotten. Informants told me proudly that there were dead from a very long time ago in their tomb, but they neither knew nor cared who they were. Those who are remembered are more important, but the recently dead are clearly the most important of all and are always mentioned with reverence. This is reflected in the tomb where the most recently dead are placed in the most honoured positions and the longest dead in the least honoured positions. Thus *famadihanas* and funerals are times of reorganization of the tomb, since when new corpses are brought the old ones must be moved to less favoured places.

Once all the bodies have been wrapped in their *lamba mena* the women

----

[1] An exception to this are certain mythical ancestors of demes who have importance. This is, however, a different kind of importance.

put them on their shoulders a second time and dance with them, going backwards and forwards, but ultimately going three times round the tomb in a clockwise direction. Their dancing becomes more and more frenzied. The skeletons are thrown in the air with shouts. Some of the women start to run and tug and pull. The joking relatives of the dead, brothers-in-law, start to play tricks on the dead and attempt to stop them returning to the tomb. At this stage, the element of ritual sacrilege which has already been mentioned becomes clearly apparent. Some of the corpses whose very contact involves a tremendous emotional strain at the beginning of the ceremony are now, along with the others, thrown up and down and the bones can be heard to crush. There is an extraordinary transformation of mood.

Finally, they are replaced in the tomb much in the same riotous spirit. The men who have replaced the bodies throw out the mats in which they were wrapped during the ceremony. Immediately the women outside fight each other for them, as the possession of these mats which wrapped the dead is greatly valued. Sleeping on them helps fertility.

This is yet another element which runs right through the ceremony. Dancing during the *famadihana* and especially with the corpses is also good for fertility. It is difficult to know, however, to what extent this is believed, and whether or not it is only said to encourage the women to dance.

Once all the corpses have been returned to the tomb the relatives go in and note the position of the dead to which they are related. They are urged to remember where they are placed for another occasion.

I now want to turn to a short description of the return *famadihana*. This becomes necessary when a *voanjo* has died away from his *tanindrazana* and has been buried temporarily. In such a case the first part of the ceremony takes place at the place of temporary burial, normally where the dead man lived.

Usually the first part of the ceremony which occurs at the place of temporary burial is a smaller affair than the tomb ceremony. This is for practical reasons. Only a small party of the *zana'drazana* can normally manage to go and fetch the corpse. The number of these "fetchers" is affected by the distance to be travelled and the price of the fare. They are joined by kinsmen who live at the place of temporary burial who in turn invite their neighbours. These people may only see this part of the ceremony. Quite clearly, therefore, a number of factors affect the size of this first part of the ceremony. It is significant that if the family of the dead man has settled in any number and for a considerable length of time at the place of temporary burial, which is normally the place of abode of the dead man, the ceremony will be more important than if this is not the case. In fact, the respective importance of the ceremony at the place of temporary burial and that at the place of the family tomb is a measure of the relative attachment of the family of the dead man to the two places. If the ceremony at the place of burial is a big affair it means that the relatives of the dead man feel that they have obligations to many people there and must invite them. If the ceremony at the place of temporary burial is small, the reverse is true. The same applies to the size of the ceremony at the tomb. We can therefore see the relative size as an indicator of the detachment or otherwise of the bereaved family from the *tanindrazana*.

On the first day there is usually a gathering of the kind that has already been described. In the evening the *zana'drazana* present go to "call the dead". The next day they go to the grave in much the same way as they would go the tomb. On reaching the place of burial the men of the party dig for the corpse while the women endeavour to dance strenuously. Once the body is found, it is wrapped up in a white linen cloth and probably placed in a new wooden box if the old one is rotten; it is then carried away and the journey back begins. If possible, it is placed at the north-east corner on the roof of a *taxi-brousse* in which the family return to the *tanindrazana*. From then until its reinhumation it is never left alone, as the nearest relatives take it in turns to stay by it. On arrival at the *tanindrazana* it is put in a specially prepared place where it is watched until the time when the party of *zana'drazana* set out to the tomb, with the corpse which they sling on a pole to which it is held fast with ropes. On the way to the tomb it is purposely swung and jolted. Those carrying it play with it, rushing it forwards and backwards. This strange practice is said by certain authors to make sure its soul does not come back to the house of the living, but my informants could not support this. It seems to me rather to be part of the general element of sacrilege which, as we have seen, becomes more and more apparent and acknowledged throughout the ceremony. If other corpses are to be exhumed at the tomb this is done first, and then the corpse which has been brought back is taken out of the wooden box, and from thereon is treated in the same way as the bodies taken out of the tomb.

A corpse which is brought back in this way is always that of a recently dead person, and it is therefore given the most honoured treatment described previously. In fact, such a *famadihana* is said to be done specifically for the returning *razana*.

Interpretation of *Famadihanas*

Any explanation of such a complex group of ceremonies as various forms of *famadihana* raises a difficulty. Either we have to explain every form separately, or we try to obtain the essence of the notion of a *famadihana*. The difficulty arises because, although the external observer may consider each kind of ceremony as different, it is clear that the actor thinks of them as essentially the same, since he has no words which distinguish one kind from another. The difficulty is aggravated by the fact that, although the actor sees all the ceremonies as essentially the same, the explanations of the ceremonies which are given apply exclusively to one or other form of *famadihana*.

First let us consider the explanations of informants and the types of *famadihanas* to which they refer, without any attempt at interpretation. Then I shall try to take these varied explanations and, by putting them in a sociological context, discuss the basis of the category *famadihana*.

It is surprising how difficult it is to get a clear answer as to why a particular *famadihana* is being held. I was often told by people who had spent huge sums on a *famadihana* that they did not know why the ceremony was performed. More commonly, I was told what amounts to much the same, namely, that this was the custom of the ancestors and so it was right. For some kinds of *famadihana*, however, a clear answer is given.

For those *famadihanas* which are held because the old tomb is full and a new one is being built part of the answer is obvious. However, when pushed further and asked why it is necessary to transfer some of the dead from the old tomb to the new one, informants seem to have very little idea. They sometimes attempt rather evasive answers, like "No one, when dead, wants to lie alone", or the proverb "An empty tomb is hungry".

When a *famadihana* is held to transfer a corpse from one tomb to another the purpose is clearly stated. This is a very rare ceremony but of great interest. It is normally carried out for women, and only very occasionally for men, who have been buried in the tomb of their still living spouse, and who are later returned by *famadihana* to one of their parental tombs. The reason given for this transfer is that the living spouse may not marry again so long as his dead wife is in his family tomb. To free himself he transfers his dead wife to her parents' tomb.

For the very much more common return *famadihana* the reason given is also fairly explicit. It is assumed that it is the deepest wish of everyone to be buried with other people, and especially with their kinsmen. The terror of being buried alone is a major obsession, and those few individuals who fear this might be their fate are continually bringing the conversation back to this topic as if obsessed by the thought. I often tried to push the point further and discover what specific unpleasantness awaited the person who was permanently buried alone, or what special pleasures awaited those buried in the family tomb. Here again one meets with no very definite ideas about what actually happens to the dead. The point implied is simply that the dead are thought to enjoy some kind of life, and no sort of life can be enjoyed without being surrounded by kinsmen.

For those *famadihanas* which only involve taking the corpses out of the tomb and returning them the reasons behind them were almost never formulated. I was told such things as, "They have not been touched for a long time". Even more general answers were obtained such as, "The neighbours will think us wicked to have money while the dead do not have new *lamba mena*". One rather cynical shopkeeper with whom I discussed the matter said that the neighbours were putting pressure on him to hold a *famadihana* as they did not want him to accumulate too much money. In this particular instance the neighbours won in spite of his cynicism. As I was about to leave the village he was planning one.

At a more general level informants told me that the *famadihanas* are performed to make the dead happy. In some cases I was told that a *famadihana* was held after a dead relative had appeared in a dream to one of the initiators and had actually asked for a *famadihana*, either because he was buried away from the ancestral tomb and wanted to return or simply because he was cold.

The ceremony is not thought to change the nature of the soul or its state as the theories of Hertz and Van Gennep might lead us to expect.[1] Nor is a *famadihana* thought to bring specific benefits to the living, such as the removal of diseases.[2]

---

[1] R. Hertz, "Contribution à une étude sur la représentation de la mort", *L'Année Sociologique*, 1907, and A. Van Gennep, *Les Rites de Passage*, 1909.

[2] I checked this point repeatedly as comparative ethnography might suggest this possibility.

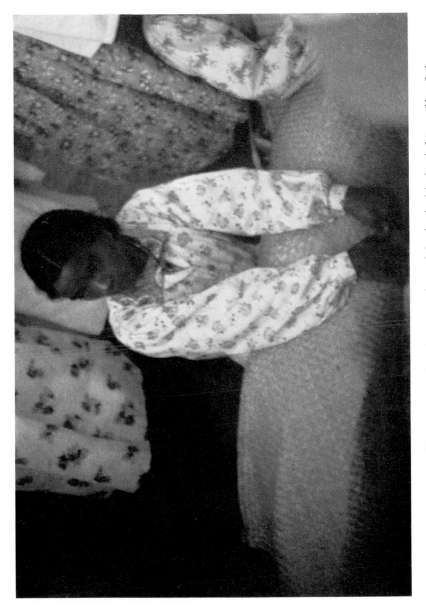

Plate 5a. *Famadihana.* Young woman listening to a eulogy of the dead with the skeleton of her father-in-law on her lap.

Plate 5b. *Famadihana*. Dancing with the corpses towards the end of the ceremony in a near Bacchanalian spirit.

It is true, however, that since the dead are happy the living take the occasion to ask for a blessing, or more exactly a *tsodrano*. The word *tsodrano* means "blowing on water" and this is what a living person does when giving a *tsodrana*. After having wished the recipient a long life, many children, etc., he blows over water in which an *ariary tsy vaky* has been placed. Today this is often modified into spraying the water with the hand in a manner clearly derived from the practice of baptism. A *tsodrana* is normally given either by a person who is very old—often in return for a small present—in which case the nearness to death is thought to give special power, or it is given by the head of a family. It may also be asked from the dead by the gift of a small libation at the tomb. At a *famadihana* it is understood that all those directly concerned are by their action asking for a *tsodrano*. Sometimes some of the dances while the corpse is visible are mimes requesting a *tsodrano*. The actual effect of receiving a *tsodrano* is again not clear. It makes the object of the blessing more prosperous, but above all it removes *tsiny* (approximately "guilt").

The removal of *tsiny* and its relation to the *famadihana* is one of the most abstract expressions of the purpose of the ceremony. This is a topic usually only approached by those renowned for their knowledge of "custom", mainly senior men who carry a great deal of authority, or astrologers. The notions about *tsiny* are therefore not general knowledge in the same way as the ideas discussed above.

The nature of *tsiny* for the Merina has been discussed at length and in great depth by Andriamanjato.[1] I can only summarize his argument by saying that *tsiny* is believed to be the guilt incurred by wrong actions, especially those against kinsmen, although there is no specific idea that a particular action is the cause of one man's *tsiny*. The incurring of *tsiny* is almost unavoidable in that one is continually failing to fulfil one's duties completely, especially towards one's kinsmen. As one goes through life one is weighed down by the inevitable accumulation of *tsiny*, and as a result all one undertakes is thwarted. The *famadihana* lightens the burden of *tsiny*. This means that it does not positively cause anything good to happen, but it removes possible unspecified future misfortunes.

Conversely, failure to carry out a *famadihana* when one is financially able to do so may increase *tsiny*. Here a clear distinction is always made between return *famadihanas* and other kinds of *famadihanas*. In the case of

---

[1] R. Andriamanjato, *Le Tsiny et le Tody dans la Pensée Malgache*, 1957.

non-return *famadihanas* there is only *tsiny* if the ceremony is not carried out while the living are getting rich. For return *famadihanas* the obligation is much more definite. I have often been told that as soon as a relative has been buried temporarily his kinsmen must start saving up to carry out the *famadihana* at the earliest possible date. If they cannot manage otherwise they must sell whatever they have, even if it means disposing of the land which is their means of livelihood, if they want to escape *tsiny*. I know of several cases in which this was done. It shows the very special place of the return *famadihana* in the Merina mind. This is my starting point for a wider discussion of the ceremony.

Let us turn now from the specific explanations given to me by informants to a more general explanation of the ceremony, which is based partly on informants' statements, partly on direct observation, and partly on general considerations of Merina society.

When we ask what the essence of the *famadihana* is and what it is that all *famadihanas* have in common the answers we obtain are not very illuminating, but a hint of what the actors think on this subject can be found in the assumptions they make when talking about *famadihanas*. All discussion of *famadihanas* in general by the peasants only refers to return *famadihanas*. As soon as the subject is raised generally, descriptions or explanations are given which only take into account the return *famadihana*. This can go to extraordinary lengths. In one particular case I remember questioning an important informant during a *famadihana*. This *famadihana* was of the type in which the bodies are taken out of the family tomb and then replaced and was not a return *famadihana*. I started to discuss the subject in general with him. Not only was what I was told applicable only to return *famadihanas*, but it was firmly denied that any other kind ever occurred. It seems to me that this attitude can only be explained by the fact that the intellectual concept of a *famadihana* is that of the return *famadihana*. Other factors, including the clearly stated fear of incurring *tsiny* if the return *famadihana* is not carried out, strongly support this assumption. There is also the fact that when the Merina feel they should defend their customs against non-Merina they are always willing to rise to the defence of the return *famadihana*, but feel a little uncomfortable when the other forms are mentioned.

The defence given on such occasions is in itself very interesting. The main point they make is that it is essential to bring together the dead of one family. The universality of this desire is taken for granted. As has already been noted, it is a basic fear of the Merina to be buried away from their kinsmen. The very strength of this feeling makes it quite clear that it involves many factors. The point is that to be without a tomb to go into really means to have no kinsmen and no family while alive or, in other words, to have no place in the continuing social structure. It means to have no kinsmen while alive, because the group of closest kinsmen is conceptually associated with the tomb group. It means to have no place in the continuing social structure because a man only has such a place in relation to a tomb. As we saw, there are no descent groups of the living, but there is a notion of descent groups in relation to the dead in the tomb. In the ideal past, the family is believed to have been a quasi corporate localized group with its tomb on its territory. Now the only thing that allows this picture to continue to live is the fact that although the family is not there any more and not a corporate group any more, it is known that when dead it will be such a group again.

Here we can look again at the concept of *tsiny*. Andriamanjato has stressed first, how *tsiny* is linked with failing to fulfil duties to Ego's kinsmen, and second, how the Merina feels it cannot possibly be escaped. It seems to me that an important aspect of this failure is that the actor feels himself continually forced for reasons of practicability to have close relations with people who are not his kinsmen. It is clearly felt that such relations should exist only between kinsmen. This is shown by the way people with whom one has contractual relationships are said to be kinsmen, even when it is obvious they are not. This means that the actor feels that by entering into non-kinship relations he deprives his kinsmen of what really should be theirs: this is *tsiny*. Therefore the dispersal of the family inevitably leads to *tsiny*. The actor makes up for the fall from kinship grace, which is due to the dispersal of the living, by spending large sums on the ritual regrouping of the dead. He thus avoids the maximum *tsiny* which would be the acceptance of the definitive break with the *tanindrazana* and his family.

The idea of the rightness of being together with kinsmen during life and death is clearly expressed in what is, without doubt, the most commonly quoted Merina proverb, which is always given as an explanation for the return *famadihana*: "*Velona iray trano, maty iray fasana*", which can be translated as "Those who live in one house should be buried in one tomb". It is interesting that this aspect was noted by Hertz in his essay on death. Most of his thesis is not applicable to the *famadihana* since he is dealing with somewhat different secondary funerals, but it is interesting to note that many of his points are relevant. He states:

La réunion des ossements du mort a ceux des ancêtres . . . constitue . . . en général, l'un des actes essentiels de la cérémonie finale. Les ossuaires dont l'existence nous est attestée par de nombreux ethnographie, appartiennent le plus souvent à la famille ou au clan. "Vivant, une seule maison, mort, une seule Tombe", dit un proverbe Malgache qui semble exprimer un sentiment profond.[1]

This proverb implies that those who live together while alive should be buried together. It refers to the traditional society when neighbours were kinsmen and it amounts to saying that kinsmen should be buried together. This is why it is quoted in justification of bringing back those who have been buried away. When applied to the present it involves an interesting paradox. Although in the past this formulation may have corresponded to an actual state of affairs, nowadays, as likely as not, the people who will be buried together probably never lived together. Instead of the tomb being a continuation of the state of affairs of the living it is an ideal of corporateness and family unity which is striven for during life, but is never achieved. The return *famadihana* is therefore a ritual regrouping. It is often described as bringing back those who have gone away. But it is not a question of bringing *back* since there is no pre-existing group, descent group or local group from which the living could have separated themselves. What really happens at a return *famadihana* is the *making* of a group which, as we saw, is an ideal model for the living.

The notion of a descent group which is associated with the tomb is also clearly to be seen in the *famadihanas* which accompany the making of a new tomb. There we saw how it is necessary to take some of the dead out of the old tomb in order to place them in the new tomb. This action obviously stresses the importance of continuity of a kinship group through time. The aspect of the *famadihana* which stresses fertility also seems to fall into place here because of its obvious link with the continuity of the group.[2]

The notion of reforming the family as a permanent group is only one aspect of the *famadihana*. It is, as we have seen, the aspect which is foremost in the minds of the actors. The other basic element is the emotion aroused in the individual by the relation of the recently dead. This

---

[1] R. Hertz, "Contribution à une étude sur la representation de la mort", *L'Année Sociologique*, 1907, p. 113. Much of what Hertz has to say of the Malagasy is not relevant here as it refers to the funeral ceremonies of the Betsileo kings.

[2] Also relevant to this argument is the rare type of *famadihana* which takes place when a corpse has for some reason been lost. In such a case a megalith representing the man who has died is erected near the tomb and a very similar ceremony is performed.

is very clear to the observer but it is an aspect much less taken into account by the actors when they talk of the *famadihana*. This relationship has two aspects. First, there is affection and respect for the dead, marked by the giving of *lamba mena* and the spending of vast sums on them, and the obvious emotion of the participants. Second, there is the aspect of sacrilege. In one way the *famadihana* is a demonstration of the kinship links of the dead to the living. The giving of *lamba mena* and the assembly of the kinsmen of the dead marks off the dispersed family centred around the dead, a bilateral web. The group of the kinsmen of the dead are the *zana'drazana*. The genealogy in Fig. 9 shows how the dead are the links which hold this group together. This is an Ego-centred bilateral group and it should be noted that the people who will be buried in the tomb are not in any way the main actors.

It follows that, bearing in mind that the kinship system of the living is a bilateral web which does not divide society into exclusive groups, and that the idea of corporateness is a concept which can really exist only in relation to tombs, the shift of emphasis from the tomb to the individual dead is a shift of emphasis from groups to interpersonal relations. We are marking this change of emphasis when we pass from the return aspect, which is principally concerned with bringing the dead back to the tomb, to the emotional aspect, which is mainly concerned with activating the relationship between the living and the individual dead. The reaffirmation of the link of the living to certain individual dead at the same time stresses interpersonal relations between kinsmen. The *famadihana* is well suited to demonstrating such links because all direct kinship relations depend on links through the dead. This is because all kinship relations are ultimately based on having a common forebear in an ascending generation. If this forebear is dead the two relatives interact directly, but if this forebear is not dead the authority vested in the senior generations means that the two relatives must go through the intermediary of their senior kinsmen. By taking the simple example of two brothers we can see what this means. If two brothers whose parents are dead want to participate in an important action then they will combine together knowing that they are linked by the dead. If their parents are living any joint action has to be directed by their living parent and the relationship between them is of one brother to the parent of the other brother. In this way the fact that the links to the dead are demonstrated ceremonially under great emotional stress strengthens all kinship links between individuals. This strengthening of kinship is the second aspect of the *famadihana*. In other words, while the return aspect of the *famadihana* is a ritual denial of the cross-cutting nature of kinship, since the grouping into tombs is a way of dividing society into non-overlapping groups by forgetting the kinship ties which do not fit into this pattern, the second aspect of the *famadihana* in contrast stresses the full spread of the individual's kinship relations. This is manifested by the fact that all relatives of the dead must participate irrespective of their tomb group and *tanindrazana* affiliations. It is, however, not simply a matter of maintaining individual ties; it is also a question of transforming them.

The aspect of the *famadihana* which seems at first most strange is the deliberate disrespect shown to the corpse. This seems to be a complete contradiction of the act of piety in giving *lamba mena* to the dead. The whole matter is obviously most complex. A similar topic has recently been discussed by Dr. J. Goody.[1] Two of his points are particularly relevant here. First, he states: "When the reversal concerns a strongly sanctioned prohibition, by the very act of breaking the social norm the initiate forges a bond with the other members of the group as against the rest of the world." In this case he is referring to associations, but a similar effect does seem to me to occur here, in the sense that in having committed a sacrilege together the bond between kinsmen is all the stronger. This is only one aspect. Dr. Goody also states for a ritual involving similar sacrilege towards the dead: "The fear of the corpse is purged by contact with the very object of disgust." This brings me to a completely new aspect.

The *famadihana* is for the actors a transformation of the living's idea about the dead. This applies for those dead for whom the *famadihana* is principally performed and who are being "touched" for the first time since their burial. During decomposition the body is terrifying because in some ways it breaks the division of those essential categories, life and death. Although it is dead it arouses in the living still the same picture and emotions as when alive. The rough treatment given to the corpse and its display as a skeleton is a clear demonstration of its complete death. It is interesting to note how, during the ceremony, the close relatives who have the most intimate memories of the dead person are forced to handle the skeleton so that the realization of death is fully accepted. They are made to come to terms with the fact that their

---

[1] J. Goody, *Death, Property and the Ancestors*, 1962, pp. 74–77.

brother, mother, etc, is nothing but a pile of dry bones, a point stressed by Hertz in a slightly different context:

Le fait brut de la mort physique ne suffit pas a consommer la mort dans les consciences: l'image de celui qui est mort récemment fait encore parti du système des choses de ce monde; elle ne s'en détache que peu a peu, par une serie de déchirements intérieurs.

p. 129

Hertz's view of the secondary funeral as an act of separation is also relevant here. Hertz saw the ceremony as changing the nature of the dead so that they were more remote from the living. In other words finally liberating the soul of the corpse from its body. At a *famadihana*, however, no drastic change is thought to occur to the dead.[1] The change which occurs is in the attitude of the living to the dead. While in the ceremonies considered by Hertz the dead are separated by being removed away from the living, in the case of the *famadihana* the living are separated from the dead by being removed away from the dead. The ritually sacrilegious attitude which is forced on the living is one which makes them consider their relatives as irreversibly dead, and consequently separates the dead from them in a definitive manner.

There is one further aspect of this contrast between secondary funerals and the *famadihana*. The separation involved in a secondary funeral is an explicit belief: after the secondary funeral the soul is said to change its state. The separation involved in a *famadihana* is subjective and not explicit. The significance of this is that the separating effect of the ceremony varies with the individuals concerned and in some cases the final separation involves more than one *famadihana*. Even when bodies are being exhumed for a second or even a third time some aspects of the element of demonstrating and breaking kinship links remain, but in such cases the emotions are much weaker and the ceremony is much smaller and of only secondary importance.

An analysis of a *famadihana* must therefore take two aspects into account: firstly, the aspect of regrouping in the tomb, and secondly, the aspect of demonstrating relationship to the dead, and through the dead to other living people. This second aspect is ambiguous, since at the same time as the individual relationships are being demonstrated they are also being broken.

---

[1] Nor is the *famadihana* linked with the end of mourning.

The concept held by the Merina of their kinship system is one of seg-mentary, corporate groups. This illusion of corporateness and locality is maintained by its demonstrability for the society of the dead. The return *famadihana* plays a major part in this. In contrast, the *actual* structure of the kinship system is no longer one of localized corporate groups. As a result of the partial breakdown in the rule of endogamy and of territorial dispersion the actual structure of kinship has become very much what we would expect in a bilateral society; that is, a web of interpersonal relationships which, because of their overlapping, do not divide the society into groups. The second aspect of the *famadihana* serves the purposes of such a system by stressing interpersonal links bet-ween the living and the dead and, by extension, between different living people.

The *famadihana* therefore combines the picture of the exclusive ideal groups by stressing the unity of the dead within the tomb (this is clear in the return aspect) and, at the same time, the contradictory bilateral dis-persed family of the dead. This is achieved by the giving of *lamba mena*, the gathering of all the relatives, and by sacrilege. What is most impor-tant is the combination of these two elements in one ceremony. This combination means that the *famadihana* becomes the articulation between the ideal kinship system and the actual system by being a significant part of the gradual process of depersonalization of the dead. Before the first *famadihana* those who have died are still often mentioned in conversa-tion and clearly their personalities and their social ties are remembered with emotion in the same way as when they were alive. We saw how the first *famadihana*, and to a lesser extent the succeeding ones, involve the gathering of the dead's dispersed family which pinpoints his place in the kinship system. However, this is only one aspect for the ceremony also involves a separation from the dead. This separation takes the form of a brutal demonstration that the dead relative is really nothing more than a dry skeleton. After the *famadihana* the skeleton is always replaced in the tomb. This, as we saw, marks the dead man's place in the ideal society. Membership of the tomb by the dead and the placing of an individual finally in the society of the ancestors implies forgetting and ignoring many kinship relations of the dead which cut across the groupings of this society. The separation aspect of the ceremony does precisely this because it is no longer as relatives of the living that those who have died ultimately become part of the society of the ancestors but as a part of the tomb. After the first *famadihana* especially the names of the dead tend to be forgotten and it is only as members of "our tomb" that they later have any significance. In this way the bilateral web of the living has been literally transformed by means of one or more *famadihana* into a system of discrete interlocking groups. This is the end of the process which began with the funeral in the village. The full funerary *rites de passage* therefore imply a ceremony involving the practical society, then a ceremony involving the moral kinship society, which ultimately means reducing the dead man to a part of the Merina model of an ideal society.

PART 3

The Break with the *Tanindrazana*

6

Marriage

In Chapter 2 we saw how in the traditional system the corporate nature of the deme is seen as maintained in part by rules of marriage. Similarly the group-like existence of the *fianakaviana* is maintained by a high degree of in-marriage. The rule of deme in-marriage has the dual purpose of not allowing rice lands to be inherited by those outside it and of maintaining rank. In the case of the *fianakaviana* the preference for in-marriage is solely designed to keep inheritance within a group of close kinsmen (*lova tsy mifindra*). These rules were probably fairly well obeyed in the past. Out of nine marriages which took place before 1905 and about which I have information, only one could not be classed as *lova tsy mifindra*.[1]

Today these rules of marriage are still recognized. As the figures which are given below[2] show, most people choose to marry within the traditional categories. None the less, it should be remembered that in the present situation the first reason for such marriages, the desire to keep land within a small local group, is unlikely to apply in the same way any more, since kinsmen are now not normally neighbours. Nevertheless it still keeps ancestral property in the hands of the group and still serves the purpose of maintaining rank. But above all, these marriages take place nowadays to reaffirm the link with the society of the *tanindrazana* and with Ego's kinsmen. Marrying back was described to me as "closing up a breach". The reason why the Merina sees a marriage within the dispersed family in this light is because each new generation which

---

[1] This information is not, of course, necessarily completely reliable.
[2] See p. 54.

reaches marriageable age is seen as a potential threat to the link with the *tanindrazana*. This threat lies in the fact that the young men or women might contract unions with outsiders and their children would subsequently have a more tenuous link with the *tanindrazana* or associated *tanindrazana* than either of the parents, since fewer of their relatives would share the same or a similar *tanindrazana*.

Up to now I have presented the link with the *tanindrazana* as permanent and unbreakable. This is certainly how it appears to the actors. In fact, most people living in or near Ambatomanoina still maintain this link. Nevertheless, the fact remains that in some cases the link is ultimately broken and marriage outside the *fianakaviana* and deme plays an important part in this break.

Marriage is therefore crucial to understanding the link with the *tanindrazana* and also how it is broken. This is because it is an act of identification with the *tanindrazana* for which, as we shall see, potentially dangerous alternatives exist. Unlike the other forms of identification with the *tanindrazana*, which are quite separate from other concerns, the choice of a marriage partner involves a choice between intensifying relations with the society of the *tanindrazana* or with another society, which in this case of course is the society of neighbours.

Preliminary marriage negotiations among the "white" Merina are started by the parents of the groom when they feel that their son is making a full contribution to agricultural work, which is usually when he is 16 or 17. If the boy is still at school marriage will be delayed until he has worked right round the year in his parents' fields. A year before the projected marriage the father will "give" his son a piece of rice land to cultivate.[1, 2] "Giving" at this stage should be understood in a special sense. The son is not given the right to dispose of the land as he wishes, but only the right to cultivate it and to consider its produce his own. This ownership of the produce and the right to cultivate the land are largely nominal. The reason for this is that, since the household is the smallest cooperating group, its members work together on all land whether "given" in this manner or not. Agricultural decisions, such as when to sow, are taken by the head of the household for all the land

---

[1] If the parents rely for rice land on land belonging to the mother, then it will be the mother who makes this gift.

[2] The place of the father in what follows may be taken by a foster father, but this depends on the details of the fostering relationship.

which is cultivated by it. Even after the harvest all the rice grown by any members of the household will be placed in the same store. This means that, apart from the *notion* that a part belongs to the son, all rice will be used in the same way for preparing the meals of the household.[1] The land given in this way is not thought of as *pre-mortem* inheritance, although it is part of the handing down of property process. It is always less than the ultimate inheritance, although in all cases about which I have information it was to become the core of the land which was ultimately inherited. Obviously, the amount of land so given varies with the amount owned by the father and a landless man cannot give this kind of gift to his son, but the ideal is to give enough rice land for the needs of a small nuclear family. In the Ambatomanoina area, where the yield per hectare[2] was low, this meant at least half a hectare of rice land. A gift of this kind is usually made to the groom, but a similar gift is often also made to the bride. The gift to a girl is made at the actual time of marriage, not before.

Although this gift is of great symbolic importance at this stage and is a promise of support after marriage, it is of little economic value to the groom before marriage. More relevant is the fact that at this stage the young man will start to cultivate some cash crops for himself. These are grown on the hill-sides which cannot be used for rice cultivation. Although individual rights over some of this land exist, there is no shortage of it and anybody can cultivate as much as he wants of it. In and around Ambatomanoina the main cash crops are groundnuts and beans, but those who live near enough to the road to Tananarive also cultivate onions and tomatoes. The money obtained in this way belongs to the future groom and will be used firstly for the expenses of the wedding, and secondly, together with the livestock he may own, as starting capital for his own household.[3]

After the parents or guardians have "given" their son rice land, and when he has shown his ability to work like an adult, they will set about looking for a bride for him. The initial choice may well come from the boy himself if he is attracted to a particular girl, but if this is the case no

---

[1] In the rare cases when rice is sold the son may be given some of the money obtained from the sale. In the two cases about which I have information in which this happened, the father gave the son 1000 FMG without attempting to work out the exact proportion of rice that was his.

[2] 1 hectare = 2·47 acres.

[3] Young men often own some cattle and other livestock. This is obtained as a reward for herding cattle when a child, or in the form of gifts from fond parents and grandparents.

hint of it will be given in the formal proceedings.[1] The boy tells his father the name of the girl he would like to marry and if she is suitable the father will then act as though the original idea had come from him.

The father who is considering the marriage of his son then employs the services of an intermediary. In the case of a marriage along traditional lines, the father will choose someone who is genealogically related both to him and to the future bride. If he has no particular prospective daughter-in-law in mind, he may ask the intermediary to look around among *his* relatives for a suitable candidate. In the case of non-traditional marriages, the intermediary may be anyone with close links to both sides and will not normally be related to them.

Once the intermediary has discovered from the girl's parents that the match is possible,[2] both sides will then go to consult the family astrologer to see if the destinies of the future partners are compatible. If this is so, then the boy (or possibly the girl) will be sent to take a look at the proposed partner to see if he likes her. Although respect for the judgement of their elders will push a boy and girl to accept the proposed partner, a very real element of personal choice comes into the marriage sequence at this stage, and very often the boy or girl will block the proceedings. In fact a boy may go to two or three families to see which of a number of girls he likes best.

Once the choice of a partner has been made the preparations for the marriage ceremony proper begin. These can only be dealt with briefly here. The parents or guardians of the couple, accompanied by a few senior relatives, meet at the house of the bride for what is called a *dinidinika* (meaning "a careful examination"). This takes the form of prolonged discussion held in private where the terms of the marriage as well as its timetable are decided upon. Most important, the amount and value of the various marriage prestations are fixed. It is at this stage that the real bargaining is done and the discussion of these matters which will take place during the actual marriage is simply acting out publicly what has already been decided at the *dinidinika*.

A Merina marriage involves two major sets of prestations (see Fig. 10). First, there are the prestations made by the groom (possibly with the help of his relatives) to the relatives of the bride. Second, there are the

---

[1] It is said that elopements occur but they seem to be fairly rare and as far as I know none took place during my period of field work.

[2] Sometimes, although rarely, it is the parents of the girl who take the initiative.

gifts made by the parents of the bride, with the help of their relatives, to the newly married couple. These I shall call the dowry. Apart from these principal gifts a marriage is often the occasion of other prestations.

The two principal prestations made by the groom to the bride's parents and relatives at the *fisihaona* and the *vody-ondry*. Of these, the

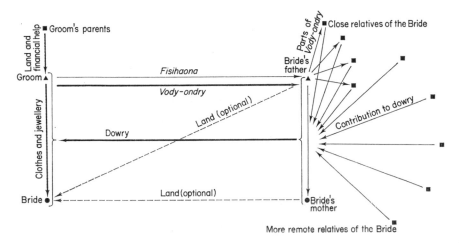

Fig. 10. Major marriage prestations.

vody-ondry is much the larger payment, and I will deal with this first, returning to the *fisihaona* later. The money for both these prestations should come from the groom himself, but it may be supplemented by his relatives in the form of a loan, gift, or payment for services rendered.

The phrase *vody-ondry* means, literally, "the hind quarters of a sheep". This is because the hind quarters of any animal is the most ritually valued part of it. It is the part given to a political superior, who is normally either Ego's father, or the head of the local family. The *vody-ondry* is always paid in cash and the name is symbolic only, although I was told that in the past it did, in fact, consist of the hind quarters of a sheep, although there is no written record of a time when anything else but money was paid.

The *vody-ondry* is given to the father of the bride as an act of obeisance to him. My informants used a phrase which can be said to mean "to show respect". When the father of the bride has received the *vody-ondry* he will then divide a part of it among the bride's mother, living grandparents, siblings of the parents, and brothers of the bride. The following example shows how this is done. A *vody-ondry* of 1250 FMG given in 1965 was divided among the relatives of the bride as follows:

> 500 FMG to the girl's parents
> 250 FMG to the mother's mother
> 250 FMG to the father's father's sister
> 100 FMG to the father's brother
> 50 FMG to each of the three older brothers.

The reason why part of the *vody-ondry* is given to other relatives is that the payment is explicitly stated to include, apart from the *vody-ondry* proper, compensation for such services as the girl would have offered to her mother, grandparents and relatives had she not married. (They include fetching firewood, pulling out white hairs, and looking for lice. These services are enumerated in the speech when the sum is actually being handed over—see below.)

The Merina stress that the *vody-ondry* is a small amount. They compare their own custom favourably with that of other peoples to the north such as the Tsimihety and the Sakalava who, if the Merina accounts are anything to go by, have a full bride price system.[1] There is great variation in the amount paid, from around 500 FMG (70p) to as much as 7000 FMG. The *vody-ondrys* about which I have absolutely certain information were 755 FMG, 1250 FMG, 1000 FMG, 2550 FMG, 4000 FMG, 5800 FMG, 1250 FMG, 3750 FMG, 5000 FMG.[2]

The dowry given by the parents and relatives of the bride is, unlike the *vody-ondry*, in kind. Broadly speaking, relatives who receive a proportion of the *vody-ondry* participate in making the gifts to the newly married couple in the same proportion. However, more remote relatives, who receive no part of the *vody-ondry*, may also make a small contribution to this gift.

The presents given by the bride's family consist of the essential movables used in the Merina house. These usually include a mattress of raffia (the more wealthy family may have one of the European type, or even a bed), a number of fine papyrus mats and baskets made by the female relatives of the girl, a trunk (an essential item of Merina furniture), plates, knives and spoons. There is also a mirror, a needle and

---

[1] It is interesting to note that the *mainty* who do not practise *lova tsy mifindra* marriages tend to give much higher *vody-ondrys*.

[2] Casual information on this subject cannot be trusted, unless verified, since government and Church propaganda has made it more respectable to pay a very small *vody-ondry*.

thread, and other symbols of the future wife's domestic duties. Rich people may include such items as linen sheets, probably embroidered by the girl herself, and a great variety of other household goods.

The total value of this dowry varies and does not seem to be related to the amount of the *vody-ondry*. If related to anything, it is to the wealth of the bride's family and other more intangible things such as how far the bride's family wants to impress that of the groom. A fairly typical dowry of such a kind which I saw given was worth around 8000 FMG. (The *vody-ondry* on this occasion was 3750 FMG.)

The intention behind the giving of a dowry is obvious. It is a contribution by the bride's family to the future joint household and a contribution to help those aspects of the life of the household which will most concern the future wife. In this way it is as much a personal gift to the bride by her family as it is a gift to the new household. This is shown by the fact that at no stage is the dowry ever given to the groom and that, unlike the *vody-ondry*, it is returnable, i.e. the girl takes the dowry back with her if the marriage breaks up. If the marriage breaks up before the birth of children all the dowry is returned. If there have been children of the marriage, and if the children stay with the father, only part is returned. The dowry is in no sense a *pre-mortem* inheritance.

Once the *dinidinika* has been completed and the general timetable of the ceremonies, as well as the amount of these two major transactions has been fixed, the families of the groom and of the bride carry on their preparations for the marriage separately, these consisting mainly in gathering the food necessary for the feast and the money for the prestations. They may, however, carry out the minor ceremony of handing over the *fisihaona*, or "demand" before the main ceremony, the giving of the *vody-ondry*. The *fisihaona* is a small payment, usually one-tenth of the *vody-ondry*, given by the groom to the girl's parents. This payment stands for exactly what it says and its acceptance is more or less an acceptance of the groom as a future son-in-law. Combined with the *fisihaona* is another nominal gift called the *tapa maso*, or "breaking the eye". This refers to the ending of the avoidance taboo whereby any young man with designs on a girl must never be seen by the girl's father. After the giving of the *tapa maso* the taboo is removed and the father of the bride ceremonially "sees" the future son-in-law in a mime where the boy stands in front of the father-in-law covered by a blanket which he then removes.

Although the giving of the *fisihaona* and *tapa maso* forms in many cases a separate ceremony, this ceremony is modelled on the ceremony of giving the *vody-ondry*. In fact, in the Ambatomanoina district the two ceremonies were merged into one and I never saw a separate *fisihaona* ceremony.[1] This is because a traditional marriage in Ambatomanoina usually involves marrying someone living quite a distance away. It is difficult enough to get both families together once, let alone twice.

The real marriage ceremony, however, is that at which the *vody-ondry* is given. The normal way of enquiring whether two people are properly married is to ask *"Efa lasa ve ny vody-ondry?"*—literally, "Has the *vody-ondry* gone?"

It is for the girl's family to ask the astrologer to fix the time and day of this most important ceremony. When told by the astrologer, they inform the boy's family of the day, but not of the exact time.

A week before the marriage relatives of the girl will visit the house of her parents, bringing their contribution to the dowry. It is then that a feature which is evident at various stages of the marriage ceremony first appears. Many of the relatives who contribute to the dowry and will receive some part of the *vody-ondry* are probably also related to the groom. This is a result of the system of *lova tsy mifindra* marriages. In such a marriage the same people often play two different roles—as relatives of the groom and as relatives of the bride. This is possible because, apart from the actual discussion of the *vody-ondry*, which only involves a few people, the ceremonies on the bride's and groom's sides are quite separate. The only difficulty is that this double role often causes those involved hectic travelling from one place to another.

Another set of gifts must be prepared before the day when the *vody-ondry* is presented. The groom, when going to fetch his bride, takes with him a complete set of clothes for her, a sunshade and some jewellery. These again can be a fairly large expense, as the only example of this prestation for which I could ascertain the cost shows:

Sunshade	800 FMG
Dress	350 FMG
Lamba	600 FMG
Jewellery	3400 FMG
Total	5150 FMG

[1] In some cases when the *fisihaona* has been given and the *vody-ondry* is delayed, as it often is, it is not unusual for the future pair to be allowed by their parents to live together at their houses for short periods.

This is a non-returnable present made by the groom to the bride. Apart from the items mentioned above, shoes and more expensive jewellery may be included.

On the day fixed for the ceremonial donation of the *vody-ondry* the first thing that happens is the gathering of a group of people at the house of the groom.[1] This party, referred to as the *mpaka*, "the takers", is led by the head of the groom's local family, unless the head of the family is also the father of the boy. (The father of the boy must never be included in the *mpaka*.) Apart from the head of the delegation there is the groom,[2] his younger brother or someone to take the place of a younger brother if there is none, perhaps a few other male relatives, a woman from the groom's family who is fairly senior, at least two women who have married into the groom's local family, and probably other close relatives. The only participant not closely related to the groom is the *mpikabary* (speech-maker). He is a respected older man (known for his abilities as a speech-maker), who is asked to perform by the father of the groom. Often he is a protestant minister. The *mpikabary* will be the spokesman for the groom's family. He is not paid, but the fact that he is asked is a great honour and is considered sufficient reward in itself. The *mpaka* party sets out, carrying the bride's clothes, either travelling on foot or by *taxi-brousse* according to the circumstances.

The *mpaka* customarily arrive too early at the village of the bride and, being completely ignored by the bride's family, have to wait outside the village. So as to make them arrive much too early they will have been wrongly informed of the time at which they should come to the bride's house. It is then indicated to them, indirectly, when they may try to enter the house, and this is usually a considerable time after their arrival. This is part of the obvious element of humiliation that the groom's family are made to go through during the first part of the ceremony. They are asking for a favour and are therefore in the position of inferiors.

After a sufficient length of time has elapsed, the head of the groom's party or the speechmaker goes, rather reluctantly, to ask for admittance. He is ignored and returns to his party, only to set out again a little while later. Admittance has to be requested seven times[3] before it

---

[1] For a description of the normative way to perform a marriage according to the custom of the ancestors, see W. E. Cousins, *Fomba Malagasy*, 1963 edition (edited by H. Randzavola), p. 24ff.

[2] Among andriana families the groom does not go to fetch the bride.

[3] Seven and three are propitious numbers. See R. Decary, "La puissance mystique du nombre 7 chez les Malgaches", *Revue de Madagascar*, Vol. 21, 1954.

is granted, and even then the head of the bride's household has to be bribed with a small sum of money (usually 50 FMG). The groom's party file in, hanging their heads in shame, to the northern room which will have been spread with clean papyrus mats. In the north-eastern corner,[1] piled up, is the dowry which the bride will take with her. The groom's party go and sit on the south and west sides of the room. The family of the bride, composed of the senior members of her local family, sit on the north and east sides.

The groom's party settle down and humbly wait to be spoken to. After a while they are welcomed as though they had come to pay a social call. At this point the game of words between both sides begins. The bride's family will steer the conversation away from the matter in hand while the speechmaker is trying, imperceptibly and without being rude, to introduce what he has to say. If he is rude, and in a situation like this he always has to be, he will be fined. The pattern of the whole proceedings takes the form of a battle of wits. The speechmaker has, in smooth polite phrases, well illustrated with proverbs and biblical references, to say what he has come for and to offer the *vody-ondry*. But all the relatives of the bride try to find fault with what he says because of alleged rudeness, as, for example, introducing the subject too abruptly, or illogically, or for not saying what he has to say sufficiently clearly. The bride's party fine the groom's party a small sum of money on any of these pretexts. It is clearly impossible to avoid being fined at least once or twice. The mention of the *vody-ondry* or of marriage would be con- sidered most offensive, and elaborate circumlocutions or euphemisms must be used. Similarly, a mention of both the groom's and the bride's name in the same sentence is taken as a suggestion of gross impropriety, and the bride's family will refuse to hear any more until they have been paid 50 or 100 FMG. Also, if the speechmaker has not stated clearly the names once the *vody-ondry* has been accepted, the bride's parents will pretend to have misunderstood his speech, and will present a little girl as the future bride, only bringing the girl in question after yet another fine has been paid.

The actual sequence of events is roughly as follows. Once the *mpaka* have settled themselves, the owner of the house where the ceremony is

---

[1] The north-east is the most valued corner where those who are senior sit; the south-west, the least valued corner, is traditionally that of the slaves, (see J.-C. Hebert, "La cosmographie ancienne Malgache suivie de l'enumeration des points cardinauz et l'importance du Nord-Est", *Taloha* I, 1965). All Malagasy houses are orientated.

Plate 6a. Marriage. The *vody-ondry* discussions. On the left the bride's family jeer at the representatives of the groom's family. Of these only the leader is visible on the extreme right.

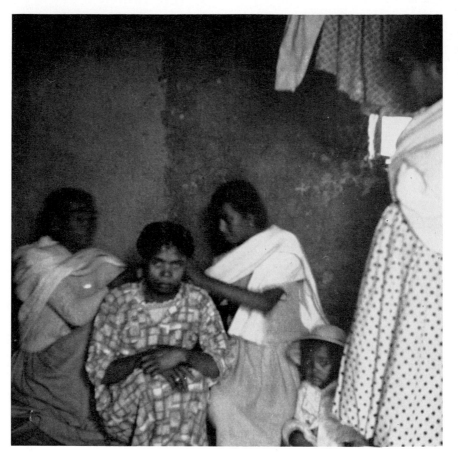

Plate 6b. Marriage. Women who have married into the local family of the groom dress the bride.

taking place addresses the speechmaker. As would be the case with any normal social call, the host eventually gets round to asking *"Inona voavoa?"* or "What is the news?" This question is invariably answered with the assurance that there is no news, but . . . and then comes the explanation why the call has been made. In this particular case, the answer is *"Tsy misy vaovao, mitsidika fotsiny"*, or "There is no news, we are simply paying a social call". This unrevealing statement is followed by the opening of negotiations by the speechmaker. He starts, head bowed, quietly, almost inaudibly, to make pious and commonplace remarks which are the usual prelude to formal Merina speeches. The difficulty for the *mpaka* is to pass from these commonplaces to the matter in hand without being fined. In all the cases that I witnessed the speechmaker recognized that he had to be fined at least once at this stage. One way out of the difficulty which is sometimes taken is to propose offering up a short prayer. Although no doubt the main motive in this is to ask for God's blessing, the move does introduce the subject of marriage in a way which cannot be objected to. No good Christian could take exception to the content of a prayer.

After the prayer and one or two Church hymns, the speechmaker begins again in what takes the form of a *kabary* (a traditional oration). A *kabary* always begins with a *miala tsiny*, "removal of offence", section. This is an apology on the part of the speaker for his temerity in talking at all, considering how junior and insignificant he is. The mood is summed up in the phrase which is always included in this section: *"Tsy zoky fa zandry, tys ray fa zaza"*, which means, "I am not an elder brother but a younger brother. I am not a father but a child". Then the speech goes on with formal acknowledgements to the local dignitaries, and usually includes a patriotic passage and a reference to President Tsiranana, the father of Malagasy independence. The speechmaker continues and his ability is judged by the interest of his speech, which is assessed mainly by the number of proverbs, stories and biblical anecdotes which he includes. He must get to the real point in such a way that the bride's family does not realize when he will arrive at it. As the speech proceeds, the girl's family continually interrupt the speechmaker, challenging him to give proof of his assertions, objecting to what he says, and making offensive remarks about the groom and his family. The speechmaker, for his part, must listen and approve all this without losing his temper and must even thank the interrupters for their remarks. This kind of verbal game is greatly appreciated by the Merina and the ability of a good orator is highly valued. The length of such speeches (they may last several hours) is not thought of as a drawback in the least.

After the speech has gone on for some time, and a number of fines have been paid, the *vody-ondry* is placed in front of the bride's father and he is urged to accept it. The money is placed in a little bundle together with a few quartz crystals and some broken fragments of pots. Quartz is called *vato velona*, which means "living stone" and is thus a symbol of life and fertility. The fragments of pot are said to have come from a *sinibe* (a large pot) which holds the water for a house and is filled daily by the women. In this way the crystals and fragments of pot are symbols of domesticity.[1]

The father of the bride does not normally accept the *vody-ondry* straight away, but leaves it on the ground in front of him. The speech-maker then goes on to point out the advantages of a marriage viewed in the abstract, and often quotes the scriptures. The bride's father asks for assurances about the treatment of his daughter if she is going to live with the groom's family. He will ask for her to be allowed to come back if she is unhappy and above all will specify that, in the case of a divorce, the joint property will be divided according to the traditional apportionment of one third to the woman and two thirds to the man. This kind of division is called *kitay telo an dalana*, or "the three bundles of firewood on the path". This refers to a traditional allegory, the gist of which is that, although a man cannot run a home without the help of a woman, a woman cannot manage without the help of a man and it is considered the man contributes rather more than the woman.[2]

In all the *vody-ondry* ceremonies I attended two particularly revealing points were made at this stage. It was specified that in the case of divorce the children would be allowed to follow their mother and would not be detained and that the right of levirate would not be insisted on.[3]

Other conditions may be laid down by the bride's father before he agrees to accept the *vody-ondry*. The groom is made to agree to help the members of the bride's family, if they need it, either financially or by

---

[1] Traditionally, when a woman wanted to show that she was leaving her husband permanently, she would break the *sinibe* before going.

[2] The text of this tale is given in the collection of passages called *Anganon'ny Ntaolo*, Ed. L. Dahle, 1962 edition, p. 176.

[3] This is one aspect of the ambiguous attitude of the Merina towards their recognition of the supremacy of patrifiliation over matrifiliation. It is accepted in principle but is in fact denied. See W. E. Cousins, *The Marriage Ceremony Among the Hova*, p. 479.

working for them. He is told to look after his parents-in-law when they are old. A special case may be made out by the bride's family for, say, an old grandmother who is particularly badly off and the groom's party will give a small sum for her, to hurry on the proceedings. Still other requests may be made such as for the son-in-law to come and help if the bride's parents are making drainage or irrigation ditches, which is a particularly arduous task.

If the conditions and requests carry on for too long at this stage, which is often the case, a member of the groom's party, usually the head of the group or the senior woman, gives an extra 100 FMG as a final encouragement. This cuts short the proceedings as it is what the bride's father has usually been waiting for, so that he can accept the *vody-ondry*.

Once the *vody-ondry* has been presented the marriage is considerep valid. It is the presentation of the *vody-ondry* which, according to custom, makes the marriage legal.[1] As soon as the *vody-ondry* has been accepted, the atmosphere changes radically and the element of rivalry between both sides which has been present disappears. Often at this stage either some coffee is drunk or there is a meal. The meal has no expressed significance as a symbol, but the groom's party may not eat during the time they are waiting to come in, or during the discussions. As a result, during the whole proceedings they become hungrier and hungrier. It is yet another of the humiliations they have to undergo, but when the meal does come it is very welcome.

Once the *vody-ondry* has been accepted the bride is called and comes to join her parents in the room where the discussions have been taking place. She will be dressed in old clothes, her hair elaborately plaited in a very complex arrangement of small, tight plaits.[2] This is the traditional hair-style of unmarried girls.

The bride and groom are then addressed in short speeches, one by the bride's father, then one by the head of the groom's family group, and finally one by any respected person present. These speeches are exhortations to the groom to look after his future wife and children, to honour parents and parents-in-law, to live frugally, etc. The bride is exhorted, in particular, to obey her father-in-law and not to forget her own family.

---

[1] It is accepted as proof of common law marriage by the courts of the Malagasy Republic.

[2] The significance of hair-styles, to which I refer here and also later, is explicit during marriage, but not at other times. Nowadays, at least, married women may wear their hair in small plaits and unmarried girls may wear it in the single "bun" of the married woman.

She is also told not to be lazy (*Kamo*—see Chapter 1). Apart from these more specific reminders, there are more general statements on the nature of marriage. These are of two kinds. First there are quotations from the Bible and other Christian sources. Then there are traditional sayings, mainly proverbs, which are illustrated with suitable examples. There are a great number of these and they have nearly all been published.[1] Some of these proverbs are particularly important and are always mentioned. The commonest is *Talakom-fosalahy, fasovavy: amoizamtsy foy hananan-tiana* ("A male crab is exchanged for a female crab. For something precious we obtain something valuable"). In other words, marriage is a bargain between two parties, each party getting something equally valuable. This is further explained by the participants in the speeches as meaning that while the family of the groom is gaining the bride, the family of the bride is gaining the groom.[2] Other proverbs such as *Omby mividy, lasan'olona* ("A bull which has been sold is lost to others") are often mentioned. This implies the irreversibility of the process,[3] but other proverbs which seem to contradict this last one, for example, those given on p. 356 of the *Tantaran'ny Andriana*, state how easily marriage may be ended.

After the exhortations comes the dressing of the bride. This is done by those women among the *mpaka* who have married into the groom's family.[4] First, the women undo the many little plaits of the girl's hair. It will have been purposely plaited by her mother as tightly as possible, and in such a way that it can only be unplaited with difficulty. Once it has been completely combed out it is replaited in big plaits which, tied together, form the married woman's bun. Then the old clothes which the bride has been wearing are removed and she is dressed in the new ones brought by the groom. The immediate aim of this is to make the bride look her best, in complete contrast to her shabby appearance when she is first presented. It is not, however, simply a matter of making her look her best, but making her look attractive in the clothes, cosmetics and jewellery brought *by the groom*.

The next ceremony is the blessing of the new couple. For this they are placed sitting down next to each other, and a plant used for binding is

---

[1] R. F. Callet, *Tantaran'ny Andriana*, 1908, p. 346ff. *Ohabolana ou Proverbes Malgaches*, Ed. J. A. Houlder, 1957, p. 149ff.

[2] *Ohabolana ou Proverbes Malgaches*, Ed. J. A. Houlder, 1957.

[3] R. F. Callet, *Tantaran'ny Andriana*, 1908, p. 358.

[4] There may be considerable variation in the timetable of this ceremony.

balanced on their heads.[1] The head of the bride's local family, her father, other older men, and lastly the bride's mother bless the couple in turn. The number of blessings must be either three or seven. The blessing is performed either by blowing on, or spraying on, water into which an *ariary tsy vaky* has been placed.[2] The new couple are wished seven boys and seven girls, wealth, possessions, descendants. For this purpose God, the *razana*, the twelve holy hills of Imerina,[3] the sacred earth and the *lolo*[4] are invoked.

While all these ceremonies are going on, the more distant relatives of the bride and the bride's parents' neighbours, who had gathered before the arrival of the groom's party, are feasting. They come to watch the bride leave with the triumphal procession formed by the groom's party. The bride is usually accompanied by her father but never by her mother, and the separation of mother and daughter is thus stressed. The other women in the groom's party encourage the bride to come by singing a daring (by Merina standards) song, telling of the pleasures of married life.

In some cases the older brothers of the bride pretend to sleep on the path in the way of the procession and only agree to move if they are given a small sum of money.

The return trip, whether on foot or by *taxi-brousse*, assumes the form of a triumphal procession, with the bride's party singing and sometimes also playing musical instruments. They carry back the girl's dowry and so are easily recognized by anyone meeting them on the path.

On arrival at the groom's village the returning party are joined by others who have caught sight of them from a distance. They all now bring the bride and groom to the groom's mother and all the senior members of her local family. At the village all the more remote relatives of the groom and the neighbours have been feasting and welcome them enthusiastically. The arriving party then go to the house of the groom's parents, normally their future house too,[5] and walk round it either three or seven times in a clockwise direction[6] before actually entering.

---

1 Often aloes fibre is used.
2 See p. 152.
3 R. F. Callet, *Tantaran'ny Andriana*, 1908, p. 1019.
4 See p. 125.
5 See p. 191.
6 See R. Decary, "La puissance mystique du nombre 7 chez les Malgaches", *Revue de Madagascar*, 1954.

Then the *mpaka* report back on what has happened. First the leader of the party, then the speechmaker, describe what has been said and how much money they have had to give. This is another occasion for the speechmaker to display his skill and as many people as possible crowd into the room to hear what he has to say, to laugh at the jokes he makes and try to memorize the proverbs and anecdotes which he quotes. The father of the groom then makes a speech thanking the *mpaka*, and in particular the speechmaker, for their help.

Most of the time after this is spent in eating and making merry, but the new couple go through another ceremony. They are made to sit down and are ritually fed with the food which is also symbolic of plenty —a mixture of rice, milk and honey. This food is given to them by the oldest woman of the household, who passes a spoon from one to the other three times. This is an explicit incorporation rite and is said to make them "one house" (*iray trano*) with the groom's parents.

A week after these ceremonies one final rite takes place. The newly married couple return to the house of the bride's parents and have there a substantial meal. They are then also made *iray trano* with that family.

Apart from the traditional form of marriage which has just been described, it is becoming usual to register the marriage with the civil authorities, when this is possible. (The partners may be too young, or one or other of them may have been married legally once before.) The marriage takes place before the mayor of the canton and is over in a very short time. It may take place before the ceremony of the *vody-ondry*, or between the *fisihaona* and the *vody-ondry*, or afterwards (sometimes some considerable time afterwards). A civil marriage is a sign of respectability and confers minor legal advantages. It is, however, a considerable added expense. It does not affect inheritance by the children and is, of course, not considered so important as the *vody-ondry*. In contrast to government marriage, government divorce is beyond the reach of the peasants and consequently, when a marriage breaks up, future marriages cannot be performed by government officials.

There may also be a marriage in church. Practising Roman Catholics are always married in church, if there is no definite bar to the marriage being performed there. Where possible the church wedding is celebrated on the same day as the *vody-ondry*. It is much rarer for Protestants to be married in church, although the new couple may well be received by the pastor on the Sunday after the presentation of the *vody-ondry*. He welcomes them into the congregation and blesses their union. A full church wedding is a sign of social status and peasants may save up for quite a time for it. As a result, it can happen that the church wedding takes place a few years after the traditional ceremony.

The marriage procedure which I have been describing is the fullest form as practised in the Ambatomanoina district. In certain cases it may be curtailed and the details may be varied. When the bride has been married before the ceremony is usually much more modest than for a first marriage.

Although the ceremonies described above are seen as the most important step in the establishment of a marriage, they can also be considered as part of a wider process. Traditionally, Merina marriage is patrilocal. That is to say, the new couple go to live in the house of the groom's parents. But this is not invariably so. It is quite common for a new couple to live with the bride's parents, with other relatives, or somewhere else independently. Although living with the groom's parents is the ideal choice it is not considered a disgrace to live with the bride's parents or to move to the bride's home village. The figures in Table 2 show the position in the first village where I worked.

TABLE 2

Sample of marriages in the canton of Fieferana

Virilocal	Uxorilocal	Not known or neolocal	*Total*
50	39	20	109
46%	*35%*	*19%*	*100%*

There are many reasons why newly married couples choose to reside with relatives other than the groom's parents, but most commonly it is a question of rice land. We saw how the father of the prospective groom gives him land which he will be able to cultivate. Land is also often given by the parents of the bride-to-be and sometimes even by other relatives if they want to attract the new couple.

If the couple live patrilocally they are normally given their own room in the house (if it is big enough) and are at first completely incorporated within the household. The groom works with his father in the same way as before the marriage, and the bride helps her mother-in-law. She is said to be "learning" to cook. The next stage for the newly married couple is when they start to keep their rice separately, something which leads, almost automatically, to their cooking separately. This may mean that after a while the new couple build a kitchen near the house. There they not only cook but eat as well.

The new kitchen becomes more and more the centre of the new couple's lives until they completely break away from the old household by building a new house. This final stage normally takes place after the birth of children, or, alternatively, after a period of around three years. It would be misleading to give the notion of a fixed timetable for these various events, as there are very wide variations from case to case. Once the final separation has been achieved the new couple are completely free to live where they like. Naturally they often remain in the local family where they started their married life, but it is also quite common for them to move to another local family, often that of the bride's parents.

The Nature of the Alliance

I have given this description of Merina marriage because of the significance of marriage in perpetuating or otherwise the link with the *tanindrazana*, and many aspects of Merina marriage have not been touched on as they would be more suitably discussed in the context of domestic institutions. It is, however, necessary before understanding how this effect of marriage comes about to see what the ceremony of marriage implies in terms of the transfer of rights over the individuals concerned in so far as this affects our theme.

Certain obvious aspects of Merina marriage are of only minor importance here. For example, some aspects of marriage are concerned with a girl's initiation into the society of women. While Merina boys go through an important initiation ceremony at circumcision, Merina girls go through no such equivalent ceremony at a similar age. It is clearly at marriage that initiation takes place for girls. It is then that they are ritually "separated" from their mother and "aggregated" to the wider sex group of the community: two very clear functions of the circumcision ceremony for boys.

This side of marriage is acted out by the way the plaits of the girl, made deliberately tight and difficult to undo by her mother, are untangled by the wives of classificatory brothers of her future husband and are then remade by them. The change of clothes also manifests this passage. The initiation aspect of marriage must be borne in mind as it

Plate 7a. Marriage. The family of the groom returns with the bride and her dowry.

Plate 7b. Marriage. The groom, bride, and groom's mother, followed by all those present at the groom's village, walk three times around the house of the groom's parents.

partly accounts for the clearly expressed change in status of the girl which is brought about by the ceremony. This is a change which otherwise could be interpreted entirely as being a matter of the transfer of rights over the girl from one group to another. Although rights are transferred it would be misleading to overemphasize this aspect, as we would do if we saw the ritual change in the girl as simply this.

Perhaps the clearest meaning of marriage is that the girl is being introduced by the ceremony to her husband's family. The girl is actually taken away from her parental home to that of her husband's parents. Marriage integrates the girl into the society of married women, but it is specifically into the society of married women in her husband's village. It should not be assumed from this that the bride is simply being handed over to her husband's family. Only certain specific rights are transferred.

A sexual monopoly over the bride is handed to her husband and adultery on her part will be punished by her husband. Also, marriage is a transference of the domestic services of the girl to her husband's family and ultimately to her husband. Both these aspects are mentioned during the ceremony. Payments are specifically made as compensation to her natal household, for the fact that she will no longer do such things as fetch water and firewood, look for lice in her relatives' hair and pull out white hairs.[1]

Much more important, however, to the structure of the society is the question of the transfer of rights over women *in genitrixem*. In the Merina case we do not find an idea that through marriage the husband's family is being given the ability to increase and continue, which is at first surprising since the desire for many children is continually stressed. The reason why the desire for children is not linked with the handing over of the bride by her parents is that children are not thought to belong exclusively to their patrilateral or matrilateral kin. This is never stated clearly but a number of facts show this. Children of widowed or divorced parents normally live with their mother's family and are very likely to settle with them, to be "given" land there, and to be buried with them.[2] Children are very commonly fostered by matrilateral kin; indeed there is a common arrangement whereby it is decided at the *dinidinika* that the

---

[1] These are usually mentioned as separate payments but are in fact merged with the *vody-ondry*, see p. 181.

[2] I was told by one informant that children brought up by their mother should return to their father when they are old enough, but in the many cases of this situation which I observed this was never done.

first one or two children of the couple will be fostered by the bride's parents. (This fostering often develops with time into something close to adoption.) Finally there is the question of the membership of permanent corporate groups by the children. This has already been indirectly dealt with. For the smallest such group, that associated with the tomb, we saw how the child could belong either to the father's or the mother's tomb group.[1] For the wider group, the deme, the problem does not normally arise at all, the reason being that marriage is thought of as taking place within the deme so that a child should belong to the deme of both his father and his mother. In fact, it is often specifically emphasized during the *vody-ondry* discussion that in the case of a divorce the children should follow the mother. (See "Raketaka" by G. Mondain, Publication de la Faculté des Lettres d'Alger, *Bulletin de Correspondance Africaine*, Tome LXI).

Finally, regarding the question of whether the bride is incorporated into the group of the groom, it is clear that this is so only in a limited way. The girl is, as we saw, ritually incorporated into the household of her husband and therefore into his local family by the ritual meal of rice, milk and honey. However, the household and the local family are not a moral group continuing through time. The right of the bride to take up residence with her parents after the marriage is never doubted. The ritual return a week after the marriage of the newly married couple to the bride's house demonstrates this and in fact in my experience married women were always welcomed if they chose to live with their parents, whether they came alone or brought their husband and children with them. The fact that, when possible, not only the boy but also the girl are "given" land at marriage to cultivate in the village of their respective parents is a clear demonstration of the alternative of local family membership which they are given—an alternative which contradicts the fact that the marriage ceremony stresses the coming of the girl to live with her parents-in-law.

It is clear therefore that the *vody-ondry* is not a "bride price", which is given principally in exchange for rights as a member of a group over a woman and her future children. In the Merina case, only certain limited rights are transferred and these are paid for by minor payments, which are separate, at least in theory, from the *vody-ondry*.

If the taking of the bride to the groom's family is one important

---

[1] See p. 115.

aspect of Merina marriage, of equal importance is that aspect symbolized by the giving of the *vody-ondry*. The importance of this prestation is fully recognized by the actors themselves since it is the giving of the *vody-ondry* which is to them legal proof of the marriage. Its significance is clear since what it stands for is quite explicit.[1] The *vody-ondry* is an acceptance by the groom of the father-like authority of his father-in-law and it is a sign that he accepts the kinship ties which this implies.

In this way the *vody-ondry* is the incorporation of the groom into his wife's family since, like the bride's brothers and their children, he gives the hindquarters of an animal to his father-in-law because whenever an animal is killed by a son and he is living in the same village as his father he has the hindquarters sent to him.

One of the results of this situation is that married men are in much the same position as women; that is, they have a double allegiance to honour and obey two different people, their own father and their father-in-law. It is not normally an allegiance to two different groups, since the more remote relatives are likely to be common to both sides. The problem, however, is there and is recognized as such by the Merina. One inform-ant told me that one should not marry a girl in the same village as oneself because, when one kills a chicken it is difficult to decide whether to give the *vody akoho* (the hindquarters of a chicken) to one's own father or one's bride's father, and this is likely to cause dispute. The *vody akoho* being, like the *vody-ondry*, the part one should give to one's senior kinsman.[2]

Merina marriage is therefore a ceremony whereby, while the bride becomes a "child" of her husband's senior kinsmen, the groom becomes a "child" of his wife's senior kinsmen. "The exchange of a male crab is a female crab. For something precious we obtain something valuable", becomes easily understandable since at a marriage both sides are gain-ing new members of their family.

This leads us to consider the kind of relationship established between both sides. Throughout the ceremony the element of controlled rivalry which we usually associate with affinal ties is manifest. After marriage there is an unformalized avoidance of parents-in-law and a joking relationship between brothers-in-law. However, apart from these factors affecting very close relatives, the relation of the two families is not that of affines in the sense which implies "rivalry in alliance". Individuals from

---

[1] See p. 179.

[2] This fact explains the rule that the groom's father should not accompany the groom. By giving the *vody-ondry* the groom is recognizing a rival "father".

either side are treated in the same way as kinsmen and are referred to as being members of their respective dispersed family. The relatives of one spouse will, if not otherwise related, address the relatives of the other spouse in terms used for relatives. It is only in the relation of the new couple to their respective parents and siblings that affinal behaviour is at all apparent, and even here it is ambiguous.

It is interesting to note that among all Merina only affinal kinship terms for parents-in-law, siblings-in-law and children-in-law are not classificatory. In this way Merina marriage is seen as extending genea-logical ties (*fianakaviana*). It does not forge a link of affinity between groups but it reaffirms a kinship link. The reason for this unusual state is quite obvious. Since marriage was traditionally practised within a small localized group of kinsmen, the people whom one marries are considered as kinsmen. Marriage in traditional terms was, as one informant told me, "closing up the breaches in the *fianakaviana*" or, in other words, strength-ening already existing genealogical ties. Even when the two parties are not previously related the same general concept applies. In this way ties of kinship and ties formed through marriage are classified together. Thus, in the traditional system, even marriage is a kinship relationship rather than a contractual one.

The Choice of Spouse and the Break with the *Tanindrazana*

It is because Merina marriage is thought of as closing the gap, and as strengthening the family (*fianakaviana*), that it is of such crucial rele-vance for understanding the relation of the society of the *tanindrazana* to the society where one lives. This follows from the fact that any notion of reinforcing the ties within the kinship group raises the question of which kinship group. The word *havana* conveys both the idea of a person with whom there are close links of practical cooperation as well as genealogical links. Although in the traditional ideal system these two sets of relationships link a man to the same people, this is no longer the case. This fact leads the Merina to refer to the people he cooperates with, but who are not genealogically related to him, as *havana mpifankatia*, implying a kind of artificial kinship. Thus for most of his life the peasant participates in two kinship systems. For nearly all activities these two systems are apparently separate and independent of each other. At marriage, however, this is not possible as marriage changes the status of the spouses in both systems and also presents the individual with a

choice between them. This unique merging of the two systems is reflected
in the way marriage ceremonies divide the participants into two groups;
on one side are the kinsmen and neighbours of the bride and on the
other the kinsmen and neighbours of the groom. This contrasts with
other ceremonies which divide the participants into a group of neighbours and a group of kinsman, e.g. funerals and *famadihanas*.

In practical terms this means that a preference for either one system
or the other must be demonstrated in the choice of a spouse. In one case
I observed the parents of the bride discussed two possible candidates
precisely in terms of the relative value of an alliance with a neighbouring
village or strengthening the ties with their *fianakaviana*.

The choice is actually made by the parents or guardians of the spouses
before the negotiations begin. When a marriage is first considered the
father of the groom turns to an older trusted kinsman to ask him to find
a bride for his son. This he normally does by looking among *his* kinsmen.
The choice of a kinship intermediary leads automatically to marriage
with people between whom some genealogical connection can be traced.
If a marriage with a neighbour, as opposed to a kinsman, is envisaged
then it is more normal to turn for an intermediary to a close *havana
mpifankatia*, expecting him to look among his kinsmen or among his
neighbours. In this way the choice between the two societies is made
even before the choice of a particular spouse.

Before seeing how the choice is actually exercised we must examine
what different advantages marriage with real *havana* and *havana
mpifankatia* has for the peasant. Also we must see what sanctions if any
maintain the rules and preferences of traditional marriage.

Obviously one of the main reasons for close in-marriage with kinsmen
(*lova tsy mifindra*) has partially disappeared. The concern with keeping
land within a small local group of kinsmen has largely lost its relevance.
Furthermore, the ambiguous nature of *lova tsy mifindra* marriages as
potentially incestuous[1] provides an excuse for not following them. None
the less the more general preference remains that one should marry
havana.

The advantages of marriage with someone within the dispersed
family are seen as much the same as the advantages of maintaining a
link with the *tanindrazana*. These advantages have already been discussed fairly fully. Marriage strengthens the existing links of kinship

---

[1] See p. 53ff.

and these links are what binds a man to his *tanindrazana*. By contrast, marriage outside the dispersed family or even outside the deme does not necessarily lead to a break with the *tanindrazana*, but it may be part of the process of breaking away since certain non-traditional marriages actually do eventually lead to this.

Traditional marriage is not practised solely because of the advantages it may bring. It is also maintained by a system of sanctions which operate against an individual who does not obey its rules.

Since the population of the Ambatomanoina district comes from many different places in old Imerina, it follows that the various local families belong to a great variety of demes of differing ranks. This relative rank between local families is relevant to the possibility of inter-marriage. In other words, even in cases where marriage with neighbours rather than marriage with kinsmen has been decided upon, it does not mean that all rules from the traditional system will be ignored. The most important of these rules is that dealing with the white–black division of Merina society. This "colour bar" is explained by the Merina as dividing the descendants of free men, who are said to be white (*fotsy*) and the descendants of slaves who are said to be black (*mainty*).[1]

The difference between the *fotsy* and the *mainty* is further deepened today by the belief that this division corresponds to a religious and political one. It has previously been described how it is widely thought that the *mainty* are predominantly Catholic and supporters of the government party, the PSD (*Parti Social Democrate*), and the *fotsy* are pre-dominantly Protestant and supporters of one of the opposition parties, the AKFM (*Ankoton'ny Kongrei'ny Fahaleovantenan Madagasikara*). In fact in the areas where I worked I obtained no valid correlation between religion and the *mainty–fotsy* division, although it is very likely that such a correlation does exist if we take Imerina as a whole.[2]

The implied correlation between political party and "colour" is very difficult to verify, but it is clear that this again is a very much more complex matter than it would seem at first.

Finally, although the *mainty–fotsy* division cannot be said to be an economic one, there is little doubt that taken as a whole the *fotsy* are

---

[1] See p. 3.

[2] Local factors are extremely important as far as religion is concerned because of the varying influence of different missions and missionaries and historical circumstances. A very large sample would be necessary to obtain a definitive answer to this problem.

better off.[1] This is particularly marked if we consider the distribution of specialists in the two groups. In the canton of Ambatomanoina where the *mainty* outnumber the *fotsy*, out of 39 relatively full-time Merina specialists (shopkeepers, blacksmiths, pastors, school teachers etc.) 31 were *fotsy*.

The division between *fotsy* and *mainty* is therefore significant in many fields and, as might be expected, marriages crossing this line are strongly disapproved of. This disapproval is mainly explained in racialist terms and the *fotsy* often describe the *mainty* as ugly (*ratsy tareha*). The clearest sanction against such marriages is that the children will be forbidden to enter the tomb of their "white" parent. Indeed the "white" partner may himself or herself be threatened with being forbidden entry by his relations. (This latter threat seems to be not normally enforced but is a deterrent used by the disgusted family when such a marriage is under consideration.) The children of a mixed marriage who are not allowed into the tomb will either be buried in the tomb of the black parent or in a new tomb outside the *tanindrazana*.[2]

In fact out of 114 marriages including at least one "white" partner only, five were marriages either of people with a high degree of education whose whole system of values was little concerned with tradition, or marriages when a man of white descent found himself isolated or belonging to a very small local family in a predominantly "black" area.

Next in importance to the "colour bar" is the division between andriana and hova. Marriages which cross this barrier are seen by the andriana in much the same way as marriages between *mainty* and *fotsy*. However, this involves neither the racial element nor the same feeling of horror. The children of such mixed andriana–hova marriages will be excluded from the andriana tomb. In such a case it is also possible that the children may not be accepted by the hova family and may therefore be excluded from both families. This is because certain demes insist that only full members be included and also certain hova groups may consider themselves superior to certain andriana groups.[3] However, marriages between andriana and hova are more common than between *fotsy* and *mainty*. Out of the sample of 114 marriages 13 were mixed andriana and

---

[1] A similar conclusion is reached in the study of a suburb of Tananarive by S. Raharijaona, *Population et Habitat dans un Quartier Populaire de Tananarive, Manarintsoa-Isotry*, 1960.

[2] See Chapter 7.

[3] This is illustrated in the story which tells how Andrianampoinimerina offered the Tsimahafotsy the possibility of becoming andriana but they refused.

hova. The reasons for such marriages are roughly similar to those between *mainty* and *fotsy* but, as might be expected, less extreme conditions can cause them.

Apart from these major barriers, marriages which are outside the deme but within these larger divisions may also be negatively sanctioned. Within the andriana demes this is particularly obvious. Some of the highest groups may frown on such marriages and normally the children will have to be buried in the tomb of the lower deme. Among the higher andriana, however, many special matrimonial arrangements exist which modify deme in-marriage and are quite acceptable such as inter-marriage between Andriantompokoindrindra and Andriamasinavalona.[1] Also it is traditional for Andrianamboninolona women to marry Andriamasinavalona men.[2] At all events, marriages between different andriana demes are felt to be excusable, unlike marriages between andriana and hova. Several times when discussing such marriages I was told that they did not matter since we are all "the same kind of people—andriana". Surprisingly, however, as far as I could judge from small numbers, such marriages were not very frequent, out of 34 andriana marriages only six were between different demes.

Among hova groups deme "endogamy" is even less firmly sanctioned. Apart from certain groups high up on the ranking hierarchy like Tsimahafotsy, Zafimbazaha and Marovatana little attempt seems to be made any more to stop marriages outside the group. Furthermore, many special marriage alliances exist between certain groups such as the Zanakandriambe and the Zanakandrianato. The high degree of in-marriage which does exist is more the result of the positive preference for *havana* than the fear of any definite sanctions. Informants agree in general terms that a rule of deme endogamy should apply, but they no longer attach great value to it since, if a marriage breaking this rule is contracted, they will not normally exclude the descendants from their tomb. Out of 62 hova marriages 38 were between people who could trace genealogical connections.

The strictness or otherwise of the application of these rules depends first of all on the parents of the spouses, since it is they who may exclude their children from their tomb if they disapprove of the marriage. In the case of a gross breach of these rules, even if the guilty party's parents do

---

[1] J. Ratsamimanana and L. Razafindrazaka, *Ny Andriantompokoindrina*, 1909.
[2] Informants' statements. The children of such a marriage belong to the group of the lower rank, i.e. the Andrianamboninolona.

Plate 8a. An important man and his wife. This is the man to whom Map 4 refers.

Plate 8b. Traders from Tananarive buying rice. This is one of the new influences to be taken into account in the future development of Merina society.

not want to take any action, the tomb management group under the leadership of its head may stipulate the exclusion of the children of such a marriage.

To conclude this discussion one can say that the rules of in-marriage which in the traditional system were motivated by the desire to maintain rank and to keep land within a small group are now concerned with maintaining rank and the link with the *tanindrazana*, although this may take the form of keeping land in the *tanindrazana*.

Having seen the sanctions which maintain traditional marriage, we must now turn to the question of why marriages outside the deme occur. One important factor in this is that a certain number of such marriages result from romantic love. Given the fact that marriages within the local family are very rare, it follows that marriages which are seen as caused by romantic love are normally marriages outside the deme. It should not be assumed that this is a new factor resulting from European contact. These marriages are fairly common and in my experience are equally common among young people who do not have much contact with Europeans. The notion of romantic love and the attempts of young people to try to get married against the wishes of their parents is a basic element in Merina folk tales. Near Ambatomanoina a stone was often pointed out to me as the place where a *fotsy* girl had eloped with her *mainty* lover and on seeing her family come to take her away had committed suicide. Almost identical stories are associated with many places throughout Imerina. However, for romance to be successful the approval of the parents must be obtained, and so we return to the question of when do the parents agree to the non-traditional marriages.

For the answer we must turn back to the brief description of social organization in the Ambatomanoina district given in Chapter 3. There we saw how the environmental and political situation forced all local families to have close links with non-kinsmen for the purposes of agricultural cooperation, common membership of villages and political influence. We saw how the close cooperation required by these activities is normally classified by the Merina with kinship. The peasants refer to the people they must cooperate with as kinsmen, *havana*, but since they are not really kinsmen they refer to them as a special kind of kinsmen, *havana mpifankatia*. These are clearly felt not to be as reliable as real kinsmen. Hence the sometimes elaborate pretences they have that such *havana mpifankatia* are really *havana tena iray tampo* ("kinsmen really of one womb").[1] This is the result of the notion that only true kinsmen can really be relied upon for the kind of cooperation which the peasant is forced to have with non-kinsmen.

The only way to transform these people into true kinsmen and to make them fully reliable is to encourage marriages between close *havana mpifankatia*, even though this is likely to break some of the rules of the traditional system. Marriage is particularly well suited for this since intermarriage is the sign both of pre-existing kinship and of the strengthening of such pre-existing kinship. Thus a marriage between two local families is a way of asserting that real kinship existed before the marriage (though in fact it really was kinship by extension) and that, at all events, this kinship now exists since the two groups are performing that typical act of genealogically related people—marrying together. Finally it ensures that the next generation will be related by completely unchallengeable kinship.

If we look in detail at the figures for marriages in the Ambatomanoina area this process becomes clear. Naturally the need to form close *havana mpifankatia* relationships is strongest for the smaller local families. The description of agricultural cooperation given in a previous chapter shows why this is. This also applies to village membership. A small local family is unlikely to form a satellite kinship hamlet, and will therefore have to live in a village where other local families also live. Finally, but less easily demonstrated, the psychological anxiety of the Merina peasant who is not surrounded by a large number of kinsmen[2] makes him all the more anxious to increase the number of kinsmen through marriage. Table 3 shows the correlation between size of local family and the frequency of marriage outside the deme.[3] The frequency of marriage between people not previously related by a definite pattern of alliance is statistically significant to 1 per 100.[4] This correlation may be somewhat exaggerated by the tendency of long established families to be larger, but I feel certain that the smallness of the local family does lead to marriage with neighbours. In the same way it can be shown that

---

[1] See p. 58ff.

[2] See p. 58.

[3] This correlation was calculated for the Kendall Bank Corporation by G. Whittington of the Faculty of Economics, University of Cambridge.

[4] I feel this correspondence would be even clearer if we took into account the amount of land possessed by the local families concerned. Although I do not have figures to show this, I am sure it would appear that it is those local families with a relatively large amount of land and few people to cultivate it who would be most likely to marry outside the traditional system.

TABLE 3

Relationship between number of out-marriages and the size of the local family as indicated by the total number of marriages

Total number of marriages	Marriages outside deme with people with whom no definite pattern of alliance has emerged	
		percentage
13	5	$37\frac{1}{2}$
11	1	9
10	1	10
7	2	29
7	2	29
7	1	14
6	1	17
5	2	40
5	2	40
5	0	0
4	1	25
4	0	0
3	2	67
3	1	33
3	1	33
3	1	33
3	0	0
3	0	0
2	2	100
2	1	50
2	1	50
2	1	50
2	1	50
2	0	0
1	1	100
1	1	100
1	1	100
114	31	

these local families living in non-kinship villages are more likely to marry outside—a fact which is linked to the greater need for cooperation in these circumstances[1] (see Table 4).

---

[1] One difficulty here is that these marriages are rarely with co-villagers. Another is that again local families in kinship villages tend to be the larger ones.

TABLE 4

The different frequency of out-marriage in kinship villages and non-kinship villages

Kinship villages		Non-kinship villages	
In-marriage	*Out-marriage*	*In-marriage*	*Out-marriage*
9	1	3	2
5	1	1	2
6	1	3	2
10	1	1	1
9	0	5	2
		1	1
39 (*91%*)	4 (*9%*)	0	1
		1	1
Number of families in		3	1
kinship villages 5		0	1
Number of marriages in		0	2
kinship villages 43 (*100%*)		2	1
		5	2
		2	0
		1	1
		3	0
		8	5
		2	1
		4	0
		3	0
		0	1
		48 (*64%*)	27 (*36%*)
		Number of families in non-	
		kinship villages 21	
		Number of marriages in non-	
		kinship villages 75 (*100%*)	

NOTE: The same is meant here by in-marriage and out-marriage as in Table 3.

Finally a leading member of a family who wants to extend his influence over a wider area is likely to encourage close *havana* type links with other local families, while they in turn might be willing to attach themselves to an influential man. I cannot illustrate this by figures, but Map 4 shows an example of this. The head of the kinship village, marked with a circle, is a particularly ambitious local politician and the lines joining his village with others show how he has established a network of relations, many of which are based on marriages outside the deme, in spite of the fact that the village in question is populated by a group of exlusive andriana.

In this way marriage with neighbours, which nearly always means marriage outside the traditional system, is seen as the extreme manifestation of the tendency to call non-kinsmen kinsmen. This tendency is the

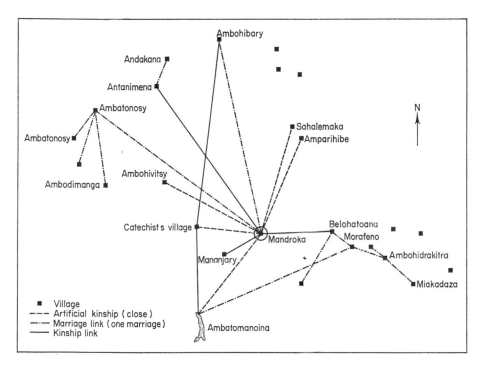

Map 4. Local kinship linkages of a politically important man.

result of the need for economic and political cooperation. In some cases this need is greater than in others and so there is more likelihood of non-traditional marriage.

Seen in greater perspective this means that certain economic and political pressures lead to actions which may ultimately break the link with the *tanindrazana*.

7

The Break with the
Tanindrazana

Other Forms of Alliances

The argument, in so far as it concerns the formation of links distinct from those associated with the *tanindrazana*, has stressed how the economic and political situation has forced the peasants in the Ambatomanoina district to forge quasi-kinship links with other inhabitants of the area. This process of artificial kinship is the logical result of the Merina premiss that living in the same village and working together are typical actions of kinsmen. It may be seen in the context of a long tradition of forming artificial kinship links between individuals who have had to cooperate through time. The most formal of these is blood brotherhood (*fatidra*) but this is of little significance for the organization of the Merina among themselves.[1]

---

[1] This is a ceremony of reciprocal blood drinking. The reason why it is not used to link people who cooperate in such everyday matters as agricultural work and co-residence in a village is that it is felt to be too strong. This throws revealing light on the nature of *havana mpifankatia* links. *Fatidra* links were, and still are, used for people who are in a totally foreign environment, usually visiting another tribe. Such a link forces the very strongest mutual obligations on the parties involved. I was told you could under no circumstances refuse anything to a *fatidra*, whatever your circumstances or the request. Indeed it is said that this mutual obligation extends to wife-sharing should this be requested by a *fatidra* partner, although I have no evidence that this is still the case. Obviously, in such circumstances continual contact between two partners would be very awkward indeed. The second reason why *fatidra* links are felt to be unsuitable is that the making of such a link supposes pre-existing emnity between the parties. When discussing *fatidra* links I was told, "We cannot do it with people with whom we live and whom we love". In fact it was often hinted to me that this was a trick of the clever Merina by which they captured the allegiance of the easily fooled "primitive" tribes of the north. This is

The process which is much more relevant is the form of artificial kinship, *havana mpifankatia*, but these artificial links are in the end felt not to be sufficient to guarantee the reliability of the other partner. The next step is to create real kinship links by marriage. Marriage does this in two ways. Firstly, it implies that the descendants of the contracting party will be kin; secondly, it forms a kinship link at the time of marriage, since for the Merina kinship and alliance links are on the whole the same kind of thing and are subsumed under the term *fianakaviana*.

However, if we can see marrying neighbours as just going further along the path which led to establishing *havana mpifankatia* relationships, there is nevertheless a great difference between the two stages.

Marriage as a Local Alliance

If marriage is traditionally seen as reaffirming already existing kinship links it is clear that marriage with non-kinsmen ultimately leads to a weakening of already existing kinship links. Marriage outside the dispersed family means breaking the link with the *tanindrazana* which is maintained by reaffirming the link to kinsmen. This is so for the children of such a marriage since most of their kinsmen will not share the same *tanindrazana*. This need not break the link since the attachment to tombs is subject to quite wide adaptation. In some cases only one marriage outside may mean the exclusion of descendants if this marriage breaks some of the more strongly sanctioned rules of in-marriage.

What I want to consider now is a further step in this process which can only be suggested tentatively because of the paucity of my material, due to the fact that the process discussed here is only just beginning in the Ambatomanoina area.

Briefly, the point is that if marriage outside the dispersed family need not necessarily break the link with the *tanindrazana*, it nevertheless means a strengthening and in the end a transformation in the link with the place where one lives, which ultimately may be the most significant result of such marriages.

As we saw, marriages with neighbours are usually made for purposes

---

little more than a self-flattering rationalization since normally such an alliance is advantageous to both parties. However, this idea shows in what spirit the connection is viewed. (The ceremonies involved and the rights and duties implied have very often been described by writers on Madagascar. The earliest and one of the fullest accounts is given by W. Ellis in *History of Madagascar*, Vol. I, 1838, p. 87ff. See also W. E. Cousins, *Fomba Malagasy*, 1963 edition (edited by H. Randzavola), p. 91.

of alliance. Isolated cases of such marriages need not imply a significant change in the general morphological pattern of Merina kinship, but, in some circumstances, these at first isolated unions may lead to such changes. This happens in the following way. Once one marriage has been contracted between local families the relation between them changes from one of artificial kinship to one of real kinship. Therefore when another child of either local family reaches marriageable age the category of kinsmen, which is the category of people among whom one may look for a spouse, includes a local element, with which in the past it had proved useful for practical considerations to forge a link which might well be usefully strengthened in the present. Obviously, a group of kinsmen to whom Ego is related by only one marriage is less close than the traditional dispersed family to which he is related in many and varied ways. However, when a marriage is being considered between two local families and a previous marriage has already been contracted, the main obstacle has been removed. In fact such marriages are fairly frequent and each new marriage makes the succeeding one easier. The process may develop until a whole network of links firmly establishes the two contracting local families in each other's dispersed family. Fig. 11

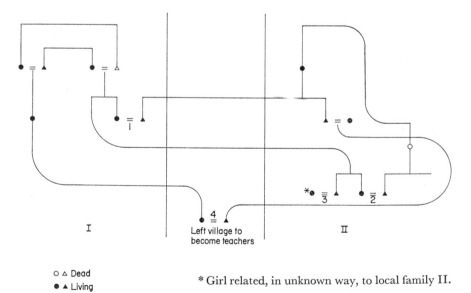

I   Left village to   II
                                    become teachers

○ △ Dead
● ▲ Living   * Girl related, in unknown way, to local family II.

Fig. 11. Pattern of marriage alliances between local families I and II. (Roman figures indicate local families. Arabic figures show order of marriages.)

and Fig. 12 illustrate two such cases from the village of Ambatomanoina itself, giving the order in which the marriages took place. These examples only involve two families each and show in a simplified way what has happened, but such strengthening of alliance and kinship may involve three or four families who are either linked in a series or each to the others.

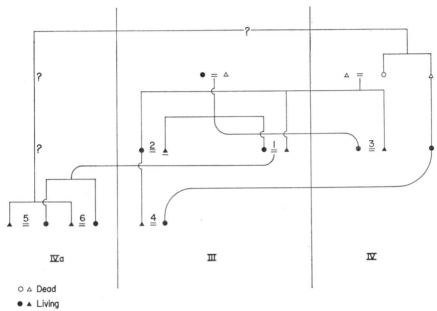

Fig. 12. Pattern of marriage alliances between local families III, IV and IVa. Some kind of relationship is believed to exist between IV and IVa. but these three focal families are no longer really distinct. They all recognize one head, ▲.

(Roman figures indicate local families. Arabic figures show order of marriages.)

It is interesting to consider under what kind of circumstances this process is likely to happen. In the same way as marriages between neighbours originate from the need to establish a moral link to strengthen political and economic ones, the continuing and strengthening of that link comes from the need to have a permanent and long lasting political or economic alliance. This usually means a long settled position in the area of colonization and a clear investment in staying there; in other words, owning a relatively large amount of land. Clearly, if two local families own extensive rice fields near each other the need to cooperate economically and politically will be a permanent feature of their relations. It is not surprising therefore to find that the four local families whose genealogies are given are all four fairly big land owners and all descendants of one of those people who founded Ambatomanoina.[1]

The Formation of New In-marrying Groups

Seen with greater perspective the process just described appears to be the process of the reformation of in-marrying groups closely associated with a territory. If in-marriage is sufficiently frequent between neighbours their descendants will be kin and will therefore automatically marry among themselves. The final stage of reproduction of the traditional pattern cannot be said to have already taken place in the Ambatomanoina area. Most villages which were founded by non-kinsmen are still clearly non-kinship villages. Some seem to have been non-kinship villages originally, but the occurrence of intermarriage has meant that for all practical purposes this is forgotten. An example is the village of Ambatonosy, seven kilometres north of Ambatomanoina. What may also happen is that belief may develop that the ancestors of local families in such a relationship were really related and kin-like behaviour may accompany such a myth. An example of this is the hypothetical link believed to exist between families IV and IVa in Fig. 12. Only one marriage ever took place which indirectly links them, probably because one family is closely associated with the Protestant church (it includes the secretary of the church), while the other is closely associated with the Catholic church (it includes two mission school teachers). To counteract this absence of kinship ties the belief has grown up that in the past their ancestors were related. This is extremely unlikely and was denied by the oldest members of the two families.

Since the Ambatomanoina region is only at one stage in the formation of in-marrying groups, and since new factors are involved in this process,[2] it is worth looking at what has happened in a few historical cases. There is reason to believe that this process had always been an element in the territorial expansion of the Merina which is known to have been taking place for at least two centuries.

When Andrianampoinimerina decided to strengthen his northern frontier he placed a group of settlers in the area near Anjozorobe. These were called the *valon-zato-lahy* or "the eight hundred men". These

---

[1] See p. 80.
[2] See p. 215.

people came from a great variety of white demes.[1] However, partly because of their isolation and partly because of repeated in-marriage, the descendants of these soldiers talk of themselves as though they were one deme and compare themselves with neighbouring groups such as the Zanakandriambe who are a traditional deme claiming themselves to be the descendants of one man, Andriambe (see Map 3).

A perhaps less well-documented example, but probably more typical of the early process of the formation of new demes, is the case of the Andrianamboninolona. Although there is no documentary evidence, the present situation, together with archaeological evidence, makes it fairly clear what must have happened. Nowadays (see Map 5) the Andrianamboninolona villages are strung out along river valleys from near Ilafy to approximately 25 miles to the north-east. Clearly, both from traditional and archaeological evidence,[2] the oldest villages of the Andrianamboninolona are all in the south-west centred around the old village of Ambohitromby which they consider as their capital (*foibe*). What has happened in the case of the Andrianamboninolona is fairly clear. Having started from around Ambohitromby they expanded in the only direction where there was available rice land, i.e. towards the then unpopulated north-east (see Map 5). What is of interest here is that the people living in these further villages are sometimes referred to as Zanakambony. In fact several informants disagreed whether the Zanakambony were the same people as the Andrianamboninolona. What seems to have happened is that as the Andrianamboninolona moved north-east they formed new villages which tended to marry together since their lands were contiguous. With time they became a group distinct from the other Andrianamboninolona whom they had left behind near Ambohitromby, and what amounts to a new deme was formed.

Their relationship to the rest of the Andrianamboninolona is explained in a myth which states that, while the Andrianamboninolona in the old area are the descendants of Andrianamboninolona himself, the Zanakambony are the descendants of one of Andrianamboninolona's relatives. Nowadays the Zanakambony are a group within a restricted territory whose tombs are all in their own villages, and where a high degree of in-marriage takes place—in other words a deme (see Map 5).[3]

---

[1] R. F. Callet, *Tantaran'ny Andriana*, 1908, p. 611.   [2] Personal communication: P. Vérin.
[3] A study of the Tsimahafotsy would reveal a similar situation on their northern frontier. This would also be the case for the Marovatana, the Zanakandriambe, the Zanakantitra and probably many others on which I do not have information.

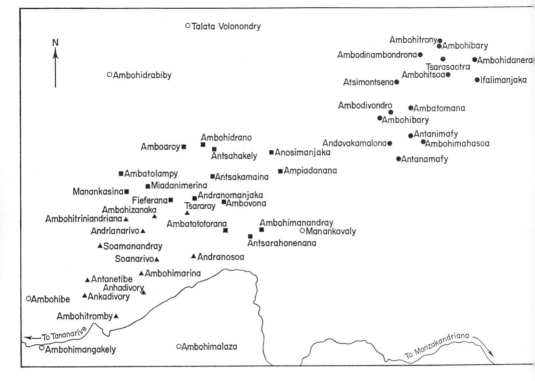

Key

Ambohitromby—Traditional place of origin of the Andrianamboninolona.

▲   Andrianamboninolona villages.

▨   Zanakambony villages.

●   Villages settled by Zanakambony and Andrianamboninolona which, just before the coming of the French, were beginning to manifest deme characteristics.

○   Large villages of other demes.

—   Road.

Map 5. The expansion of the Andrianamboninolona deme from the densely populated south-west towards the under-populated north-east.

The Movement of Tombs

If what I suggested happened in the case of the Zanakambony and the Andrianamboninolona is the way new demes seem to have been formed, we can now examine how far this process corresponds to what is happening now in the Ambatomanoina region.

The similarity between the Ambatomanoina situation and that of the Andrianamboninolona is that in both cases new colonists moved from their own villages to previously unoccupied areas in order to cultivate new lands. This put the colonists in the situation where the old traditional marriage alliances, linked as they were with the concept of maintaining land within a local community, became irrelevant, while similar alliances, but with new neighbours, were becoming desirable. Here, however, a major difference arises. While in the case of the expansion of the Andrianamboninolana the new neighbours of the colonists were also Andrianamboninolona, the neighbours in the Ambatomaniona situation are not. Therefore, while in the old situation there were no major obstacles to marrying neighbours, since they were all of the same rank, in the new situation there usually are such obstacles because of the different deme origins. This means that the formation of new in-marrying groups leads to breaking the rules associated with the traditional order. The formation of new demes as a development of the appearance of in-marrying local groups is, as a result, more difficult in the Ambatomanoina area. Furthermore, the process is clearly incomplete so long as members of these new groupings still attach themselves to their original demes through *tanindrazana* and tombs. Even this is in some cases showing signs of breaking down. In the Ambatomanoina area a few tombs are being built for "white" families.

This possibility is only really considered when the tomb management group segments.[1] It is an almost inevitable result of the movement of part of the old tomb group to a new area and the formation of a new local family because in such cases nobody is able to make the tomb group reach decisions. This is even more so if the new local family stops strengthening its ties with the *tanindrazana* by marrying neighbours. Segmentation need not necessarily mean a break with the *tanindrazana*, since it is normal to build the new tomb in the *tanindrazana*. However, the fact that a new tomb is being built raises the possibility of moving the tomb.

Although I have only very few cases with which to support this point, it seems to me that there are two kinds of reasons why the tombs are moved to the new area.

As we saw in Chapter 4, the link with the *tanindrazana* and the link with true kinsmen are thought of as two aspects of the same thing. In

---

[1] See p. 117ff.

a very real sense it is through meetings, and the participation in common ventures at the *tanindrazana*, that a man keeps in touch with his relatives. However, in a case where a man's family have been contracting marriages outside the traditional system, the kinsmen he contacts at the *tanindrazana* become with each generation more and more remote. On the other hand, many of his closest kinsmen will not belong to his *tanindrazana*. The emotional tie to the *tanindrazana*, which is largely maintained in terms of the emotions of kinship, thus disappears to a great extent, and it is really only the rank giving aspect of the *tanindrazana* which remains of value.

Consequently it is not surprising that those families which have many kinship ties in the area where they live are the ones which have moved their tombs.[1] Although it would be misleading to say that the reason given above is consciously evaluated when the choice is made, it is implicit in many of the things said on this subject. In this way a young man whose family had built a new tomb near Ambatomanoina explained to me that he had moved the tomb because he did not know anybody in the *tanindrazana* and that in the new village they now had many kinsmen. Often the matter is more simply put in terms of distance and difficulty in arranging funerals and *famadihana*.

In spite of this there remains the problem of how rank is to be demonstrated if the tomb is not in a village in traditional Imerina. The difficulty is partly avoided by stating that the people who have moved their tomb are still associated with the old *tanindrazana* since, if they wanted to, they could still be buried in the old *tanindrazana*. It is in fact a fiction but having this hypothetical link might actually be more useful to the kind of family I am talking about here than the more common straightforward link. The reason is as follows. As we saw, marrying neighbours often means breaking more or less seriously the traditional rules of marriage. Such breaches are punished by forbidding entry to the tomb to the children of such marriages. Now, such exclusion is a clear demonstration that the people excluded do not have the rank associated with a particular *tanindrazana*. Rather than risk this the descendants of such mixed marriages are likely to avoid the disgrace and build themselves a new tomb in a new territory where they can claim the association with the old *tanindrazana* without having actually to demonstrate it. Thus

----

[1] Of the four families whose genealogies are given two have tombs in the Ambatomanoina area. (They are the two with the widest network of kinship in the area.)

many of the people who have built a tomb in the new area are people who would probably not have been accepted in a tomb in the territory of the deme of which they claimed membership.

The movement of tombs should not be dismissed just as a manifestation of rank assertion by those of uncertain status. The point is that the occurence of such a situation is itself linked with the much more deeply significant tendency to marry neighbours.

The brief examination of the movement of tombs to the new area and the appearance of in-marrying groups suggests at first sight that the older pattern of demes is reproducing itself. This would be the kind of process which, although disruptive to particular groups, is really governed by an unchanging system.

It seems very probable that new demes formed by the process which it was suggested led to the formation of the Zanakambony were structurally similar to the groups from which they came. For the case in hand such an assumption seems bound to be dangerous. Although the process is not yet sufficiently advanced in the new area to show clearly what is happening, it seems to me that the various in-marrying groups which are emerging differ one from the other in economic and educational status, while demes do not. That is, richer, better educated families tend to intermarry while the same is true of poorer, less educated families. This means that what is now developing in the idiom of the traditional system may in fact be closer to a class system.

Even if this suggestion is merely tentative one thing is clear. These now in-marrying groups differ in kind among themselves as far as religion is concerned, some being Catholic, others Protestant.

8

Social Change and Descent

In the introduction to this book I suggested that one of the major features of present-day Merina culture was the way in which it considered the world as being divided between the past—*Malagasy* times—and the present—European times. This distinction takes on special importance in the social life of the modern Merina who really sees himself acting in two separate systems, the society in which he lives and the society of his ancestors. Both these societies make incompatible claims on him and, since he cannot be socially in two places at once, he compromises for his departure from the ways and the place of the ancestors by preparing his ultimate and final reintegration as a corpse. In this way the placing of a corpse in its ancestral tomb is the final act of atonement by at last transforming the social being into an actor in the imaginary society of the ancestors.

This behaviour implies a philosophy of social change, an attempted answer to the problem which lies in the fact that we consider ourselves to have a continuing identity irrespective of our actions and that at the same time we are only what we appear to be to others at a particular time. It would clearly be totally misleading to consider the beliefs we have been examining as simply an interpretation, a classification, of an already existing external world. The Merina act as they do because of the way in which they see the world and by this means they create it. The material we have been examining shows this clearly. The Merina who organizes a *famadihana* is not just returning his dead kinsmen to the ancestral fold, he is creating the ancestral fold. Only thus can we understand his ability to create a different type of ancestral fold attached to the place where he lives.

The problem of the establishment of identity in change is not unique to the Merina and the Merina answer, or attempt at an answer, is comparable to other answers. In the same way the social circumstances the Merina system both interprets and creates are also comparable with other examples.

A comparison which has been touched on already in this book is that with systems having unilineal descent groups. Professor Fortes has recently stressed the way in which such institutions as totemism have value for defining identity in societies with unilineal groups (Fortes, 1968). The similarity of the material presented here with that for many societies with unilineal descent groups is indeed very great. The association with ancestral villages and tombs offers a classification of people, and gives them the impression of belonging to a group which has always existed and which has pertinence beyond the immediate events of the moment. The value of this sort of system in a rapidly changing situation has been shown by Jones (1961) and in an even more striking way by Marshall Sahlins whose study of segmentary lineages can be seen in one respect to imply that the framework of lineage links enables the members of the society to foray far and wide and still be able to overcome the insecurity involved in predatory territorial expansion by maintaining a safe organizational base (Sahlins, 1961).

The great difference between systems with unilineal groups and the Merina situation is that, while in the former case the descent belief is relevant to the organization of political and economic life, this does not seem to be so here. Admittedly the relevance of the descent belief for organization varies from such societies as the Tallensi, where territorial organization depends on it, to the Nuer where the social uses to which it is put are much more limited. However, the Merina case is much more extreme in that here the groups on which allegiance is founded turn out, on closer examination, simply not to exist in action terms at all.

One way of dealing with this situation would be to adopt what has recently become a fairly common point of view. That is to say that under the label "descent" two quite different phenomena are grouped: one is a descent ideology, the other a set of actions leading to the formation of groups. Following this distinction the argument would run thus: we could say that the Merina have a descent group ideology but no descent groups. I have suggested that we can consider the behaviour associated with tombs and ancestral villages as an answer to the problem of identity in flux which in the short run is the flux of life in society and, in the long run is the flux of social change. All men are faced with this problem since it logically follows from the notion of society itself, and it is therefore not surprising if the answers of many societies to the same problem are similar. However, this is an intellectual problem and societies also have organizational problems which they answer independently. If some societies link up their answer to the intellectual problem with their answer to the organizational problem, as do societies with unilineal descent groups, this is quite reasonable and economical, but it is also perfectly understandable that some societies keep their answers to these two problems separate. Such a society would be Merina society where the descent ideology is of little relevance to social action.

This conclusion which seems to fit in well with the present sociological vogue for separating ideology and action is, in spite of its preliminary helpfulness, in the end misleading. The difficulty is two-fold, or rather, has two sides. Firstly, we must know what ideology divorced from action is and, secondly, define this action which is divorced from ideology. I can well understand how one comes to talk of ideology when dealing with such things as the Nicene Creed or an election manifesto, but this is not the sort of thing that anthropologists normally study. Schneider in a book on American kinship justifies separating ideology (here called culture) from action in the following terms: "This book is concerned with American kinship as a cultural system; that is, as a system of symbols. By symbol I mean something which stands for something else, where there is no necessary or intrinsic relationship between the symbol and that which it symbolizes" (p. 1). However, on page 5 he goes on to expand his statement thus: "The cultural symbols are *different* from any systematic, regular, verifiable pattern of actual, observed behaviour. That is, the pattern of observed behavior is different from culture. This is not because culture is not behavior. Culture is actual, observable behaviour but of only one specially restricted kind." (Schneider 1969.) Surely this last point nullifies the attempt to keep behaviour and culture (corresponding to action and ideology) separate. If culture is a type of behaviour the first question to ask is why certain types of behaviour (culture) are regularly contrasted with other types of behaviour. Our task is to analyse what is different between these two types of behaviour—an impossible task if we consider culture and behaviour as different sorts of "things". Indeed, I hope that the data which is the basis of this book illustrates the point clearly.

It has been shown how some Merina behaviour, directed towards the tombs and the ancestral villages, is governed by formal expressed rules (culture or ideology) while some Merina behaviour is governed by values directed to life in the place where one lives, values governed by direct notions of maximization of satisfaction (action, behaviour), but it will be obvious that it would be wrong for the anthropologist to follow the actor's sharp separation of these different types of values by using an ideology–action dichotomy. This is firstly because these different actions draw on the same store of resources and secondly because they are, as we have seen in the preceding chapter, sometimes alternatives between which the actor must choose. It also follows from this that a study of action irrespective of "ideology" would for the same reasons be meaningless.

Equally difficult would be the suggestion that action apparently un-affected by the traditional attachments could be in some way analysed apart from ideals. We have seen how agricultural cooperation and terri-torial organization are governed by beliefs about *right* and *best* forms of relationships even if these are different ideals.

Having said that the contrast between the world of the *razana* and the world of either the *vazaha* or the village in which one lives is not best treated as a contrast between ideology and action but rather as a con-trast between different types of action, we are thrown back on the ques-tion of what makes these types of action different. In the introduction I pointed out the different values given to these two worlds, but here I want to stress another difference; that is, a difference in the time scale relevant to the decisions taken in respect of these two worlds.

The time scale relevant to decisions connected with the world of the ancestors is prolonged. It is characteristic, for example, of true kinship as opposed to artificial kinship in that the relationships involved in true kinship do not lapse if they are not cultivated continually and only need to be activated occasionally. The period between prestation and contra-prestation is much greater and therefore lends itself to strategies in-volving one or several lifetimes. The notion of the land of the ancestor is not just a matter of a place where a man's forebears lived but also of a place where, if the gamble of everyday life should turn against him, it will always be possible for him to return to live in the family house and to cultivate the family lands. This is not just a vague notion, as bank-rupt shopkeepers or disgraced politicians have in fact come back to their *tanindrazana*, although usually not for long as they do not really have enough to live on there. Equally relevant is the relation to the category of people associated with the *tanindrazana* and here the importance of the time scale is even more obvious. The processes which we have considered maintain a link between a group of people and a number of ancestral villages and tombs. We have seen how having the same or a related *tanindrazana* is enough to enable a social relation to be presumed as pre-existing. What is actually happening is that a relationship which dates back many generations, because of its particular "of the *razana*" nature, has survived to the present day. This contrasts with such relationships as the obligations of neighbourhood. Once these are broken, that is when neighbours move away, they almost immediately lose any binding force. Here we are speaking of two extremes. There are types of relationships which operate over an intermediate time scale and really we are concerned with a continuum. However, when we try to look again from an external point of view at the difference between the relationships which are classed by the Merina as "of the ancestors" in contrast to those classed as "of the present", it will be seen that it is the degree of permanence of contracts which forms their basis. Naturally, like all attempts to transform what is in fact a continuum into a binary opposition, there are certain manifestations which are difficult to place. We saw how the Merina deal with these ambiguous relations, the *havana mpifankatia* link and the marriage link, and how in different contexts they place them in different categories. The *havana mpifankatia* are at the time of the funeral true kinsmen, at the time of the *famadihana* non-kinsmen.

More generally I would suggest that the contrast I have just underlined in the time scale between different types of relationship is really what underlies the contrast many anthropologists make between descent ideology and social action.

Social Change and the Concept of the Person

Throughout this book I have considered the phenomena under examination from a sociological angle; that is, as explanations of social relations or as social relations. This has been because of the necessity of concentrating on one topic only. However, it must be remembered that this is only *one* side of things. By way of conclusion I want to suggest how if the phenomena described can be seen as the result of a philosophy of social change they are also intimately linked to a philosophy of the place of man. In other words rather than concluding I would like to open up a further avenue for work on this topic.

The analysis of the *famadihana* ceremony has formed, so to speak, the pivot of the analysis of Merina society, but clearly this very important ceremony could be considered from many other angles. Let us consider one aspect of the ceremony which has only just been touched on.

If the *famadihana* is a ceremony concerned principally with death, there is another aspect of it which is concerned with birth. As has been pointed out, taking part in the ceremony at all helps towards fertility and, in particular, fighting for the mats in which the bodies have been wrapped is seen as a direct aid to fertility. These beliefs have been linked with the sociological side of the ceremony but clearly the ways of dealing with death and birth are not limited to this aspect. This is especially so in Imerina where the opposition between living and dead is continually brought out. For example, nearly always when the word for people, *olona*, is used it is further qualified by the adjective *velona*—"living". This means that people continually talk of *olon-belona* in most everyday matters as well as in most serious ones and at the same time imply the other type of existence of people as being dead. The *famadihana* is a time when this most essential relationship between living and dead people comes to the fore. This goes even further, as the *famadihana* implies that death properly treated leads to future life. In fact this argument is not only implicit in the *famadihana* but is also present in circumcision, the other main ritual of Merina life, which I have not discussed. I hope to deal with this ritual and its implications elsewhere, but here it can be noted how at a highly abstract level the circumcision ceremony is a *famadihana* in reverse in that, while the dominant theme of the *famadihana* is the handling of death and the fertility side of this is left as an unelaborated background element, circumcision is principally concerned with the creating and handling of fertility, while the implication of the place of death is left unelaborated and minor although clearly present.

Taken together therefore *famadihana* and circumcision stress the relation of fertility and death and develop it into a central concern of Merina culture. The logical link that life necessarily implies death and death implies life is one which many cultures choose to exploit. Indeed the importance of the subject matter makes it more or less inevitable that this will always be of some concern, but cultures vary in this respect and Merina culture is one which has invested a particularly large number of its beliefs in this potential anchor of human experience.

Even among those cultures which particularly stress the relation of new life and death there is variation of interpretation. Basically there are two alternatives: since something is lost at death and the same thing is gained at birth, it is either that this thing which is lost at death is lost permanently and that which is formed at birth is being continually created, or, on the other hand, it is possible that that which was lost at death is not really lost but is used again. Of this latter type of belief the most famous examples are beliefs in reincarnation or the philosophy of Heraclitus. Such religious systems as that of the Nuer would represent the former type. It seems that most systems are a compromise between these alternatives. In Merina belief, whether traditional or Christian, something is lost: the *fanahy*. However, it seems clear that that other quality of living beings which is transformed at death, the *ambiroa*, is in some way preserved. This view of the *ambiroa* is found throughout Madagascar, but takes various forms. The royal mortuary rituals of the Betsileo show particularly elaborate devices for keeping the *ambiroa* of a king, as is so well demonstrated in the description and analysis of R. P. Dubois in his *Monographie des Betsiléo*, and similar principles underlie the *tromba* of the Sahalava (see Russillon). Yet by contrast with these beliefs which are concerned with royal personages, the Merina ceremonies transform the *ambiroa* before its quality can be transmitted to a further generation. It is not a question of transmitting the *ambiroa* of a particular individual and indeed, as we saw, placing in the tomb is a depersonalizing process in which a particular individual becomes merged with all the ancestors, the unnamed *razana*, and ultimately the tomb itself. It is the dead as a whole and the tomb which retain this power of life and the ability to transfer it. It is participating in a *famadihana* at a tomb and touching things which have been in contact with the dead which encourages fertility, but not the *famadihana* of a particular person or touching a particular corpse. In the same way appeals in blessings are made to all ancestors irrespective of who they are and indeed the Merina remember the names of very few ancestors. Occasionally Merina will leave bottles of water to stand on their tombs to capture the power of the ancestor group and so that the water can be sprinkled around the house to transmit good luck and fertility to the inhabitants. Again it is the contact with the tomb and the dead in general which produces the effect. We are therefore dealing not with a clear dogma but with beliefs which stress the omnipresence of death and therefore the scarcity of life, and above all the paradox that it is the dead who have been and will be the suppliers of life.

Glossary of Malagasy Words

(Only a brief translation is given here. A fuller translation will be found in the text where the words are first mentioned.)

Andevo	Slave
Andriamanitra	God
Andriana	The higher demes in the traditional ranking hierarchy
Andrianam-poinimerina	A Merina king
Angatra	Ghost
Ankizy	Child (minor)
An tsaha	In the fields
Ambiroa	Soul
Ariary tsy vaky	An uncut coin
Avelona	Soul
Canton	Administrative unit of around 5000 people
Dinampokon'olona	Act of the *fokon'olona*
Dinidinika	Conference
Famadihana	Ceremony involving exhumation
Fanahy	Soul
Fandroana	A chess-like game
Fasana mandrosoa	A grave at the entrance to a tomb
Fianakaviana	Family
Fianakaviana be	Big family
Fisihaona	A present marking betrothal; a demand
Firelomana	A living
Fokon'olona	A local group; a local council
Fomban'-drazana	The custom of the ancestors
Fomban vazaha	The custom of the Europeans
Fotsy	White

Havana	Kinsmen
Havana mpifankatia	Quasi kinsmen; neighbours
Hena ratsy	Meat eaten at funerals; lit: bad meat
Hova	The Merina belonging to demes of the lower half of the traditional ranking hierarchy. Also sometimes used to mean Merina
Imerina	The land of the Merina
Inona masaka?	What is there ready to eat?
Iraytampo	Of one mother
Iray trano	One house in the sense of "living together in one house"
Kabary	Formal speech
Kamo	Lazy
Karazana	Species
Lamba mena	Shroud; lit: red cloth
Lolo	Butterfly; spirit
Lova tsy mifindra	Marriage between havana; lit: inheritance not going away
Mainty	Black
Malagasy	Not *vazaha*
Mamadika	To turn over
Marofotsy	A people to the north of the Merina
Merina	A person having an ancestral village in Imerina
Métayage	A form of leasing land
Mpifakatiavana	People who love each other
Mpaka	Those who take away the bride
Mpakafo	Heart thieves
Mpamosavy	Witch; incest
Mpikabary	Speechmaker
Olon-belona	Living people
Paraky	Tobacco
Radama I	Merina king
Ralambo	Early Merina king
Ranavalona I	Merina Queen
Razana	Related dead; ancestor

Sampy	Cult object
Sihanaka	A Malagasy people
Sinibe	Water storage jar
Tanindrazana	Ancestral village; land in ancestral village
Tapa maso	Removal of avoidance
Taxi-brousse	Small bus
Tenin-drazana	Proverb
Toko	Part
Tompon'jama	The organizer of a ceremony
Tompo-tany	Owner of land
Tsara va tompoko?	Greeting used for andriana
Tsiny	Guilt
Tsodrano	Blessing
Vahiny	Stranger; guest
Vazaha	European; crafty
Vazimba	Mythical early inhabitants of Imerina
Vatovelona	Quartz
Voanjo	Seed; groundnut; settler
Vody akoho	The hindquarters of a chicken (a mark of respect)
Vody-ondry	The hindquarters of a sheep (a mark of respect)
Zana'drazana	The dispersed family at a *famadihana*
Zazarano	Infant

References

Abinal, R. P. and Malzac, R. P. (1888 and subsequent editions). *Dictionnaire Malgache-Francais*. Éditions Maritimes et Coloniales. Paris.

Andriamanjato, R. (1957). *La Tsiny et le Tody dans la Pensée Malgache*. Présence Africaine, Paris.

Arbrousset, F. (1951). *Le Fokon'olona à Madagascar*. Domat Montchrestien, Paris.

Beattie, J. (1960). *Bunyoro—an African Kingdom*. Holt, Rinehart and Winston, New York.

Bloch, M. E. F. (1966). "Aspects psychologiques et culturels de l'attitude du paysan Merina envers les Grands Hopitaux". *Bulletin de l'Académie Malgache*. Nouvelle Série. Vol XLIV–2.

Bloch, M. E. F. (1967). "Notes sur l'organisation sociales de l'Imerina avant le régne de Radama." *Annales de l'Université de Tananarive*, 119–152.

Bloch, M. E. F. (1968a). "Astrology and writing" in *Literacy in Traditional Society* (Ed. J. Goody). Cambridge University Press, London.

Bloch, M. E. F. (1968b). "Technique employées pour l'étude sociologique d'un village Merina." *Civilisation Malgache*, 2.

Bloch, M. E. F. (1971 forthcoming). "Decision making in councils in Madagascar" in *Councils in Action* (Eds. Richards, A. I. and Kuper, A.) Cambridge Papers in Social Anthropology, Cambridge University Press, London.

Callet, R. F. (1908). *Tantaran'ny Andriana*. 2 Vols. Imprimerie Officielle, Tananarive. [Translated into French as *Histoire des Rois* by Chapus, G. S. and Ratsimba, E. 1953, 1956, and 1958. Académie Malgache, Tananarive. 4 Vols.]

Condominas, G. (1960). *Fokon'olona et Collectivités Rurales en Imerina*. Berger-Levrault, Paris.

Cousins, W. E. (1875). "The ancient theism of the Hovas." *Antananarivo Annual*, I, 5–12.

Cousins, W. E. (1896). "The abolition of slavery in Madagascar." *Antananarivo Annual*, XX.

Cousins, W. E. (1963 edition). *Fomba Malagasy* (Ed. H. Randzavola).

Dahl, O. C. (1951). *Malgache et Maanjan: une Comparaison Linguistique.* Studies of the Egede Instituttet, 3, Oslo.

Dahle, L. (1962). *Anganon'ny Ntaolo, Tantara Mampiseho ny Fombandrazana sy ny Finoana Sasany Nananany* (Ed. Sims, L.). Imprimerie Luthérienne, Tananarive.

Danielli, M. (1947). "The witches of Madagascar." *Folk-Lore,* **58** (June), 261–276.

Decary, R. (1951). *Moeurs et Coutumes des Malgaches.* Payot, Paris.

Decary, R. (1954). "La puissance mystique du nombre 7 chez les Malgaches." *Revue de Madagascar,* **21**, 40–48.

Decary, R. (1962). *La Mort et les Coutumes Funéraires à Madagascar.* G.P. Maisonneuve et Larose, Paris.

Deschamps, H. (1959). *Les Migrations Intérieures Passées et Présentes à Madagascar.* Berger-Levrault, Paris.

Deschamps, H. (1961). *Histoire de Madagascar.* 2nd edition. Berger-Levrault, Paris.

Dez, J. (1965). "Les baux ruraux coutumiers à Madagascar" in *Etudes de Droit Africain et de Droit Malgache* (Ed. Poirier, J.) Etudes Malgache. Faculté des Lettres et des Sciences Humaines, Université de Madagascar.

Dubois, H. (1929, 1934). "L'idée de Dieu chez les anciens Malgaches." *Anthropos,* **24**, 1/2 Jan.-Apr., 281–311; **29**, 5/6 Sept.-Dec.,757–774.

Dubois, H. (1938). *Monographie des Betsiléo.* Institut d'Ethnologie (Travaux et Mémoires, 34), Paris.

Durkheim, E. (1912). *Les Formes Elémentaires de la Vie Religieuse: le Systéme Totémique en Australie.* Félix Alcan, Paris.

Ellis, W. (1838). *History of Madagascar.* 2 Vols. Tolles, London.

Evans-Pritchard, E. E. (1937). *Witchcraft Oracles and Magic Among the Azande.* Oxford University Press, London.

Evans-Pritchard, E. E. (1951). *Nuer Religion.* Oxford University Press, London.

Falck, K. (1958). "L'ancien village au Vakinankaratra." *Historisk-Antikvarisk Rekke,* **IV**, 1–27. University of Bergen.

Faublée, J. (1946). *L'Ethnographie de Madagascar.* Nouvelle Edition, Paris.

Faublée, J. (1954). *La Cohésion des Sociétés Bara.* Presses Universitaires de France, Paris.

Fortes, M. and Dieterlen, G. (Eds.), (1965). *African Systems of Thought.* Oxford University Press, London.

Fortes, M. (1949). *The Web of Kinship among the Tallensi*. Oxford University Press, London.

Fortes, M. (1949). "Time and social structure: an Ashanti case study" in *Social Structure* (Ed. Fortes, M). Oxford University Press, London.

Fortes, M. (1953). "The structure of unilineal descent groups." *American Anthropologist*, **55**, 17–51.

Fortes, M. (1966). "Totem and taboo." Proceedings of the Royal Anthropological Institute for 1966, 5–22.

Frazer, Sir J. G. (1890). *The Golden Bough*. Macmillan, London.

Fustel de Coulanges, N. D. (1864). *La Cité Antique*. Durand, Paris.

Van Gennep, A. (1909). *Les Rites de Passage*. Emile Nourry, Paris.

Goody, J. (Ed.) (1958). *The Developmental Cycle in Domestic Groups*. Cambridge papers in Social Anthropology, No. 1. Cambridge University Press, London.

Goody, J. (1962). *Death, Property and the Ancestors. A Study of the Mortuary Customs of the Lodagaa of West Africa*. Tavistock Publications, London.

Goody, E. and Goody, J. (1966). "Cross-cousin marriage in northern Ghana." *Man, The Journal of the Royal Anthropological Institute*, I. 343–355.

Grandidier, A. (1886). "Des rites funéraires chez les Malgaches." *Revue d'Ethnographie*, Paris. [Translation in Sibree, J. (1896).]

Grandidier, A. and Grandidier, G. (1892). *Histoire Physique, Naturelle et Politique de Madagascar* (including *Ethnographie* (4 vols) and *Histoire Politique* (1 vol)). P. Brodard, Paris.

Harris, G. (1957). "Possession 'hysteria' in a Kenya tribe." *American Anthropologist*, **59**, 1046–1066.

Harrison, T. (1962). "Borneo death." *Bijdragen tot de Taal-landen Volkerkunde*.

Hartland, H. S. (1911). "Death and disposal of the dead" (introductory section) in Vol **IV** of *Encyclopaedia of Religion and Ethics* (Ed. Hastings, J.), 1908–1926. Edinburgh.

Hebert, J.-C. (1965). "La cosmographie ancienne Malgache suivie de l'enumeration des points cardinaux et l'importance du Nord-Est." *Taloha, Annalles de l'Université de Madagascar*, **I**, 83–195.

Hellot, F. (1900). *La Pacification de Madagascar*. Berger-Levrault, Paris.

Hertz, R. (1907). "Contribution à une étude sur la représentation de la mort." *L'Année Sociologique*, **10**, 48–137.

Houlder, J. A. (1957). *Ohabolana ou Proverbes Malgaches*. (Translated by Noyer.) Imprimerie Luthérienne, Tananarive.

Isnard, H. (1954). "Les bases geographiques de la monarchie Hova." *Etudes d'Outre Mer*, Apr. 1954, 165–175.

Isnard, H. (1955). *Madagascar*. A. Colin, Paris.

Jones, G. I. (1961). "Ecology and social structure among the N.E. Ibo." *Africa*, **31**, 117–134.

Julien, G. (1909). *Institutions Politiques et Sociales de Madagascar*. 2 Vols. Guilmoto, Paris.

Kluckhohn, C. (1951). "Values and value orientations in the theory of Action" in *Towards a General Theory of Action* (Eds. Parsons, T. and Shils, E.). Tree Press, Cambridge, Mass.

La Fontaine, J. S. (1970). *City Politics—A Study of Leopoldville* 1962–63. Cambridge University Press, London.

Leach, E. R. (1961). *Pul Eliya, A Village in Ceylon: A Study of Land Tenure and Kinship*. Cambridge University Press, London.

Levi-Strauss, C. (1962). *Le Totémisme Aujourd'hui*. Presses Universitaires de France, Paris.

Levi-Strauss, C. (1963). *La Pensée Sauvage*. Plon, Paris.

Lewis, I. M. (1966). "Spirit possession and deprivation cults." *Man, The Journal of the Royal Anthropological Institute*, **1**, 307–329.

Mantaux, C. and Vérin, P. (1969). "Traditions et archeologie de la vallée de la Mananara." *Bulletin de Madagascar*, No. 283.

Matthews, T. T. (Translator) (1897). "Among the Fahavalo" (from "A native account"). *Antananarivo Annual*, **XXI**. Tananarive.

Mayer, A. C. (1960). *Caste and Kinship in Central India*. Routledge & Kegan Paul, London.

Mayeur, N. (1777). *Voyage au Pays d'Ancove*. (Reprinted in *Bulletin de l'Académie Malgache*, Vol **XII**, 2nd Partie, 1913, pp. 13–42.)

Miles, D. (1965). "Socio-economic aspects of secondary burial." *Oceania*, **XXXV**, 161–174.

Molet, L. (1956). *Le Bain Royal à Madagascar*. Imprimerie Luthérienne, Tananarive.

Mondain, G. (1925). "Raketaka". Publications de la Faculté des Lettres d'Alger, Bulletin de Correspondance Africaine, **61**, Paris.

Murdock, G. P. (1949). *Social Structure*. Macmillan, London.

Parker, G. W. (1883). "On systems of land tenure in Madagascar." *Journal of the Anthropological Institute*, **XII**, 277–280.

Rabemananjara, J. (1958). *Nationalisme et Problèms Malgaches*. Présence Africaine, Paris.

Radcliffe-Brown, A. R. and Forde, D. (1950). *African Systems of Kinship and Marriage*. Oxford University Press, London.

Radcliffe-Brown, A. R. (1952). *Structure and Function in Primitive Society*. Cohen & West, London.

Raharijaona, S. (1960). *Population et Habitat dans un Quartier Populaire de Tananarive, Manarintsoa-Isotry. Resultats d'une Enquête Socio-Economique* CNRS, Tananarive.

Ramilison, R. (1951–2). *Ny Loharanon'ny Andriana Nanjaka teto Imerina etc., Andriantomara-Andrianamilaza*. Ankehitriny, Tananarive.

Ratsamimanana, J. and Razafindraazka, L. (1909). *Ny Andriantompokoindrinda*. Imprimerie Volamahitsy, Ambohimalaza.

Razafindraibe, C. (Ed.). *Fokon'olona* (Journal).

Rudd, J. (1960). *Taboo*, Allen & Unwin, Oslo and London.

Russillon, H. (1912). *Un Culte Dynastique avec Evocation des Morts. Chez les Sakalava de Madagascar*. A. Picard et Fils, Paris.

Sahlins, M. (1961). "The segmentary lineage: an organisation of predatory expansion." *American Anthropologist*, **63**, 322–345.

Scheffler, H. W. (1965). *Choiseul Island Social Structure*. University of California Press, Berkeley.

Schneider, D. M. (1968). *American Kinship: A Cultural Account*. Prentice Hall, Englewood Cliffs, New Jersey.

Sibree, J. (1870). *Madagascar and its People*. Religious Tract Society, London.

Sibree, J. (1880). *Madagascar, the Great African Island*. Trübner, London.

Sibree, J. (1896). *Madagascar before the Conquest*. Allen & Unwin, London.

Smith, R. T. (1956). *The Negro Family in British Guiana*. Routledge & Kegan Paul, London.

Standing, H. F. (1887). "The Tribal Divisions of the Hova Malagasy." *Antananarivo Annual*, **XI**, Tananarive.

Stöhr, W. (1959). "Der todesritual der Dayak." *Ethnologica*, New Series, I.

Thompson, V. and Adloff, R. (1965). *The Malagasy Republic*. Stanford University Press.

Valette, J. (1965). "De l'origine des Malgaches." *Taloha, Annales de l'Université de Madagascar*, 15–32.

Vansina, J. (1961). *De la Tradition Orale: Essai de Methode Historique*. Musée Royal du Congo Belge, Tervuren.

Worsley, P. (1958). *The Trumpet Shall Sound*. McGibbon & Kee, London.

Index